"DE LAWD"

Richard B. Harrison. Courtesy of the Moorland-Springarn Research Center,
Howard University.

"DE LAWD"

RICHARD B. HARRISON
AND *THE GREEN PASTURES*

—————— Walter C. Daniel ——————

Contributions in Afro-American and African Studies, Number 99

Greenwood Press
NEW YORK • WESTPORT, CONNECTICUT • LONDON

Library of Congress Cataloging-in-Publication Data

Daniel, Walter C.
  "De Lawd" : Richard B. Harrison and The green
pastures.

  (Contributions in Afro-American and African
studies, ISSN 0069-9624 ; no. 99)
  Bibliography: p.
  Includes index.
  1. Connelly, Marcus Cook, 1890-   . The green
pastures. 2. Connelly, Marcus Cook, 1890-   —Stage
history. 3. Harrison, Richard B. 4. Actors and
actresses—United States—Biography. 5. Afro-Americans
in literature. 6. God in literature. 7. Creation in
literature. 8. Bible in literature. I. Title.
II. Series.
PS3505.04814G733   1986   812'.52   86-7588
ISBN 0-313-25300-5 (lib. bdg. : alk. paper)

Library of Congress Catalog Card Number: 86-7588
ISBN: 0-313-25300-5
ISSN: 0069-9624

First published in 1986

Greenwood Press, Inc.
88 Post Road West, Westport, Connecticut 06881

Printed in the United States of America

The paper used in this book complies with the
Permanent Paper Standard issued by the National
Information Standards Organization (Z39.48-1984).

10 9 8 7 6 5 4 3 2 1

Copyright Acknowledgments

We gratefully acknowledge permission to print extracts:

from THE MEMOIRS OF MARC CONNELLY by Marc Connelly. Copyright © 1968 by
Marc Connelly. Reprinted by permission of Henry Holt and Company;

from THE GREEN PASTURES by Marc Connelly. Copyright 1929, 1930 © 1957, 1958 by
Marc Connelly. Reprinted by permission of Henry Holt and Company.

CONTENTS

PREFACE

As a young boy living in Macon, Georgia, I remember distinctly the large green and white billboards advertising *The Green Pastures* that I saw on the walls of a railroad overpass. The title itself made an indelible impression on me. I do not recall reading reviews of the performance or of any of the festivities honoring its principal actor, Richard B. Harrison, that must have taken place in the town. Somehow, though, I sensed some element of mystery and racial accomplishment in the announcement. At that time, Harrison was not featured as the star of the cast. The next year, I remember attending a recital sung by the world-renowned black tenor Roland Hayes. That time, I was in the segregated audience. My mother had found out we could buy tickets and had secured three for us—herself and her two young boys. I recall that our seats were in the roped-off section of the new Municipal Auditorium. A quiet pride arose in me as I listened to the tenor sing art songs in French and Italian and German. I could not understand a single word he was singing, but the sound was sweet and pleasant. And I knew an event of social and artistic importance was taking place and I was part of it.

These impressions at so young an age motivated me to seek to understand black American culture as it has been forged and delivered within the peculiar image of a native people's own rendition of the external elements of the literature and music and religion of a majority culture of which they were a part but alongside which they played out their own roles as black Americans.

Memory of these impressions has led me to many years of scrupulous research into those black men and women who have performed on America's concert stages and theater platforms in the excruciating tasks of maintaining their personal integrity and performing their art. Nearly half a century ago, Leslie Collins wrote his doctoral dissertation at Western Reserve University; entitled *A Song, a Dance, and a Play*, it was a performance biography of the singer Marian Anderson, the dancer Kathryn Dunham, and the actor Paul Robeson—a work intended to indicate some of the cultural dilemma of which I speak and how each of these artists dealt with it.

In my own way, I add *"De Lawd": Richard B. Harrison and "The Green Pastures"* as my contribution to this dimension of American culture.

Many persons have helped make this work possible: The Office of the Associate Provost for Graduate Studies and Research at the University of Missouri-Columbia provided small grants; librarians in many American cities have assisted me in gathering reviews of the play; and the documents at the Lincoln Center collection of theatrical materials of the New York Public Library have been particularly important.

My students in American dramatic literature have been insightful as they have developed interest in the study after I introduced them to American playwrights of the Depression era in seminars that I have conducted at the University of Missouri-Columbia. Articles I have written about *The Green Pastures* and Richard B. Harrison for the *Negro History Bulletin* and the *Journal of American Culture* have brought forth notes of comments from many parts of the country. All these persons have helped me to believe that the subject is worthwhile. I have been particularly pleased with the personal notes that librarians have placed on the bottom of my request letters to them, sending along the copies of reviews, and telling me they remember seeing the play when it played in their hometowns.

I am grateful, too, for the help Dr. Eva Jessye and Dr. O. Anderson Fuller, personal friends of Harrison and fellow performers with him, have given me in sharing their memories of the 1920s and 1930s.

Ms. Valerie D. White and Mr. Mark Reger have been exceedingly helpful in working with me to copy-edit the manuscript.

"DE LAWD"

1

INTRODUCTION

Some fifty years after its introduction into American culture, Marcus Cook Connelly's *The Green Pastures* appears in few anthologies of American plays. Bennett A. Cerf and Van H. Cartnell included it in their *Sixteen American Plays*.[1] That volume's introduction, written by Brooks Atkinson, praises the play highly, as Atkinson had done from the night it first appeared on Broadway. He wrote in his essay that at the moment Richard B. Harrison, "a broad-shouldered man of many years," walked onto the stage, *The Green Pastures* became a classic. And he noted that when Harrison died, five years after his first appearance at the Mansfield Theatre in the role of "De Lawd" in Connelly's play, it became impossible to keep *The Green Pastures* on the stage.

John Gassner, in his monumental *Masters of the Drama*, devotes four-fifths of his text to non-American works. He gives a few lines to *The Green Pastures*, calling it a "stunning pastiche of remarkable humor and nobility" which might be rightly regarded, despite some mixture of style, as "one of the outstanding chronicles in the history of the theatre."[2] Darwin Turner, perhaps the most outstanding scholar of the development of Afro-American drama, slants his interest in the play toward the Black Nationalist Movement of the 1960s; in doing so, he dismisses Connelly's play as a vehicle for "religious superstition which should be too familiar to require serious study."[3] Gassner probably saw the play in terms of its time and place in the comprehensive scope of modern world drama, notwithstanding his tenuous praise. Turner wrote from the perspective of the popularity of the drama of black consciousness and the agitprop purposes of the "angry" black writers. Neither Gassner nor Turner explores the play's impact on the theatergoers of the 1930s. The mixture of styles that Gassner found improper actually proved one of the play's strengths and the basis of appeal for thousands of Americans who crowded theaters to see it. And contrary to Professor Turner's statement, neither the play nor its history-making production is in any respect too familiar to require discussion. Its life on the stage, together with the life of the play's principal character, "De Lawd," and the man who brought life to the text of the play, deserves telling in detail.

From February 26, 1930, the night he stepped for the first time onto a commercial stage, until March 2, 1935, the afternoon he found himself too physically weak to go before the footlights and perform his 1,658th time as "De Lawd," Harrison's name dominated news and reviews about the American acting profession. In the darkest years of the Great Depression, his regal bearing and sonorous, kindly voice met thousands of Americans who came first to the Mansfield Theatre on Broadway in New York City and then to dozens of auditoriums and high school gymnasiums throughout the United States and parts of Canada to see *The Green Pastures*. Sixty-five years old, a man who had made his living working at whatever jobs were available while he performed when he could secure an engagement as an elocutionist and as a teacher of dramatic art, Harrison gave the nation a few hours in the theater that served as surcease from crumbling economics and harrowing fears about communism, fascism, and nihilism that crept ever closer to the sinews of America's political and moral fabric. And outside the theater, moving into the pulpits of both white and black preachers in the nation's churches, he taught, through his speeches and conversations, a faith and hope and simple beauty as a substitute for disillusionment and despair.

The Green Pastures was Richard B. Harrison. When he died, the play died. The understudy who followed him in the role could not sustain the play's appeal in the theater for long—nor could the Warner Brothers film version of the play, nor could the cast in a 1951 revision. Connelly and Harrison won significant accolades for their accomplishments in the theater. The playwright was awarded the Pulitzer prize for drama in 1930. Harrison received the NAACP's prestigious Spingarn Medal the next year as the black American who, in the estimation of a committee, had made the most important contribution to the edification of the Negro race during the year.

Even though few anthologies of American drama include Marc Connelly's play that brought him fame and fortune and captivated the hearts of the nation in some of its darkest moments, little notice has been taken of Richard B. Harrison's contribution, through the Connelly play, to acting in the American theater in a native drama.

This book is written as a biography of Harrison's role as "De Lawd" in *The Green Pastures*. Without textual criticism, or any attempt to confirm or to refute any contemporary attitudes toward the play, this book purports to present an objective story of the actor's part in the play. The chapters explore and discuss the literary and social tradition out of which the play emerged, its making, its staging, its opening and first New York run, its tours across the United States from coast to coast, and its return to New York as a valedictory for the man who gave it its importance.

NOTES

1. Bennett A. Cerf and Van H. Cartnell, *Sixteen American Plays* (New York: Garden City Publishing Co., 1941).

2. John Gassner, *Masters of the Drama* (New York: Dover Publications, 1954), p. 686.

3. Darwin T. Turner, *Black Drama in America* (Greenwich, Conn.: Fawcett Publishing Co., 1971), pp. 5-6.

2

BEFORE
THE GREEN PASTURES

Black theater is an unclear term of classification. It can suggest either theater *about* blacks or theater written, acted, and directed *by* blacks.[1] Marc Connelly's *The Green Pastures* is theater about blacks; it was acted *by* them in roles written for them. It is not about their sociocultural search for identity as is the bulk of theater that examines and expresses the historical conflicts associated with living black in the United States; nor is it theater of the black community. Actually, it is the theater of Judeo-Christian man. Its text is, primarily, the first two books of the Old Testament, written in what its author considered an American Negro idiom. It does not follow the long tradition of black stage drama in the United States. But *The Green Pastures* belongs to an important group of early twentieth-century plays written by white authors about black American life to be acted by black performers. Ridgely Torrence, Eugene O'Neill, and Paul Green are the principal figures in this tradition. Some of their best-known works were the precursors of *The Green Pastures*. In fact, *The Green Pastures* essentially marks the end of the epoch of white playwrights writing about black American life in a way that was edifying to both black and white groups. Connelly's *The Green Pastures* also marks a significant change within that tradition. For before Connelly, Torrence, O'Neill, and Green had written and produced plays that focused on the American Negro as a feeling and thinking human being, living in black/white America. As a psychological drama about people striving valiantly, and often unsuccessfully, for identity and for their own voice, these playwrights contributed to the rich fabric of American culture most significantly in breaking with the nineteenth-century minstrel tradition. They created characters that moved beyond the prevailing stereotype, but their practice was not as liberating as it might at first appear. These white playwrights—along with white producers, directors, set designers, and audiences—established what Harold Cruse has called "a tradition of white cultural paternalism."[2] According to Cruse, this cultural paternalism preempted the development of black ethnic theater—theater written, directed, and performed by blacks. In its place it offered white patronage. But white patronage did not aim at producing black community theaters. Such a development had to wait until the 1960s. The white playwrights Torrence, O'Neill, and Green saw the potential for drama in the myths and images of the American Negro and used them effectively. And their work did make American audiences take a new look at black people. But they undertook to present black life on the American stage more for their own advancement than for black America's. "As a result," Cruse writes, "a most intense (and unfair) competition was engendered between white and Negro writers; the whites, from their vantage point of superior social and economic advantage, naturally won out." Some details of this aspect of American theater history seem an appropriate discussion for placing The Green Pastures into the milieu out of which it arose.

During the first decades of the twentieth century, some black playwrights reached the commercial stage, among them Garland Anderson, Willis Richardson, Frank Wilson, and Wallace Thurman; but their works were minimally effective.[3] The black community in Harlem, however, which was fostering a literary renaissance, was also supporting a community theater. Through literary contests sponsored by The Crisis, the house organ of the National Association for the Advancement of Colored People, the NAACP had nurtured a black writing community. The contests were largely the result of the personal effort of W.E.B. Du Bois, the magazine's editor and an eminent artist-scholar who made racial uplift his life's work. The National Urban League, through its magazine Opportunity, edited by the sociologist Charles S. Johnson, also held literary contests and provided space in its columns for aspiring black writers. Both Du Bois and Johnson used their considerable contacts with white philanthropists and personalities in the publishing industry to spawn the Harlem Renaissance. A. Philip Randolph and Chandler Owens, two young black migrants from the American South to Harlem in the early 1900s, published independently The Messenger, their monthly magazine that promulgated the "New Negro" concept of the World War I and Harlem Renaissance period. They brought to the reading public writings by the young black authors who, to some extent, created a rebirth of the vitality of that small but powerful literary movement William Wells

Brown, Frederick Douglass, and Charles Chesnutt—in particular—had established between the end of the Civil War and the turn of the century. Theophilus Lewis, the first black writer for a black publication, who sought to establish drama review and criticism in Harlem, wrote columns for *The Messenger* and for the *New York Amsterdam News*, a weekly national newspaper published in Harlem. His work sought to establish aesthetic standards for theater in Harlem during the Renaissance.[4]

Du Bois played a key role in the Renaissance not only as editor of *The Crisis* but also as a writer. Most familiar are his prose essays and sociological and historical studies, but Du Bois had a strong urge to be a creative writer. He produced several novels and, most important for this discussion, wrote plays and pageants. He also organized the Krigwa Players as a little theater group in 1926, bringing into black artistic circles some of the activities that had been generated by the little theater movement among white people in major cities in the nation. Krigwa's members—both playwrights and actors—believed that there was a need for a new American theater. To them, although the Negro had long been in the theater, his role had not been a normal one. Actors had played before largely white audiences who had considered the performers merely "entertainers." Demands and ideals of whites and their conception of Negroes had set the norm for black actors, Du Bois and his associates complained. They rejected the roles that black actors had played in the most popular of the "serious" plays because these works operated on the defeatist motif by ending in lynching, suicide, or degeneracy. Krigwa Players promoted a native black theater that issued from black people who acted out their dramas on stages within their communities. There the audiences and the players would validate the salutary image of living black in the United States. Krigwa's playhouse was the basement of the 135th Street Public Library in the middle of Harlem. There the fifty-five members, directed by Charles Burroughs, invited anyone who had written a play or any group that wanted to present one to do so. Beyond Broadway, what little there was of black theater enjoyed some measure of success in Harlem's Lafayette Theatre, Chicago's Pekin Stock Company, and Karamu House in Cleveland. Black colleges and universities, the setting in which one would have expected black drama to flourish, faithfully produced conventional white plays.

But without the resources of the white theater, black community theater in Harlem could not develop with vigor. Into the breach stepped the white playwrights. Ridgely Torrence is usually accorded the distinction of having written the first plays that used Negroes as subjects for serious dramatic consideration and employed black actors. O'Neill's reputation in the theater was established with *The Emperor Jones*. Paul Green won a Pulitzer prize for his *In Abraham's Bosom*, an honor that

Connelly won three years later with *The Green Pastures*. All of these white playwrights except for Connelly shared a common heritage: each was at some time related to the social and cultural reform movements that blossomed during the first decades of the twentieth century. Without an interest in the revolutionary sentiments of these movements, none would have created the theater that is the subject of this book. Each profited by his choice of Negroes as subject matter, and each literally changed the course of American theater history by his plays about Negro life in the United States. Marc Connelly benefited most, although he was not an active member of the Provincetown Group, as were Torrence, O'Neill, and Green.

They were part of a group of young intellectuals who established a colony on the tip of Cape Cod in Massachusetts, led primarily by Hutchins Hapgood and his wife, Neith Boyce, with Lincoln Steffens. Their meeting place in Manhattan was the Fifth Avenue "Salon" of Mabel Dodge, wealthy patroness of the young radicals to whose luxurious apartment came the playwrights under discussion here, as well as Sinclair Lewis, Michael Gold, Dorothy and Du Bose Heyward, and Robert Edmond Jones. In recalling her involvement with the "younger spirits," who had by the summer of 1914 become a distinct community of kindred souls, Dodge wrote:

> In time there came Steffens (Lincoln), and Emma Goldman, and Berkman, that group of earnest native anarchists, Reed, Lippman, Bobby Jones, Bobby Rogers and Lee Simondson, these but lately out of college; Max Eastman and Ida [Rauh], Frances Perkins, Gertrude Light, Mary Heston Vorse, and the Sangers—and all of the labor leaders, poets, journalists, editors and actors.[5]

The point here is not so much that most of the group were in some way related to a radical philosophical-political position, but that they were, by and large, the playwrights who participated in the enterprise between white writers and black performers. They were either the playwrights themselves or those who influenced them. Mabel Dodge's Salon was an extension of the association between black and white artists that had taken place in the theater of the 1890s, when Bob Cole, James Weldon Johnson and his brother, J. Rosamond Johnson, Will Marion Cook, and Paul Laurence Dunbar had been the leading figures in this circle. A few of the Negro creative artists of the time, including both Johnsons, were occasionally invited to the Salon.

Emilie Hapgood, sister-in-law of Hutchins Hapgood and wife of Norman Hapgood, the drama critic for the *New York Advertiser* and the *Evening Post*, produced the Torrence one-act plays that have been so often praised as having initiated the new trend that brought serious plays about Negroes before white audiences. She, who had financed productions of John Galsworthy's *Justice* and G. K. Chesterton's *Magic*, sponsored the performance by black actors of Torrence's *The Rider of the Dreams*, *Granny Maumee*, and *Simon the Cyrenian* at the Garden Theatre in Madison Square Garden in New York on April 5, 1917. On the eve of President Woodrow Wilson's declaration of war on Germany and its allies that brought the United States into World War I, Robert Edmond Jones, who was emerging as the brightest star among stage and costume designers, actually directed the Torrence plays.

Three years earlier Torrence had presented *Granny Maumee* in the winter of 1914 for the Play Society of New York. Mostly theater people attended that performance, which was on a double bill with Thomas Heywood's *A Woman Killed with Kindness*. Carl Van Vechten, who later became one of the principal white guiding spirits for many of the black writers of the Harlem Renaissance period, wrote in the *New York Press* that *Granny Maumee* was a "serious play entirely about Negroes from the Negro point of view." He went as far as to claim that the little play presaged the beginning of a native black American drama like the Irish theater movement in Dublin. But the production, for all its reality, used white, not black, actors. In May 1914, the white Manhattan Players performed *Granny Maumee* at the Lyceum Theatre in Rochester, New York. On the basis of the reception the play received in these public showings, Torrence seemed to realize that he had discovered a viable subject for his literary talents and ambitions. He now turned to efforts to produce his Negro plays with black actors.

But he did not know any. He wrote to his mother: "This afternoon I am expecting to go out to Groton to talk over 'darky' plays with Bobby Jones [Robert Edmond Jones] who wants to put on the stage and costuming [*sic*] some pieces of mine." With calculating candor, he wrote in the same letter: "I and my scenic man, Robert Edmond Jones, are going up to Harlem to attend a performance of colored people so that we may look over the ground." He had already made arrangements with Emilie Hapgood to put on his plays at the Garden Theater April 5, 1914, but as late as March 12, he was still wondering whether he could bring off the presentation. Apparently, Du Bois introduced Torrence to James Weldon Johnson ostensibly for the purpose of helping the playwright to find actors for his plays.[6] The cast for the three plays was chosen from black performers billed as The Coloured Players. They included Jesse Shipp, formerly a minstrel player who also joined the cast of *The Green Pastures*; Alex Rogers, who also came down through the Williams and Walker minstrels and musical comedies; Blanche Dees, who had performed with the Cole and Johnson shows, an organization of stage performers that was established by James Weldon Johnson and J. Rosamond Johnson and

Robert Cole; and Inez Clough, who was a member of Harlem's Lafayette Players and also joined the cast of *The Green Pastures*. Because the plays remained at the Garden Theatre for ten days, they must be called reasonably successful. They were moved to the Garrick Theatre, where they remained on the board for several weeks.

Invitations to the opening night were extended by the New York Centre of the Drama League of America. Robert Benchley wrote a promotional article for the performance for the *New York Tribune*. Expressing some cautious optimism about the reception the Torrence works would receive, he wrote:

> It may be that Thursday night will see the beginnings of a new involvement on the American stage. Potentially it is as rich in possibilities as any that have preceded it. It all depends on the spirit in which the public receives it. If they go expecting to see burlesque they will not only be disappointed; they will be ashamed. If they go with a sympathy for the attempt and an appreciation of its difficulties and aspirations, they may be witnessing the first stirrings of a really distinctive American drama.[7]

The plays were well received, at least by the small audiences of regular theatergoers who saw them. And they were, indeed, the first financially supported departures from the minstrel revue of blacks in the commercial theater. Clearly, the star of the performance was Robert Edmond Jones. Reviews and promotional material focused on him. Critics spoke of Torrence's "large vision" in the plays and expressed hope that the works would lay a foundation that would lead to a national Negro theater. After opening night, the *Herald Tribune* carried a full-page feature that praised Mrs. Hapgood and Jones. The *Dramatic Mirror* called the presentation the most significant feature of the season. James Weldon Johnson tied the performances back to the black community that the plays were intended to represent. He wrote in his popular and well-read column in the *New York Age*, Harlem's most prominent weekly black newspaper that was also circulated throughout the United States:

> We do not know how many colored people of greater New York realize that April, 1917, marks an epoch for the Negro on the stage. Mrs. Emily [sic] Hapgood in presenting a company of colored players in three plays by Ridgely Torrence, the poet and playwright, has given the American Negro his first opportunity in serious, legitimate drama. Of course, colored people have made attempts in serious drama before this, but

only as amateurs or before restricted audiences. Never until now have they had the opportunity to appear as a part of the professional world before the regular theatre going public.[8]

Both white and black Americans praised the slight plays. Lester A. Walton, an editor of the *New York Age*, shared Johnson's estimation of the importance of the plays in ushering a new epoch in black theater. But he criticized the use of Negro dialect in the plays, especially that of a Dr. Williams, a character in *The Rider of Dreams*, who is college-educated. Torrence simply never thought of making a distinction between the language of characters in his "darky" plays. Walton reserved most of his praise for Mrs. Hapgood for her courage in producing the plays, for "doing something no other theatrical manager of standing would ever think of attempting."[9]

These three one-act plays established Torrence's reputation as an author. Eugene O'Neill, on the other hand, is generally recognized as the foremost playwright the United States has produced. He is credited with bringing the American theater into the mainstream of modern drama. Born in the theater as the son of James O'Neill, one of the most successful actors on the American stage in Shakespearean roles, particularly, he came to playwrighting and to a knowledge of Negroes from quite a different route from that Torrence followed. O'Neill knew the theater and theater people. Whereas Torrence thrashed about between writing poetry and poetic drama, seeking a worthy metier for his interest in playwrighting, O'Neill, after trying his hand at journalism, enrolled in George Pierce Baker's famous "English 4," a course at Harvard University aimed at providing young writers with an opportunity to produce plays and learn the craft of playwrighting. His association with like-minded young persons in that course and with the small avant-garde group in Greenwich Village brought him into contact with John Reed and Louise Bryant, who told him about the Provincetown Players that emerged from a group of artists on Cape Cod. One of his earliest efforts with the group there was a sketch called *The Thirst*, which had a role in it for a Negro. O'Neill played it himself. When the group and he returned to New York after the summer of 1916, during which time the colony engaged in writing, producing, and acting in plays among themselves on the Cape, O'Neill's *Bound East for Cardiff* became the opening bill at the Playwright's Theatre in Greenwich Village. Critics liked it. Within a few years, beginning in 1920, O'Neill had been praised as at least a promising playwright.

The Dreamy Kid, O'Neill's first fairly well-known play about Negroes, was produced by Ida Rauh, a member of the Mabel Dodge Salon, during the fourth season the Provincetown Players presented plays in New York. Legend holds that O'Neill heard the story of the play's plot from a

Joe Smith, who was the "boss" of an area in Greenwich Village known as "Cocaine Alley." Rauh secured the cast from a Harlem stock company. What O'Neill had observed firsthand or heard talked about in Joe Smith's bar, called the "Hell Hole," may very well have provided the germ for *The Emperor Jones* and *All God's Chillun Got Wings*. Brutus Jones, the "Emperor," O'Neill said at one time, was patterned after Adam Scott, a Negro deacon on Sunday and a bartender during the week, whom he had known when he worked as a newspaper reporter in New London, Connecticut. The plot reflects some historical outlines of the story of Henri Christophe, the Negro slave who made himself king of a section of Haiti in 1811 and ruled despotically until he became ill and, fearing for his life, shot himself in the head before he could be killed by his subjects. Quite possibly, some ideas for the controversial *All God's Chillun Got Wings* came directly from Joe Smith's interracial marriage. Smith's white wife, Miss Viola, was a "big blonde who blazed with supposedly hot diamonds."[10] Because O'Neill was an uncommonly close friend to Joe Smith and because he spent many days and nights sitting, talking, and drinking there, O'Neill's uses of Negro subject matter in the most successful of his early plays seem authentic. He exploited his relationships, not necessarily by consciously gathering material from them to be used later as plots of plays or as stock for characters, but he wrote often from the wealth of experience he gained from his association with urban blacks in the North. One need not analyze all of his plays about Negroes in order to show clearly that he does fit well into Harold Cruse's definition of those white playwrights who created a "cultural paternalism" in their works about Negroes for the American theater.

In his *The Confident Years: 1885-1915*, the American cultural historian Van Wyck Brooks titles his chapter on O'Neill "Eugene O'Neill: Harlem."[11] And he makes the seldom-mentioned observation that O'Neill's marked interest in Negro life was "symptomatic" at a time when the so-called Negro Renaissance was also beginning, a counterpart of the renascence of poetry and the renascence of the stage of which the Provincetown Players were so notably an emblem. He recalls also that *The Emperor Jones* was "the first all-Negro play in which Negro actors took all the parts."

Paul Green, the native North Carolinian who sought to create a theater based on the American folk drama about white and black rural people, held an abiding interest in portraying the tragedy and the comedy of black and white folk. He was, moreover, specifically interested in advancing a Negro theater. Montgomery Gregory, a professor of drama at Howard University, reported that when Kenneth McGowan, an editor of *Theatre Arts* magazine, asked him to name a one-act play that accurately depicts the life of the American Negro, he immediately named *No 'Count Boy*, which he called:

an excellent demonstration of a charming play wrought from the homely materials of the Southern Negro. Here is fidelity to the actual life of these people, yet an artist, not a reporter, has painted the picture. I am of the opinion that it is the most creditable drama of its type yet written with the possible exception of Ridgely Torrence's *The Rider of Dreams*. The four characters are immensely human, and for that reason, familiar, for we recognized in them qualities that are both universal and indigenous.[12]

Gregory considered the "Boy" in the play "a certain race-type, emotional, musical, garrulous, venturesome, trifling." Therefore, he is authentic. Moreover, Gregory compliments Green, who, in contributing this one-act play to the public, had joined Ridgely Torrence and Eugene O'Neill in having done for Negroes that which they "are too blind to do for ourselves." As was the case with *The Emperor Jones* for O'Neill, *In Abraham's Bosom* won national acclaim for Green. Published in 1926 and presented intermittently for three separate runs, adding up to approximately two hundred performances, this play was awarded the Pulitzer prize for drama in 1926. Black and white critics praised it as a continuation of the new direction that Torrence was said to have set for black subject matter and black performers in the commercial theater. James Weldon Johnson called *In Abraham's Bosom* "a beautiful though terrible play" that was "closer and truer to actual Negro life and probed deeper into it than any drama of the kind that had yet been produced."[13] Sterling Brown, then a young professor of English at Howard University, who was destined to become perhaps the most distinguished literary scholar and teacher among Afro-Americans, brushed aside complaints by some Negroes that works like *In Abraham's Bosom* are depressing or that they show that Negroes never win and that most ambitious efforts to improve themselves are futile. He praised the drama for showing "a man's heroic struggle against great odds, showing the finest virtue a man can show in the face of harsh realities—enduring courage." Brown saw in Green's play a truly significant turn away from the aristocratic concept of the stage Negro as the lowly clown. Conceiving the Negro as a tragic figure, he wrote, represents a "great advance in American literature." He was writing about the Promethean struggle the mulatto Abe makes to use the property his white father has given him as the site of a school for his black neighbors, who fail to share his enthusiasm for education and the aspiration for racial uplift that motivates him. Having lost the property and having become totally frustrated in his perhaps unwise but sincere effort to make education available to his people, Abe eventually murders his white half-brother and the Ku Klux Klan beats him to death. In his last moments of life, Abe calls on God to defend him,

expressing a pathetic appeal to the Christian religion he has been taught
by the American white strain in his heritage.

Frederick Koch placed Green's early works into the matrix of white
playwrights who made profitable use of black subject matter for their
drama when he wrote:

> Since Green won the Pulitzer Prize in 1927 for his epic trage-
> dy, *In Abraham's Bosom*, there has been remarkable develop-
> ment in the Negro theatre and the beginnings of an authentic
> Negro folk drama. After *Abraham* came Du Bose and Dorothy
> Heyward's *Porgy*, representing a whole neighborhood in Cat-
> fish Row, Charleston. As done by the New York Guild Thea-
> tre, this play proved to be a production of vivid, poetic quality.
> Then came *The Green Pastures* with its sensational run on
> Broadway and its triumphant tour of the country. And one of
> the significant events of the New York season last year was a
> Negro folk-play, written by a Negro, Hall Johnson, *Run Little
> Chillun*. It was hailed by critics with loud acclaim. The wheel
> had come full circle. A native Negro folk drama, written by a
> talented Negro playwright, had arrived.[14]

The movement Professor Koch detailed also illustrates how American
native drama found the vitality that gave it distinction.

Slowly and unsteadily, the Negro as a subject for the commercial
theater moved forward alongside the earliest movements toward a native
American drama. Pioneering geniuses in its development recognized
Negro life and folkways as potential sources of native idioms for which a
major contribution could be developed. Americans were fascinated at
the time with the accomplishments that William Butler Yeats, Lady
Augusta Gregory, and John Millington Synge had realized with their
Irish National Theatre. But the national situations were not sufficiently
congruent for American playwrights to follow precisely the Irish
example. The United States was a melting pot. Ireland was an insulated,
self-conscious nation. Its many coats, as exploited by Yeats and Sean
O'Casey, was an image for its political diversity. The melting pot that the
United States considered itself was little more than symbolic language
for a many-faceted people from many nationalities and folkways. Who
were Americans? Were they not also Europeans? Did they not relate to
the Stage Irishman metaphor in their concepts of entertainment on the
stage? Did they really consider the Negro an American? Could the soul
and heart of what makes drama for the stage issue from the black
American's struggles within himself and with his socioeconomic environment without embarrassing and, even more seriously, offending the
sensitivities of white Americans as potential producers and audiences for

a native drama about deprived people? Could those who had been thought of only as "entertainers" ever become actors in a serious drama, even about themselves? Yeats and his associates could write and produce plays in their Abbey Theatre about Irish folklore and infuse their people's history with half-mythical sagas about the leaders who fought the hated English and the labor leaders who fought the businessmen in the 1913 Lockout and the Easter Rebellion, and bring forth Irish War plays of Sean O'Casey, with their mixture of comedy and tragedy, that reflect human life in the midst of the national "troubles." The mean life of the Irish country could give rise to Synge's *The Playboy of the Western World* and *Riders to the Sea*. Irishness contained coherence and division, and tensions between the two could produce a vital national drama. People could riot in the theater over *Playboy* and O'Casey's *The Plough and the Stars*. But it was still Irish theater drawn from the prism of what it means to be Irish in Ireland. The best of what these playwrights wrote and how audiences reacted to their plays gave a unique character to an American drama that was struggling to be born from the World War I era to the eve of World War II. It passed through problem plays that troubled the conscience of the nation. And at the same time it reached down into its own roots to give status and cultural respectability to the black idiom and lifestyle that was prevalent in the nation, albeit it had been a source of embarrassment owing to the ravages of the institution of slavery and the bitter years of the Civil War and Reconstruction. The black idiom proved elastic enough to provide problem plays for the social conscious and to show that in the plain life of the black rural folk lies fresh, honest, dramatic material for the "heroics" that Yeats said appears in the folk. Without these playwrights and their turning their talents on the black American as a fit subject for the theater far beyond buffoonery, the American drama might still remain in limbo, waiting for its birth on the stage.

NOTES

1. I am indebted to Genevieve Fabre for this distinction. See *Drumbeats, Masks and Metaphors: Contemporary Afro-American Theatre* (Cambridge, Mass.: Harvard University Press, 1983), p. 1.

2. Harold Cruse, *The Crisis of the Negro Intellectual: From Its Origins to the Present* (New York: William Morris & Co., 1967), pp. 36-37.

3. See Fannin S. Belcher, Jr., "The Place of the Negro in the Evolution of the American Theatre, 1769-1940" (Ph.D. dissertation, Yale University, 1945). This encyclopedic work is the most comprehensive source on its subject. Also see Doris E. Abramson, *Negro Playwrights in the American Theatre 1925-1959* (New York: Columbia University Press, 1967); Frederick W. Bond, *The Negro and the Drama* (Washington, D.C.: Associated Publishers, 1940); James Weldon Johnson, *Black Manhattan* (New York: Atheneum, 1969); and Loften Mitchell, *Black*

Drama: The Story of the American Negro in the Theatre (New York: Hawthorn Books, 1967).

4. See Theodore Kornweibel, Jr., "Theophilus Lewis and the Theater of the Harlem Renaissance," in Arna Bontemps, *The Harlem Renaissance Remembered* (New York: Dodd, Mead & Co., 1972), pp. 171-89.

5. Mabel Dodge (Luhan), *Movers and Shakers: Intimate Memoirs*, 3 vols. (New York: Harcourt, Brace, 1936), 3:2.

6. Letter from Ridgely Torrence to W.E.B. Du Bois, dated 20 February 1913, in which Torrence thanks Du Bois for "bringing me in touch with Mr. Johnson through whom I may be able to secure a good actress" in *The Papers of W.E.B. Du Bois*, reel 4, frame 548 (New York: Microfilming Corporation of America, 1981). The reference to the letter that Torrence wrote to his mother appears in John M. Clum, *Ridgely Torrence* (New York: Twayne Publishers, 1972), p. 109.

7. Ibid.

8. James Weldon Johnson. "The Negro and His Drama," *New York Age*, 19 April 1917, sec. 2, p. 4.

9. Lester A. Walton, "Negro Actors Make Debut in Drama at the Garden Theatre," *New York Age*, 12 April 1917, sec. 2, p. 4.

10. See Arthur Gelb and Barbara Gelb, *O'Neill* (New York: Harper & Row, 1962), pp. 347, 381, 439, 657, for discussions of Eugene O'Neill's relationship with Joe Smith and possible sources of plot material and character outlines for plays.

11. Van Wyck Brooks, *The Confident Years: 1895-1915* (New York: E. P. Dutton, 1952), pp. 539-53.

12. Montgomery Gregory, "The No 'Count Boy" Review, *Opportunity*, April 1925, pp. 121-22.

13. Frederick Koch, "The Negro Theatre Advancing," *Carolina Play Book*, 6 (December 1933):101.

14. Ibid.

3

MAKING OF
THE GREEN PASTURES

Fortunately, Marc Connelly recorded several times his own version of how he came to write the one play that brought him fame and fortune in the theater. It became, on the spot, a significant part of the canon of American drama for its day. Brooks Atkinson called it "the divine comedy of the modern theater." Alexander Wolcott wrote that it was "the finest achievement of the American theater in the hundred years during which there has been one worth considering."[1] After several years of living frugally in New York, working sometimes for the *Morning Telegraph*, writing occasional magazine articles, trying his hand at play-writing, and becoming familiar with the personalities of the theater in New York, Connelly collaborated with George Kaufman, drama critic of the *New York Times*, on half a dozen plays and musicals during the 1920s. *Duley* was the first one of such works of theirs that enjoyed any degree of financial success. Owing to his good fortune in this venture, Connelly was able to move from the two-room "warren" he shared with five or six other artists and writers and take an apartment in which he could also accommodate his mother, who had been widowed since Marc's childhood. His new resource base also allowed him to, as he said, "get to Europe fairly often." He became a *bon vivant* and a wit both in American communities in Paris and in New York at the Algonquin Roundtable, a group of artists who met regularly at the Algonquin Hotel for fellowship and discussion about their works and what was taking place in the world of art.

Writing *The Green Pastures*, Connelly often said, was pretty much by chance. The sequence of events that led to the making of the play began, as he wrote it, in a most casual manner:

> One day late in 1928 I was walking along Fifty-seventh Street when I ran into Rollin Kirby, the cartoonist, who was a friend of mine. "I've just read a book you ought to read," he said. I don't know whether he saw me considering it as a play or not, but I said what was it and he told me it was Roark Bradford's *Ol' Man Adam an' His Chillun*. It was a fanciful retelling of some of the stories in the first five books of the Bible. Bradford's technique was like the old-time preachers'. They'd set the stories in familiar terrain—Cain would flee to, say, Nod Parish, and the prodigal son's spree was in New Orleans. They were charming sketches. Well, I read it, and I began thinking of it in terms of theatre the moment I finished it.[2]

He considered the sketches a wonderful device for making an inquiry into man's spiritual hunger—something that was part of the classic pattern of theater. And he was reminded, as he read the work, that in its earlier day, when man exorcised in a religious rite, he had an altar right there in the middle of the theater, so to speak. For example, Aeschylus did little to change the physical circumstances of the satyr plays, and Euripides' *Bacchae* is little more than the coordination of the bacchic rites by a great dramatist. These were some of the bases on which Connelly reasoned that drama based on the Bradford sketches was part of what he called "the classic thing." He saw in the work man still trying, theatrically, to relate himself to the gods. He conceived right then of a religious play that would be expressed in terms of naive, childlike myth. He saw the possibility of writing and staging a play that would have for its theme the same one that runs through the whole of the Old Testament—man's search for the divine within himself. The play he contemplated would be a confirmation of man's finding the object of his quest.

Almost immediately upon having finished reading the Bradford book, Connelly telephoned Richard Walsh, one of the editors of Harper's, who had published the sketches, and asked about the author. Walsh told him that Bradford was a young journalist living in New Orleans who might be interested in basing a play on the work. Roark Bradford (born Roark Whitney Wickliffe Bradford) descended from the family of Governor William Bradford of Massachusetts, but he was closely related to the South. His ancestors moved to Virginia shortly after the Queen Anne Wars, and his grandfathers and their brothers fought in the Confederate Army. Bradford received a bachelor of law degree at the University of

California before entering World War I. When the armistice was signed, he was a first lieutenant in the coast artillery, although he remained in the military and carried out several assignments until his formal discharge in 1920. Moving then to Atlanta, Georgia, he worked for the *Atlanta Journal* for two years before beginning to edit a country daily newspaper in Louisiana. He worked briefly as copy reader, night city editor, and Sunday editor on the *New Orleans Times-Picayune*. When he turned from journalism to fiction and began to write short stories, his first published work in a magazine was "Child of God," which won the O. Henry Memorial Award for the best short story of 1927. He said his childhood experience gave him material for newspaper feature writing and his collection of sketches, *Ol' Man Adam an' His Chillun*, published in 1928. He followed it with similar works, including full-length novels, *This Side of Jordan* (1929) and *Ol' King David and the Philistine Boys* (1930). He contributed frequently to the *Saturday Evening Post, Collier's,* and other popular American periodicals.

Shortly after his first conversation with Harper's about the Bradford book, Connelly signed a contract for the dramatic rights to *Ol' Man Adam*. It was understood that his intention was not simply to string together and present a theatrical production of what Bradford had written as a collection of individual sketches. He wanted to use them and their manner of telling in a play that would have its own dimensions. And he planned to write what would be essentially a religious drama for which the sketches would form a loose framework. Connelly realized that he should make a trip to New Orleans to consult with Bradford and to tell him about his concept of a black, anthropomorphic, paternal God that he had decided would be the major voice and image of the play, moving through a great deal of the Old Testament stories. He had already decided on using a Sunday school scene as exposition. It would give the childlike, naive vision he conceived as the conduit for the play's action. Moving back in time to the Greek satyrs he believed to be the basis of all drama in Western civilization and expressing its Modern Age projection through rural, southern, American Negroes, Connelly thought he had found a project for his talent that would engage his time and his best efforts at writing a play and bringing it to the stage. He veered sharply from the use of Negro subject matter that Eugene O'Neill had placed in *The Dreamy Kid, The Emperor Jones,* and *All God's Chillun Got Wings,* and that Paul Green had used in his prizewinning *In Abraham's Bosom.* Their Negro themes particularized black frustration and aspiration and culminated, as Du Bois complained bitterly, with a Negro central character who either committed suicide or became mentally deranged. Even if he were not thinking about the dimensions of a native black drama that Du Bois and other black intellectuals envisioned on the Broadway stage, Connelly saw in the black American religious folk metaphor the potential for effective stage drama that was, at once, an interpretation of black Americans striving for what might be divine in their social and personal lives and the time-honored historical character of religious drama. Admitting candidly that he was not himself a religious person, even perhaps an agnostic, Connelly wanted to eschew any attempt to be funny for fun's sake in his play. He wanted to remain circumspect in his faithfulness to black religious fundamentalism as he understood it.

When he booked passage on the S.S. *Dixie*, a passenger and freight vessel sailing between New York and New Orleans, Connelly had fairly well developed the skeleton for the play. He had gone so far as to plan eight writing periods each day of the voyage. When he reached New Orleans, he had written more than half of the script. He and Bradford immediately took to each other. Bradford liked what Connelly had written and took the responsibility of guiding him around New Orleans for him to observe firsthand the churches and night spots in Negro neighborhoods. Bradford introduced Connelly to a Mrs. Edna Mae Hubbard, a black church pianist, who explained to him the variety of music sung in black churches. In his going to churches he also refined his knowledge about the Sunday school class he would write into the play. After he had gained what he considered sufficient material about the folk who would inhabit the stage of his drama, Connelly returned to New York to complete his writing in the summer of 1929. But no producer would accept *The Green Pastures*. Connelly wrote about his disappointment:

> Literally everybody turned it down. I don't know, I guess it was the idea of a black God that frightened them off. One producer said he liked it all right and would love to do it if only he could see how to, whatever he meant by that. One sent it back saying, "It's got lots of laughs in it." That really hurt. Anyhow, they turned it down, so I just put the thing on the shelf.[3]

It might have remained on the shelf had it not been for an incident that took place while Connelly was on a Mediterranean cruise later in the summer of 1929 as the guest of John and Alice Garrett. John had been the American ambassador to Italy. When some passengers on board the ship learned that Connelly had just finished a play, they invited him to read it. That was the first hearing *The Green Pastures* ever had. The reaction was heartening, Connelly reported. It also stimulated him to seek more diligently to find a producer when he returned to New York. Chapter four discusses the details of bringing the play to the stage and the unqualified success it enjoyed.

Quite appropriately, a discussion of the making of *The Green Pastures* requires detailed examination of the essential variations between

Bradford's and Connelly's writing. Moreover, critical comments about the relationship between the sketches and the stage play are in order.

The published version of the play contains a reproduction of the program of the first performance of *The Green Pastures* as presented at the Mansfield Theatre in New York City on Wednesday evening, February 26, 1930:

LAURENCE RIVERS presents

THE GREEN PASTURES

A FABLE

by

MARC CONNELLY

Production Design by Robert Edmond Jones

Music under the direction of Hall Johnson

Play staged by the Author

The Green Pastures was suggested by Roark Bradford's Southern Sketches, *Ol' Man Adam an' His Chillun*

As we shall see, the question of the degree of Connelly's debt to Bradford emerged often throughout the five years the play appeared on American stages. One way to discuss the making of *The Green Pastures*—its author's stated purposes and his dramatic method—is to contrast its tone and content with the book that "suggested" it and to include comments that critics made about the play in these terms.

The finished product was indeed "suggested by Roark Bradford's Southern Sketches," but *The Green Pastures* is Connelly's own creation as folk drama. Its dramatic ancestor is the medieval mystery play, in which works the common man, usually illiterate, dramatizes his faith for all to see. They were originally performed in the church. They gradually moved into the marketplace. Connelly's purpose envisioned a close bond between the traditional English medieval play and *The Green Pastures*. Both tell Bible stories and both represent similar stages of development in the lives of people. Both the medieval tradesman and the Southern plantation Negro—as Connelly believed he saw him—had a basic religion that was grounded in a deep personal relationship with God. *The Green Pastures*, however, is not a direct expression of a people's faith. It is a work of conscious art, created by an educated and sophisticated playwright who sought to understand that faith and the terms in which it was formulated. And it gives it voice on the stage. The image of "De Lawd" may be said to conform to a rational life of historical presentation. The Bible teaches that God created man in His own image. White people who considered God an actual person pictured him as a venerable old man with a white beard. He was a prototype of the wise patriarch of Judeo-Christian civilization. Christian artists, including Michelangelo, followed that tradition. On Connelly's terms, black Christians at the time in the development of their faith that he wanted to portray perceived God in terms of the wise man in their social group also. That corollary was the preacher. Such is the principal character in *The Green Pastures*. In this sense the play is folk drama in the simple terms of the definition.

The Green Pastures possesses the "charm" and "local color" of a folk play, indigenous to American culture. It brings a condescending smile to the sophisticated reader or theater audience. After all, it was written for them. But it also concentrates on the problem of good and evil, particularly as it relates to man's developing conception of God. Part 1 covers the stories of the Creation, Adam and Eve, Cain and Abel, and Noah and the Flood. Part 2 includes Moses and the Exodus from Egypt, the Fall of Babylon, and a scene concerning the destruction of the Temple of Jerusalem. Some scenes take place on earth and others in heaven. Negro spirituals link the scenes and make a bridge from one to another. Sometimes they comment on the dramatic action. The play cannot be considered a musical, however, although choral music is necessary for the theater the play presents. Although the opening of *The Green Pastures* on February 26, 1930, at New York City's Mansfield Theatre brought forth lively debate as to whether Bradford or Connelly should be credited with success for the play, one can see at a glance that the texts of the two works are radically different. Bradford wrote twenty-two separate stories in the Negro dialect that render a primitive, black American folk version of the folk stories making up the Hebrew Bible. They begin with "Eve and the Snake" and end with "Nigger Demus." The latter is a curious mixture of several Bible stories and contemporary problems about jim crow laws and voting. It is low comedy at best, but Connelly probably culled from it the humorous idea of a God who performed miracles all the time. In his sketch, "De Lawd" says to Nigger Demus, "When my disciples gits hongry, I jest passes a miracle on a rock and turns it into vittles." Connelly's heavenly fish fry might well have been suggested by this portion of Bradford's "Eve and the Snake" that explains that "De Lawd" preached all day every day except Saturday when there was no earth. Saturdays everybody went to the fish fry, "eatin' fish and b'iled custard and carryin' on, 'til all at once de Lawd swallowed some b'iled custard which didn't suit his tas'e." It needed a "bit more firmament," "De Lawd" declared. So he "r'ared back and passed a miracle to create more firmament." Then he had to "pass another miracle" to make a place for the firmament to drain off into. That was the earth. Bradford's first tale gets him through the Creation and the Adam and Eve story. Then he moves into "Populatin' the Earth," "Sin," "Steamboat Days," and "The Flood."

William Bolitho, writing in the *New York World* two weeks after the play opened, raised the question about Connelly's debt to Bradford. He explained that Bradford's is "a very good book," but that Connelly's play "is a masterpiece."[4] That, to him, was enough to say about the debt. The real potent, he wrote, belonged to Negro people more specifically than it did to either author or playwright, especially to black preachers and behind them, to the inspired prophets of the Hebrew people who "gave the glory to history, to the angels, and to God." Connelly practiced "the ancient alchemy of art" in writing his play, the critic wrote; "he changed good bread into a banquet for Kings." And Bolitho was the first to lay James Weldon Johnson's *God's Trombones*, first published in 1927 and reissued in 1929, alongside Connelly's play. "This remarkable work supplies the element which Bradford's (not Connelly's) representation of the Negro's Protestantism leaves out; that is his Christianity," he concluded. But he does not blame Bradford for the omission. For "not only is a question of delicacy involved, the socal taboo, which even non-Christians feel quite strongly," but also artistic taste would hardly permit Negro Old Testament and Negro New Testament to be put into the same box. Bradford gives a picture of the memory part of the Negro religion—its tenderly comical version of the Old Testament as Bolitho expressed it. Connelly improves on the portrayal by hinting at the sorrowful, comforting tragic heart of that folk realization. Johnson's poems express exclusively the Christian orientation in his preacher, who articulates the folk perception of the Judeo-Christian documents. Bolitho believes, however, that Connelly deserves the power and the glory of rendering black Christianity in dramatic presentation. He has gone far beyond the limits of what Bradford's sketches suggested. And in doing so, as the critic wrote, he succeeded in a task that Paul Claudel and William Butler Yeats had failed to accomplish twenty years earlier in trying to write mystery plays for their ethnic groups. Connelly had succeeded in presenting on the stage what the critic called "a Negro cosmogony," which no black playwright had been able to bring to the stage. *The Green Pastures* had been written by an artist who turned, not to the European, but to native Americans for the material for a miracle play—"the secrets of that strange, poor people who make you cry when they sing and laugh when they talk."

Further delineating the accomplishment that had been solely Connelly's and not even remotely related to Bradford's, Bolitho once more turned his keen discernment to telling what Connelly had done with his play:

His path first led straight through that incredibly narrow channel, the truly vulnerable spot in the heart. His heaven, that is, had made you laugh in a peculiar way—the way you laugh at a baby, or the walk of an elephant, or any other innocent yet venerable natural creation. It is prodigious to have conceived and executed that first scene in heaven, the walk of the angels, that celestial strut; to have understood Gabriel and known what his mysterious horn looks like; to have known that the everlasting banquet is a fish fry (Heine's intuition of the Talmudic menu was leviathan cooked with garlic); to have summed the Apocalypse into that magnificent line, "Gangway for the Lord!"[5]

John Mason Brown had complained about Connelly's choice of scenes from Bradford's, judging that he had not been logical in his construction, that he had left out some of the best of them, and that he failed to justify most of them. And he was the first of the critics to admit that the drama gained because of Richard B. Harrison's admirable acting, without which, Brown felt, the play would have been a failure because of its slow action and uncertainties in its construction and production. Bolitho noticed not so much the acting of Harrison as an isolated factor, although he certainly praised it. Seeing the play as an organic whole, though, he wrote:

In the role of the Ancient of Days Himself are both the height of the peril and the apex of the achievement. How does Mr. Connelly know so utterly that the withdrawn shape of their [rural Negroes'] anthropomorphism was just this subtle balance of attributes: an octoroon, not a full-blooded Negro, with a frock coat, an office? By what working of infallible intuition do we know without the possibility of doubt that he is right?[6]

Jonathan Daniels, writing one of the early reviews in the *Saturday Review of Literature*, thought any comparison between Bradford's work and Connelly's would be unfair. Yet comparisons would be made. One distinction, Daniels wrote, lay in Connelly's work as a playwright, together with the "elaborate details of direction and staging, the work of the actors, and the subtle interplay between audience and actor."[7] The differences between the two works were so substantial, Daniels claimed, that Bradford had assisted with *The Green Pastures* "only by paper and ink." Bradford had written, in his *Ol' Man Adam* and the works that followed, sketches that were composed chiefly of dialogues between a strangely altered Jewish God and strangely altered Jewish prophets, kings, and heroes. And these interchanges had contained fine, simple humor that was primarily fun making. All of them, under their biblical names, are familiar comic characters among the Negroes of the South. But Connelly adds to them what Daniels calls "an element of aspiration." In his simple presentation of the fundamental change of Hosea in Jewish theology from belief in a God of wrath to belief in a God of mercy, Connelly added "imagination and feeling to Mr. Bradford's keen surface observation of the ludicrous, with the result that he has made literature out of a very superior kind of vaudeville." It is, however, the conception of the character of God that marks the most fundamental difference between Bradford's God and Connelly's. Connelly's God has abandoned man because of his sin, but He cannot be happy in the face of prayers rising from the earth.

Daniels concludes that *The Green Pastures* rests on things more fundamental than Bradford's humor and Connelly's gentle imagination, for:

> It takes a vitality from the vitality of the Old Testament. Much of its appeal, too, lies not in the pathos of the Negroes but in an unconscious pathos of the whites. The Negro has translated the Bible and his theology into terms of his own life. The white men of Europe who have made the Christian world have never made Christianity a part of their lives. They have tried, instead, to reverse the process. The Englishman became, or attempted to become, an Old Testament Jew, whom he called Puritan, because he lacked the mass imagination to make God an Englishman. These Puritans have kept their religion in the metaphor of the Jew and the East. They have worshipped God but their religion has always been a foreign religion shaped in foreign customs and full of mysterious alien meanings. Among the Negroes, God has ceased to be a foreign god and has become an intimate, personal god who understands his people and whose people understand him. The whites of America, still worshipping an alien Eastern Deity whom they do not understand and who could never understand them, pour into Mansfield to see *The Green Pastures* to laugh and cry together at the simple Negroes who in their simplicity understand their god.[8]

Unlike Bradford's sketches, *The Green Pastures* dramatizes the development of the Jehovah of the Old Testament into the God of Mercy in the New Testament. It does so by making human even the wrath of the ancient God, making His creation of the world a comic incident—actually an accident brought on by God's own self-indulgence—that proved to be a mistake until the opportunity for the quality of mercy that even God never knew redeems both man and God. Thus, Connelly takes Bradford's incident of the "firmament" and moves it from a burlesque of a Negro God who abounds in malapropisms into a God whose image is rendered intelligible by a full company of black Americans. Mr. Deshee, the Sunday school teacher, explains the Bible to his young students in his own version. His simple faith is expressed in terms of the mysteries of the Bible. He simply does not know the answers to the questions some of the children in his class raise. It is in the Bible and that is good enough for him and should be good enough for them. Through this stage voice, Connelly is able to signal that his frame of reference for the play will be a simple one, that it will transcend debate and theological theories. The first scene—totally lacking in the Bradford sketches—gives unity to the play. The Bible stories that would have followed, had Mr. Deshee appeared throughout the drama, appear throughout the work. Connelly has exercised strategic choice of the ones he would include in his play in order to make his statement and to permit full theatrical impact. In choosing Genesis 5:3-8, 22, 27 and Genesis 1:1-2 as his "text" for *The Green Pastures*, Connelly is able, throughout the scenes that follow the first, to continue the consideration raised by the Sunday school class. What God looks like is an appropriate question for young, black, rural children and for the sophisticated theologian who wants to make Christianity real to his parishioners. In order to talk about what God looks like, one has to project a concept of God. And, given the setting of the play, that concept has to be personal and relevant enough to carry the perception of those seeking it to be a Negro man. Mr. Deshee tells the children he thinks God might look something like their pastor. Who else, besides the pastor of the congregation, might most closely resemble God in the eyes of the Sunday school children?

Marilyn M. Montgomery makes the seldom-mentioned observation that the heaven of part 1, scene 2 has antecedents in literary tradition.[9] The primeval history of the creation of the world as reflected in Christianity is the book of Genesis. Moreover, the expressionist playwright Gerhart Hauptmann, in the play *The Assumption of Hannele*, and the Hungarian Ferenc Molnár, in his *Liliom* (adapted, in part, by Oscar Hammerstein II for his musical *Carousel*), moved the setting of their plays from earth to heaven on the stage. Hauptmann's *Hannele* is the first play in the world theater to have a child as its heroine. The circumstances of the children in *The Green Pastures* and those in *Hannele* are widely different. Hauptmann's heroine is an illegitimate child, who, brought up in a pauper's home, was taken by Mattern, the mason and drunken ruffian whose cruelty killed the young girl's mother. In her attempt to escape from him, Hannele tries to drown herself. In delirium, life in heaven obtrudes on her a vision just before she dies—that heaven offers the things Hannele has missed on earth. She has plenty of food, a white robe, Cinderella slippers, and a mother's undying love. The picture is compounded of fairy tales and a child's naive notions of religion.[10] The circumstances are different between the plots of *Hannele* and *The Green Pastures*, but both present on the stage a child's vision of heaven. To that extent they are similar, especially as one continues to remember that Connelly places the whole concept of heaven and God into the purview of the children in Deshee's Sunday school class in the first scene of the play. Molnár's *Liliom* begins with a naturalistic setting and moves into a fantasy that is the only heaven the central character could have ever imagined. This time it is a celestial police court. There, the unregenerated Liliom is sentenced to sixteen years in the purgatorial fires, after which he is allowed a day to return to earth and try to atone for his crime of attempted burglary. On that day he brings to his daughter, Louise, a star he has stolen from heaven.

Neither of the plays discussed here was particularly successful in America in terms of box office appeal. Eva Le Galliene and Helen Westley played in the cast of *Liliom* when it opened in New York on April 20, 1921. When it was revived in 1932, Burgess Meredith was in the cast, as he was when it came to the stage again in 1940 with Ingrid Bergman. It would be specious to claim that Connelly was imitating Hauptmann or Molnár in writing *The Green Pastures*. One cannot overlook, however, the fact that he knew both plays and that staging a play that moved from Mr. Deshee's Sunday school class in rural Louisiana to heaven might have grown out of Hauptmann's and Molnár's experimental dramaturgy. In each case, too, we have the logical execution built on the theory that a character's vision of heaven is a natural following of that person's earthly life and views. With that concept Connelly could make the fish fry a community picnic with the boiled custard as the dessert. Surely a God based on the role of the preacher in the rural black church would be consistent with a kindly, folksy, miracle-loving ruler of his folk, who might be the authority symbol in a primitive religious cosmology. His heaven is a community of busy activity and loquacious angels. It is a utopia. Surely it suggests the surcease from sorrow that primitive folk accept in heaven. Its inelegance probably is one of the non-realities of the folk vision. On Connelly's stage, heaven is a peaceful place that transforms the lowly folk into angels and inhabitants of a heaven that is above and beyond earth. They want no memory of or concern about an earthly existence. Yet the angels are mundane in all of the good ways. They eat what those who created them in their own image eat, and talk like them, and frolic like them. Only now there is only good fun and good food and good relationships. There is no malice or doubt or cynicism. It is as if Connelly was fashioning a heaven after the Negro spiritual he must have heard that sings about the peace and joy "in that land where I'm bound."

The principal problem Connelly faced as a dramatist was how to get God on the stage. Bradford could keep his God in the narrow confines of fiction as a prose sketch. There God does not have to have an appearance, nor does he have to become a dramatic character. He is little more than a voice kibitzing with men in the days God walked the earth as a natural man. On the stage, though, God has to appear before the audience and to the other members of the cast. Connelly solved his problem by contriving the first fantasy scene in the play with God's entrance. Only an archangel would be appropriate to announce God. He is Gabriel, roughly equivalent to a head deacon in the church. He is second in command in heaven. Actually, Gabriel is not a biblical character with any distinction. It is merely a description of the angelic office. In the ordinary Christian and Jewish traditions, Gabriel is spoken of as one of the archangels. In Scripture he merely represents the angelic nature in its ministration of comfort and sympathy to man.[11] Nevertheless, Gabriel is one of the two highest-ranking angels in Judeo-Christian and Mohammedan religious lore. He is the angel of annunciation, resurrection, mercy, vengeance, death, and revelation. Apart from Michael, he is the only angel mentioned by name in the Old Testament. In Mohammedan lore, Gabriel is the spirit of truth. In Jewish legend, he deals death and destruction to the sinful cities of Sodom and Gomorrah. And according to the Talmud Sanhedrin 95b, he smote Sannacharib's host with "a sharpened scythe which had been ready since Creation."[12]

Connelly enlarges upon Bradford's causal character of Gabriel, who in *Ol' Man Adam* appears in the "Eve and That Snake" sketch, the first of the twenty-two. After "De Lawd" performed the miracle of creating the firmament and it "sloshed all over ev'rything so de angels and cherubs couldn't fly, and ev'rybody was standin' round, knee deep, shiverin' and chatterin' and squirmin' round," it was Gabriel who came up with the idea that another miracle would create a place for the firmament "to dreen off to." Then Bradford's God "r'ared back and passed a miracle and said, 'Let hit be de yearth to hold dis firmament.' " And there was the earth. Also Gabriel reminds God that somebody ought to go to earth and work the new land because it is not going to work itself. Because the angels are busy with their heavenly chores, God creates man. In this telescoping of time and action, Bradford gets the world and man created. Connelly uses his Gabriel in a dual role. He is the archangel who talks with God and walks with Him like two natural men, and he has the responsibility of blowing a horn that will signal the destruction of mankind; but he is also the one ally of God who is the angel of annunciation. That role makes him one of the significant characters in *The Green Pastures*. Patterned after the drawings of Gabriel rendered by Paul-Gustave Doré, the nineteenth-century illustrator, as Connelly suggests in the stage directions for the original play, Gabriel heralds the arrival of God on the stage. Brooks Atkinson, one drama critic who heaped praise on Connelly and *The Green Pastures* from the first night until it closed, called Gabriel's line, "Gangway! Gangway for de Lawd God Jehovah!" "the greatest entrance cue in modern drama." Another critic wrote that Connelly "summed the Apocalypse into that magnificent line." Still another remarked that up to the point at which Gabriel appears on stage with his announcement, the play has elicited only light laughter from audiences. After that, he wrote, "there came a great silence and better than that a rigidity."[13] Connelly and Bradford use the single verse in Genesis 1:6—"And God said, Let there be a firmament in the midst of the waters . . . "—and give it a wide range of literary possibilities. It is one of those words in the Bible that confuses the common folk, so they might interpret it as they choose. The use of it to mean boiled custard at a fish fry, however, is farfetched even for the theater.

But with this use and the stage action that accompanies it, Connelly is able to set the characteristics of the God of his play: that God is basically a magician, but He is also kind and benevolent. The genius of Connelly's play lies in his novel suggestion that creation of the earth was totally an accident and that God could not possibly know the consequences of His act. That image of God is foreign to the folk whose religion Connelly was trying to portray, but the image provides dramatic sequences that could lead to the more critical matter of folk sin and how it displeases God. Afro-American religious folklore does not encompass a God of precisely that nature. It holds that God is, indeed, omniscient and omnipotent, but merciful and totally paternalistic.

How that God relates to man on earth begins to unfold in part 1, scene 3. It begins with the traditional Adam and Eve story. The action follows the Bible rather closely—Genesis 2:7-22. But unlike Bradford, Connelly does not emphasize the introduction of sin into the world through Adam and Eve. He moves also from the Hebrew history of the Bible into parallels of life for Negroes in the South. Without any reference to the serpent so typically represented in adaptations of the Genesis legend, Connelly revels in telling about the creation of Eve as a helpmate for Adam and the beginning of the human family. He has no interest in the conventional occupation with the introduction of sin into this part of the Creation. Such a pattern allows the play to move into a series of circumstances in which man is the source of his own sins. The influence of Satan is hardly mentioned. As a stage strategy, Connelly brings Mr. Deshee and his Sunday school children back into the dramatic action as they consider the story of Cain and Abel. God speaks directly to Cain for the sin of killing his brother and, in a role somewhat confused as to whether it represents the earlier attributes of God or of the Southern sheriff, tells Cain to leave the county and settle down and raise a family in some other part of the earth. God threatens him with the chain gang. But the slowly developing concept of a God of mercy as well as one of justice begins to take form at this point. Cain is guilty of a sin that offends God and His creation. He is willing, however, to forgive the son of the man and woman He has created as the first to populate the earth. One sees here for the first time the theological concept that man has free will and that his sinning saddens God; that God is the judge and can do as He wishes with His creation, but that He takes a somewhat naive attitude toward man's ability to correct himself.

God learns from Cain about man, His creation, and what tempts man. For as Cain goes into the Land of Nod, east of Eden, his sin and Adam's fall become complex for God and man. Cain exercises his free will, but his actions—his choices—grieve God. Referring to the biblical Land of Nod as "Nod Parish" localizes the play, keeping it within the physical cosmos of rural Louisiana and within the ethereal imaginings of the lowly folk who are the characters. These transgressions allow Connelly to invent another of his precious touches that distinguish the play from Bradford's sketches as well as from any other representation of the deity. God has a small, modest office in heaven. At the risk of again violating the concept of luxury that their God possesses, according to the rural folk of the play, Connelly works into the action a unique role for Gabriel. He becomes the pre-Christian advocate man has before God. When Gabriel learns that God is sorrowfully displeased with the way man has lived on earth, he reminds God that man is praying to Him from earth, even if he is sinning and disappointing God. The richness of Christian lore assists Connelly in his use of Gabriel and God and their conversations about the Last Judgment. While Gabriel does remind God of man's prayers, he is, at the same time, standing ready to do his duty and blow the "trump of God." God begins to wonder whether He can make a mistake. In his role, he deviates from the folk belief that God is incapable of error. Having shown that the world was created by accident, Connelly has prepared his audience for the inevitable question about the limits of God.

Once Connelly had determined the image of God he wanted to portray in his play, the working out of the rest of the action fell into place. The sins men and women commit are particularized: dancing, violating the keeping of the Sabbath, dishonesty, adultery, bootlegging, incest, black magic, and lack of respect for the family as it was first conceived of by God when He created Adam and Eve. God vacillates between wrath and mercy. One homely incident sets the stage for the traditional Flood and destruction of the earth as told in the Old Testament. God is walking the earth like a natural man when He comes upon the preacher Noah, who has been going his way calling men to repent of their sins. That story, as it appears in the sixth chapter of Genesis, is fairly faithfully followed. Building the ark after God's specifications, bringing the chosen people into the building, and the two-by-two procession of the animals in order that they might repopulate the earth after the Flood occupy the remainder of part 1 of the play. Even in the midst of the preparations, men still sin. Human foibles of the good and evil among mankind—including the family of Noah—abound during the two scenes that present the preparations for the Flood and the final landing of the ark on dry land. The Mississippi River is the waterway that provides the realistic setting. Folkways in the area center around the occasional floods that take place from time to time on the river levee.

When the dove has been released, according to tradition, and returns with an olive branch and the promised rainbow appears in the sky, a new era of good feeling among mankind is evident. Gabriel appears again at this point. Unlike Bradford's rendition of the Flood in terms of the conventional excitement and the usual incidents, Connelly brings part 1 of *The Green Pastures* to a close with the new chance God has given man. Gabriel still has little faith in mankind, but God seems pleased with His new confidence in His creation. One gets the impression that Connelly's God is primarily concerned with proving to Himself that He has not made a mistake by creating man. When Noah renders his prayer of thanks for the preservation of the human race, God is deeply touched.

The principal voice in *The Green Pastures* is God's. The essential conflict lies in God's mind. Whether He has made a mistake in creating man and what He should do about the error is the cause that generates the dramatic action once the *agon* has been set. Ironically, human beings, understanding as they do critical elements of their own nature and their experiences, teach God the answer to His own dilemma. Ramifications of such a plot can be numerous and varied. One reading of the play might lead Americans to question whether the "gods" of the nation— those who have created the social and economic world—have made a mistake. And it raises the even more important question of what those makers of reality can and should do to create out of the present chaos a better world that would please them and those who suffer from what has been created.

In making his play, Connelly selected from Bradford's disconnected sketches certain images he wanted to use for his play, wrote some of his own creation, and fashioned an organic work of art that consciously discusses God's relationship to human beings. He has looked through the fantastic humors of Bradford's book and drawn from them—where he used them—folk and religious significance.

He turned the material from the intellectual enjoyment Bradford provided and the caricature that permeates his sketches into the vision of an artist. Brooks Atkinson wrote, in the heat of the discussion as to whether author or playwright could make the greater claim for the play:

> What Mr. Connelly has engendered out of his own imagination in the composition of the play is not incidental patchwork but the warp and woof of his fable. The Sunday school scenes

are his invention and they are not comic interludes but prel-
udes to the main theme. . . . All the scenes in the Lord's private office in heaven are Mr. Connelly's. They are not only
delicately written but they give *The Green Pastures* its significance as a Negro miracle play by showing the Lord on His
own celestial terms apart from the world's humanity.[14]

Moreover, as John Hutchens wrote in a major review of the play, "the
Bradford sketches were instinct with the poetry and child-like intimacy
with and love for a personal God." But, he continued, it was Connelly
who grasped "with dramatic and creative intuition that here was
material which in the theater, and by the theater's essential mediums,
was to be enlarged into an all-enveloping emotional experience."[15]

His imagination and artistry made the play. For Connelly had practically no close relationship with Negroes. He had not used them as
subjects or characters in any of his other plays. Curiously, he did
precisely what Benjamin Brawley had asked white authors to do if they
must write about blacks. He rebuked them for writing about what he
called their tendency to "embalm old types and work over outworn
ideas" in their fiction. The day of Uncle Remus, he declared, was over
and that for Uncle Tom as well. No one can legitimately assume that in
1929, Connelly was writing on the mode of the "New Negro" that was
the hallmark of black authors of the Harlem Renaissance period, which
was beginning to wane by the end of the decade of the 20s. But
Connelly's play does transcend the hostility or pathos that characterized
most American portrayals of Negroes in fiction or drama. It was not
quite what Brawley and Du Bois advocated, but it was an innovation.

The Green Pastures might be looked at as dividing the traditions of
images of the Negro in literature into halves. The first part of the play
might be assigned to the patronizing smile about the simpleminded
Negro that characterized the Plantation School of American letters. Part
2, however, gives *The Green Pastures* its universality, though it is expressed in terms of a Negro world and heaven. Although part 1 might
have brought the smiles, part 2 brought forth the tears Daniels wrote
about.

Part 1, scene 6 begins the dramatic nexus between Old Testament
Yahweh and the developing God of mercy, although Connelly's "Lawd"
is never frightfully vengeful. Gabriel's role figures prominently in the
metamorphosis. He is with God in the private office in heaven, furnished in lowly materials characteristic of the black South:

There is a battered roll-top desk. On the wall next to the
window is a framed religious oleograph with a calendar at-
tached to it underneath. . . . A hat rack is on the wall above

the door. There are two or three cheap chairs beside the window and beyond the door. In front of the desk is an old swivel armchair which creaks everytime God leans back in it. The desk is open and various papers are stuck in the pigeonholes.

Connelly explains in the stage directions that "the general atmosphere is that of the office of a Negro lawyer in a Louisiana town." As the lights go up, God takes a fresh cigar from a box on the desk and begins puffing it without bothering to light it. Gabriel, who until this point has always commented on God's mircles, says nothing this time. Bradford's image of God as a showoff who "rears back" and performs miracles at will begins to fade. God has given Gabriel the orders for the day. The archangel, once God turns His back, takes his trumpet from the hat rack and burnishes it with his robe. He wets his lips and puts the mouthpiece in his mouth. Without turning around, God admonishes him: "Now, watch yo'self, Gabriel." Gabriel says he just does that to keep the feel of the trumpet, suggesting that he intends to keep ready to announce the Last Judgment. God has already, in the previous scene, said He does not like the way things are going on earth, and the Choir has sung "You Better Mind." God explains the petty gripes angels are making. Some of them said the moon is beginning to melt because the sun is too hot. "It's goin' 'roun' 'cordin' to schedule, ain't it?" He asks. Seeking to end His conference with His deputy about maintenance in heaven, God asks whether there is anything else He ought to be reminded of, and Gabriel answers quietly, "De prayers, Lawd." Swinging around in His chair, puzzled, God asks, "De prayers?" and Gabriel answers, "From mankind. You know, down on de earth." Oh yes, God does remember now. He says He had almost forgotten about "poor little earth." He had not been there for three or four hundred years. Cain's slaying of Abel and the sins of his descendants had soured Him on His creation. Gabriel says, laughing, "You know you don' make mistakes, Lawd." To which God responds, soberly with introspective detachment, "So dey tell me." This is the introduction of the theory that God can make a mistake and the concept of process theology. "De Lawd" tells Gabriel He is going back to earth again and see how the humans are making out. He does not like the idea that He has made a mistake by creating men to inhabit the earth He made by accident, caused by the miracle of the firmament.

When He returns to earth, God finds young women singing the blues, violating the Sabbath, and committing adultery. The children of Cain grieve Him, even as they had done when He last visited the earth. The old morality has, indeed, disappeared from the earth. Only the birds, flowers, and children He created are going on about the way He intended. In a fit of anger, "De Lawd" decides He would rather have His earth peopled with a bunch of channel catfish than with mankind and sin. "I just cain't stan' sin!" He exclaims as He meets Noah, the country preacher, who is the one righteous man He finds on earth. The Noah scenes follow fairly closely the narrative in Genesis chapters 6, 7, and 8. Connelly's image is rendered in Negro images. He uses four scenes of the tightly knit plot to illustrate the sins that, according to people in Mr. Deshee's church, would offend God. Yet God believes man has inherent goodness that will make him fit to inhabit the earth. But He has to find a way to stop the sinning. Clearly, Noah's faithfulness becomes the basis for God's decision to continue His interest in mankind. That decision and His attempt to find a way for His divine plan to work become the theme of the rest of the drama.

The broad comedy of arguments in Noah's family as the members grow impatient from living for forty days and forty nights in the ark with pairs of every conceivable animal of the earth gives way as God appears on the deck of the ark. Two mountains can be seen in the distance. The ark has landed on dry ground. The deluge is over. Noah's prayer of thanksgiving—"Thank you, Lawd, thank you very much indeed. Amen" —and the "Amen chorus" of the Choir show rapprochement between God and man. God and Gabriel observe the new world, this time created on purpose. The old sinful one has been destroyed by God's wrath because of man's disobedience. God's limitation, though, comes back into the dialogue between God and Gabriel that closes part 1:

God: [*Looking at him suddenly*] Don' seem to set you up much.
Gabriel: Well, Lawd, you see—[*He hesitates.*] 'Tain't none of my business.
God: What?
Gabriel: I say, I don' know very much about it.
God: I know you don'. I jest wanted you to see it. [*A thought strikes him.*] Co'se, it ain' yo' business, Gabe. It's my business. 'Twas my idea. De whole thing was my idea. An' every bit of it's my business 'n nobody else's. De whole thing rests on my shoulders. I declare I guess *dat's* why I feel so solemn an' serious, at dis particklar time. You know *dis* thing's turned into quite a proposition.
Gabriel: [*Tenderly*] But, it's all right, Lawd, as you say, it's did.
God: Yes, suh, it's did. [*Sighs deeply. Looks slowly to the right and the left. Then softly*] I hope it's goin' to work out all right.
                                   CURTAIN

The *tour de force* that is totally Connelly's is the character Hezdrel, who is not in Bradford's sketches or in the Bible. This character becomes the agent through which Connelly's true theatrical genius and his deep understanding of religion, American style, are projected. Hezdrel's role violates the simple spirit of the play by moving into an essential tenet of Christianity—the dividing line between God of the Old Testament and God of the New Testament. And, although the issue executes well on the stage and elicited serious comment from the most active theologians and philosophers of the day, it does diminish the folk quality of the play. It is the everlasting question in theology that leads to the climax of *The Green Pastures*. Because the subject matter of the difference between Jehovah and Christ is suffering, one can deal with part 2's denouement on both religious and sociopolitical grounds.

Salem Tutt Whitney, who played Noah in *The Green Pastures*, wrote before the drama opened at the Mansfield that "many will consider Mr. Connelly's adaptation rather daring because for the first time within our knowledge he will have God impersonated on the stage." Bringing God to the stage in the person of one who walked the Mississippi delta was, to Whitney, no more daring than "the role played by our ministers of the gospel as they stand in their pulpits every Sunday and preach to their congregations." They are then representing God.[16] The book of the play will entertain, bewilder, and fascinate, Whitney predicted, and he continued:

> Mr. Connelly assures us that there is no intention of burlesque or ridicule, that he has the highest regard for the unquestioning faith and pure-hearted religion of the simple delta folk. He thinks the world would be a much better place in which to live if it took Christianity as seriously and practiced it as faithfully and wholeheartedly as these delta folk he learned to know and to respect.[17]

The truth is, Connelly knew little about Southern Negroes, rural or urban. As we have seen, he went to Louisiana to talk with Roark Bradford about making a stage adaptation of *Ol' Man Adam an' His Chillun*. The book was published in 1928. According to his memoirs, Connelly first read the book in the fall of that year. Within a few days after having read it, he wrote, Connelly signed a contract with Harper's for the dramatic rights to the Bradford sketches. A year later the play had been completed, a producer had been found, and *The Green Pastures* was in rehearsal. It opened February 26, 1930. Connelly had not been South before he went to New Orleans to meet Bradford. His knowledge about the people in his play was limited. He gained some of it in Louisiana as he worked on the play. The scenes in God's office, the nightclubs, and the court of Pharaoh followed the extravagant stereotypes of the Amos and Andy vintage of the 1920s and 1930s. Part 2, scene 3, the throne room of Pharaoh, "suggests a Negro lodgeroom." The parade banners leaning against the plain board walls read: "Sublime Order of Princes of the House of Pharaoh," "Mystic Brothers of the Egyptian House Guard," "Supreme Magicians and Wizards of the Universe." They closely resemble Amos and Andy's lodge hall office of the Mystic Knights of the Sea. And God's office, patterned after the office of a rural Southern black lawyer, as the stage directions read, mimics Lawyer Calhoun's of Amos and Andy. One would be hard pressed to find a rural, black lawyer in Louisiana in the 1920s. The sashes and banners with gold fringes and tassels might well have been seen in the old funeral marches in New Orleans that Bradford might have introduced to Connelly. Whether they are authentic is not the question here. But it is remarkable to note that the wizardry of the Court of Pharaoh in the Old Testament is not essentially different from the Negro lodge hall room Connelly places in the play. Magic and wizardry and color and pomp characterize both. And both are more show than substance with respect to what is important in the world. This scene offended many Negroes. Theophilus Lewis, the insightful black drama critic, complained about it bitterly. Twenty years after his initial impression appeared in his weekly column in the *New York Amsterdam News*, Lewis recanted his earlier criticism that Connelly's main purpose in making *The Green Pastures* was to ridicule the Old Testament stories by presenting them through the eyes of Negroes. He had thought they were intended to show Negroes as clowns even when they worshiped God. But he came to consider these scenes of bawdry and revelry in the context of reverence that were intended to suggest God's inherent patience with His wayward world.[18]

Connelly uses the Pharaoh scenes to move forward his biblical story, and he chooses for his properties and language the characteristics of the cast of the play. He compresses the ten plagues that appear in Exodus, chapter 5, into three in *The Green Pastures*. In them, God is still vengeful and a showoff. His representative, Moses, who is pleading for deliverance of the enslaved Israelites, becomes incensed when Pharaoh says he can outtrick God and Moses. The wicked ruler has to learn that he is no match for God. For that purpose Moses threatens to perform his crowning trick. Moses can strike down the oldest boy in every household in Egypt. "Listen, I'm Pharaoh. I do de strikin' down yere," Pharaoh retorts. Once more Moses asks the ruler to set his people free. Failing to get his request granted, Moses calls on God and his brother Aaron to perform the final "trick." And to the accompaniment of thunderclaps, darkness, and screams, the young men on the stage fall to the ground or into the arms of their horrified elders. Four men enter bearing the stricken body of King Pharaoh's own son. Only then does the king relent. God does not appear on the stage in the scene; therefore, His dignity is preserved. Moses' parting admonition is instructive: "I'm sorry, Pharaoh, but you cain't fight de Lawd." God has not walked the earth as a natural man in the scene, but His human agent has helped to restore the proper order between the deity and man on earth. He has performed His role as the Lord of Hosts, still an early concept of God in His relationship to man. And the action has set aside two nations of mankind —the Israelites and the Egyptians.

Although Connelly chose not to dramatize the other most familiar legends of emancipation—the parting of the Red Sea and the passing of the commandments from God's hands into Moses'—the audience is expected to place those parts of the biblical course into context. The drama moves from Pharaoh's court to the Exodus. That is the principal spectacle of the drama. Its theatricality allows Connelly to show off the technical devices he and Jones had devised for the play. The tension of the scene comes in concern about the aging and tiring Moses and the significant movement in the development of the Hebrew religion from the single-minded vengeance of God into a deity who rewards men for their service to God's cause, even when they have fallen short of divine expectation.

Scene 4, the Exodus, demonstrates God's eternal patience and His power over all of the forces of darkness. The stage directions express the grandeur of the scene that is both a *tour de force* in theater and a significant segment of the theme of God's everlasting search for reconciliation with man. The full text of the directions seems appropriate here:

> The children of Israel are marching on the treadmill and now singing fortissimo. They are of all ages and most of them are ragged. The men have packs on their shoulders, one or two have hand carts. The line stretches across the stage. It is nearing twilight, and the faces of the assemblage are illuminated by the rays of the afternoon sun. The upper treadmill carries a gradually rising and falling middle distance past the marchers. The foot of a mountain appears; a trumpet call is heard as the foot of the mountain reaches stage center. The marchers halt. The picture now shows the mountain running up out of sight off right. The singing stops.

A babel of "What's the matter?"—"Why do we stop?"—"What's happened?"—"What's goin' on?" rises from the throng, and the answer comes in a murmur: "It's Moses." And as their leader enters on the arm of his brother Aaron, the audience sees him now as an old and tired man. He walks slowly, seats himself on the rock at the foot of the mountain, and the dialogue between them relates that part of the story concerning God's covenant with Moses that he would lead the Israelites to the Promised Land. In his infirmity, added to by his failing eyesight, Moses speaks the words to Aaron that remind the audience of the biblical story. He says God promised him he could lead his people to the Jordan and that he would *see* the Promised Land but could not enter it because he had broken the laws back in the desert.

His vision of the Promised Land becomes a reality as Joshua, the new young leader, enters and tells Moses that the scouts have returned and reported that, indeed, the river Jordan lies just ahead, and beyond, "the pretty land on the other side." Only the city of Jericho lies in the path of the Exodus marchers. Moses makes the battle plan for taking it and assures the young leader that the Lord will take charge, "jest as he's took charge ev'y time I've led you against a city. He ain't never failed, has he?" he asks. And then he prays, as all of the Israelites bow with him:

> Oh, Lawd, I'm turnin' over our brave young men to you, caize I know you don' want me to lead 'em any further. [*Rises*] Jest like you said, I've got to de Jordan but I cain't git over it. An' yere dey goin' now to take de city of Jericho. In a little while dey'll be marchin' 'roun' it. An' would you please be so good as to tell 'em what to do? Amen.[19]

Giving the signal to march and ordering the soldiers to take care of the ark of the covenant, Moses bids Aaron good-bye. Here God returns to earth to remind Moses that although the old leader cannot go into the Promised Land, he can have a reward of a different kind. Because he has been a good man, God tells him, he has a special place among men. He has angered Him once—indeed—and at that time God was a God of wrath. That same God, though, is helping Moses up the hill to see the land "a million times nicer dan de Land of Canaan" that God gives him as a reward for his faithfulness. That faith is also what is helping the young soldiers take the city of Jericho, as the grand Choir sings the joyous spiritual, "Joshua Fit de Battle of Jericho." Moses transcends the earth, and his human frame blends in with the personage of God, presumably as the two of them proceed toward heaven.

In the midst of this surrealism and high drama of the depiction of the apotheosis of Moses, Mr. Deshee can be heard telling his Sunday school class: "But even dat scheme didn't work. Caize after dey got into the Land of Canaan dey went to de dogs again. And dey went into bondage again." His narration bridges the scene of the Exodus into the wickedness in the city of Babylon.

Connelly's Babylon represents the ultimate transgression of the Israelites against God's law. It is the playwright's own creation, in no way suggested by any portion of Bradford's sketches. It is the nexus between the God of wrath and the emerging God of mercy who comes to understand man—His own creation—and what has happened to man in his development. Man's disobedience is conceived in the form of the nightclub scene that, in the point of view of the drama, is the way Mr. Deshee's world might envision ancient Babylon. Some critics have complained that the scene resembles a Harlem nightclub more than it does a cabaret in Louisiana. That criticism is valid. But it does not diminish the effect of the point of view of the drama. For rural, Southern black folk viewed the sins of their own cities and those of the North in terms of wayward behavior. James Weldon Johnson, in his "Prodigal Son," one of the sermon poems in *God's Trombones*, refers to a mythical Babylon. Johnson's preacher admonishes his congregation to avoid that lifestyle that one finds in such settings. One familiar with the black culture could hardly avoid knowing that the content of Connelly's Babylon scene is consonant with the black preacher's visions of wickedness. Connelly probably took his models as he fashioned this scene from his own knowledge of Harlem nightclubs. Sophisticated New Yorkers visited Harlem often to patronize the nightclubs. In fact, the most successful of these establishments catered almost exclusively to whites. Bradford had shown Connelly the "barrelhouses" of New Orleans. They were far less resplendent than the scenes in *The Green Pastures*, but they remain compatible with the point of view of the dramatist.

More importantly, it furthers the narrative of the development of the Hebrew concept of God. And in this purpose it parallels the Scriptures closely enough. Showing the extravagant violation of their covenant with God that was rampant among the Hebrews, Connelly gives his own rendition of the integration of the Jews into the moral pollution they found in Babylon. The nightclub scenes provide him with the dramatization of that decline. The confrontation between God's representatives and the Babylonians begins with the entry of the High Priest into the company of the King of Babylon. In the midst of the revels, "the door at the left opens suddenly, and the Prophet, a patriarchal, rugged figure, enters." By simply calling him "Prophet," Connelly follows the historic mode of one who speaks for God. He follows the pattern of the character of Noah earlier in the play and of Moses at the court of Pharaoh. He comes, in the manner of the biblical prophets, to denounce the sinful ways of men. He takes up the responsibility of the High Priest, who, if he were carrying out his role, would be denouncing sin. Instead, he has allied himself with the King of Babylon. When the Prophet gets the attention of the crowd, which, at the request of the King of Babylon, becomes quiet to hear what the strange-looking Prophet has to say, the messenger from God cries out: "Listen to me, King of Babylon! I've been sent yere by de Lawd God Jehovah. Don't you dare lay a hand on de Prophet!" He appeals to the children of Israel, who, he says, have given themselves over to the evil ways of their oppressors; who are wallowing like hogs in sin. The wrath of God will not be held back much longer. His own people must repent of their sins before Jehovah casts "down de same fire dat burned up Sodom and Gomorrah."

Angered by the Prophet's denunciation of them and their sinful ways, the King orders the intruder shot. There is a sound of a shot and the Prophet falls. As he does, he exclaims, "Smite 'em down, Lawd, like you said. Dey ain't a decent person left in de whole world." The sobered High Priest says to the King that perhaps he should not have shot the Prophet. The King feels secure. Babylon is protected by its own gods, he explains. Further, he offers the High Priest of the Israelites "a couple hund'ed pieces of silver" to arrange to persuade his god to keep his hands off Babylon. In his greater sin of betraying Jehovah, the High Priest prays weakly, "Oh Lawd, please forgive my po' frien' de King o' Babylon. He didn't know what he was doin' an'—" He is interrupted by a clap of thunder and darkness. When the lights go on again, God is standing in the center of the stage. He renders His voice of renunciation of mankind in a voice of doom:

> Dat's about enough. I's stood all I kin from you. I tried to make dis a good earth. I helped Adam, I helped Noah, I helped Moses, an' I helped David. What's de grain dat grew out of de seed? Sin! Nothin' but sin throughout de whole world. I've given you ev'y chance. I sent you warriors and prophets. I've given you laws and commandments, an' you betrayed my trust. Ev'ything I've given you, you've defiled. Ev'y time I've fo'given you, you've mocked me. An' now de High Priest of Israel tries to trifle wid my name. Listen, you chillun of darkness, yo' Lawd is tired. I'm tired of de struggle to make you worthy of de breath I gave you. I put you in bondage ag'in to cure you an' yo' worse dan you was amongst de flesh pots of Egypt. So I renounce you. Listen to the words of yo' lawd God Jehovah, for dey is de last words yo' ever hear from me. I repent of dese people dat I made and I will deliver dem no more.[20]

This scene brings to a striking climax the characterization of the Hebrew Yahweh. In this stage of the development of the deity, the Jews had accepted a national god. He was regarded as not the only god, but merely the most powerful one, as is evidenced by the return of Connelly's God to earth to denounce mankind. Babylon's gods cannot redeem mankind, nor is there any discussion about that possibility. Clearly, Yahweh, at this stage, is also a "jealous god" who does not tolerate rivals. He was not omniscient, however. He made mistakes and regretted them. He was petulant, vengeful, and, at times, bloodthirsty. With this final speech of the scene, Connelly whets the curiosity of his audience. How will the play end? What will God do now that He has totally renounced man, his favorite creation? Will the Israelites merely turn to another god, and thereby move away from their developing concept of monotheism?

Answers to these and other questions come in the final scene of the drama. Also, the response poses the most critical demand on the person playing the role of "De Lawd." Now comes the fusion of some loose aspects of the Old Testament and the keen genius of Connelly's dramatic vision. The God of wrath—He of the Old Testament and the Ten Commandments, demanding nothing less than complete obedience to His expectations of the man He has made—now becomes the champion of the poor and oppressed, the guarantor of freedom.

Not content to rest the implications of the denouement of his drama on the Hosea known to Bible scholars, Connelly devised the final scene as the crowning glory of *The Green Pastures*. He makes his own private apocrypha. Richard Watts, Jr., called that final scene the one point at which the playwright "loses his objective viewpoint; when you suspect he is stepping out of character and showing you something, not as it appears to the old Negro preacher, but as the more sophisticated playwright has fabricated it."[21] In that apocrypha, Connelly creates the character Hezdrel, whose name sounds like a biblical character but who is not one. Watts calls him Connelly's Judas Maccabaeus, who debates with the Lord. Hezdrel is also the same person who played the character of Adam early in the drama. That duplication is purposeful. He stands in the same position Adam held when first discovered, Connelly explains in the stage directions. But now he holds a sword in his right hand and a sling in his left. He is the new Adam. Connelly felt compelled to create Hezdrel, for no other character or combination of symbols could carry the purpose needed at this point in the drama.

The scene opens with Hezdrel standing among several prostrate bodies of his fellow soldiers. Pistol and cannon shots ring out and a trumpet sounds. Six young men enter in command of a corporal. They are armed. Hezdrel is in command of the fighting force. These are the men fighting to retake Jerusalem. Presumably, the setting of this struggle is the siege of Jerusalem in 733 B.C. According to legend, in that battle, the plague-driven Assyrian hosts, fighting under the direction of Sennacherib, brought forth Isaiah, King Hezekiah's chief counsel. From that crucial battle for Jerusalem, the late Old Testament accounts held that the Hebrews came to know they had only to look to their own moral conduct and to justice and compassion in order to find favor in Yahweh's eyes. Isaiah's prophecy as God's representative contained many injunctions to his people. One major tenet of his was for them to put away evil and relieve the oppressed.

Connelly projects this part of the history of the development of Hebraism on the way toward one God and a refinement of the old God of wrath by compressing all of these years of activities into the one scene with Hezdrel as the operative symbol and the speaking character. His staunch defense of the Temple at Jerusalem brings God back to earth in the heat of the battle, this time not to perform a miracle as in the old days. He comes in disguise, as He had done to Noah in the Genesis, but Hezdrel does not recognize Him. When He asks whether Hezdrel is afraid, the young warrior ridicules Him. "Look yere, who is you, a spy in my brain?" he asks. "How is it you is so brave?" "De Lawd" asks, pushing further for understanding of this new breed of man on earth. "Caize we got faith, dat's why!" Hezdrel replies. "(Faith) in our dear Lawd God," he further explains. "But God say he abandoned ev' one down yere," God reminds him. "Who say dat? Who dare say dat of de Lawd God of Hosea?" This conversation reveals the new concept of God. The *fait accompli* of the development comes in the exchange between Hezdrel and God that follows:

God: De God of Hosea?
Hezdrel: You heard me. Look yere, you *is* a spy in my brain!
God: No, I ain't, Hezdrel. I'm jest puzzled. You ought to know dat.
Hezdrel: How come you so puzzled 'bout de God of Hosea?
God: I don' know. Maybe I jest don' hear things. You see, I live 'way back in de hills.
Hezdrel: What you wanter find out?
God: Ain't de God of Hosea de same Jehovah dat was de God of Moses?
Hezdrel: [*Contemptuously.*] No. Dat ol' God of wrath and vengeance? We have de God dat Hosea preached to us. He's de one God.
God: Who he?
Hezdrel: [*Reverently.*] De God of mercy.
God: Hezdrel, don' you think dey must be the same God?
Hezdrel: I don' know. I ain't bothered to think much about it. Maybe dey is. Maybe our God is de same ol' God. I guess we jest got tired of his appearance dat ol' way.[22]

As their conversation continues—ironically one in which God learns about the properties of God the Hebrew people have now fashioned for themselves in their own times—Hezdrel says that the old God who walked the earth in the shape of man lived with man so that all He saw was the sins in man. Hosea taught, he said, that their God was no longer fearsome. And how did Hosea learn that? The only way he could find out. The way Hezdrel found out. The only way anyone finds out—through suffering. That unshakable faith motivated Hezdrel and his men to defend the Temple with their lives. And what if they are killed by Herod,

God asks. Hezdrel has a ready answer. That God of Hosea's will be waiting for each of them. As the Lord withdraws from His conversation with Hezdrel He thanks Hezdrel for telling Him so much. "You see I been so far away, I guess I was jest way behin' de times," he says to Himself as well as to the young warrior.

This scene of recognition has been called by some critics the most beautiful and eloquent rendition of the transition from the vengeful deity of the Old Testament to the merciful God of the New. And it is totally Connelly's creation. Nothing in *Ol' Man Adam an' His Chillun* comes near to the sensitivity or the historicity of this scene.

The final scene of *The Green Pastures* returns to heaven. The setting is the same as the first. God is seated in an armchair near the center of the stage, the Choir is still singing the "March On" that it broke into singing during the battle scene with Hezdrel's warriors. The surface action comes full circle. Gabriel goes to the table, accepts a cup of custard, and chats with the angels briefly. Then, he approaches the "Lawd" with: "You look awful pensive, Lawd. You been sittin' yere, lookin' dis way, an awful long time. Is it somethin' serious, Lawd?" "Very serious, Gabriel," the Lord answers. Gabriel asks whether it is time for him to blow his trumpet, sounding the Day of Judgment. "Not yet, Gabriel. I'm just thinkin'. 'Bout somethin' de boy tol' me. Somethin' 'bout Hosea, and himself. How dey foun' somethin'." "What, Lawd?" Gabriel asks. "Mercy. [*A pause.*] Through sufferin'," the Lord says. "I'm tryin' to find it, too. It's awful impo'tant. It's awful impo'tant to all de people on my earth." And then, in deep bewilderment: "Did he mean dat even God must suffer?" And the scene and final curtain come as God continues to look out over the audience from His armchair in the center of the stage. A look of surprise comes over His face. He sighs. And in the distance a voice cries:

> Oh, look at him! Oh, look, dey gon' to make him carry it up dat high hill! Dey gon' to nail him to it! Oh, dat's a terrible burden for one man to carry![23]

God rises and murmurs "Yes!" in recognition of what is being described by the voice and in acceptance of the new intelligence He now has gained. As He smiles, all the heavenly host break forth in singing "Hallelujah, King Jesus."

Christian doctrine is presented on stage succinctly and from several approaches. God cannot desert the world He created, is one. Another is that God actually came to earth in the person of Jesus of Nazareth, and that He could redeem mankind only by partaking in the sorrows man knew. That suffering causes anyone—even God—to find mercy rather than strict justice. The Green Pastures will not mean the Promised Land

to which Moses led the Israelites, nor that which God prepared for
Moses, despite his transgressions; it is the state of being arrived at
through suffering and redemptive love. To that extent, *The Green
Pastures* is indeed a modern miracle play. And expressed in the simple
folk language and perception of Mr. Deshee's world, it is acceptable for
the stage, even if the characters are Negroes. Perhaps accepted *because*
they are. Choosing them as his medium gave Connelly the opportunity to
make a social comment with double entendre. He could speak eloquent-
ly of the need a nation had for a religion that was expansive and as
meaningful in the current day as Hezdrel's was to him. In a wider sense,
and in an approach Connelly probably would not have been able to
stage, Negroes would have been as familiar with suffering as the Israelites. He would, then, have followed the lead of the many black authors
of the Harlem Renaissance, referred to in an earlier chapter, who used
the language and symbols of suffering and the crucifixion to express and
amplify their social condition in a highly racially segregated world.

Suffering, though, becomes the heart of the drama, notwithstanding its
broad humor. Placing it at the climax of the development of Hebraism
lends validity to the play, for experience with suffering is both a
common lot of humanity and a part of the concept of God. Judging it
from a religious point of view, one is reminded that the Old Testament
considers the deeper cause of suffering to be any disturbance of the relationship between God and man through sin, and the anger of God
thereby incurred. It always implies temptation, and even the devout
man turns against God for a time and rebels under it. The illustrations
are copious in the Old Testament. Perhaps the best known is the story of
Job. Men who suffer make bitter reproaches against God with the leading questions: "Why?" "How long?" But, in the final analysis, suffering
breaks down resistance against God so that the sinner and rebel is
brought to reflect on his transgressions and to repent. It is precisely in
the hour of bitterest suffering that the longing for union with God makes
itself felt. The wrath of God brings suffering on man in the view of the
Old Testament, but one has to remember that God is still moved to compassion by man's suffering so that He forgives and comes to man's aid.
God richly rewards those who are devoted to Him, especially when they
are faithful in enduring suffering. The Old Testament teaches that
suffering is intended to compel a man to decide which position he will
take, for or against God. It is intended to draw him out of his self-
confidence, to remind him of his fault against God, and to introduce the
process of healing needed after sin. It is often a means of chastisement
that comes from the hand of a loving father. That is essentially the lesson
of Hosea, as we have seen. The suffering of the devout is a means of
atonement that, through a process of substitution, absolves the guilt of
the sinner and of the whole people of which he is a part. Thus, the

sufferer mediates salvation to others. This is the essential creed of the image of the Suffering Christ of the New Testament. The vision of his suffering and its place in the long history of mankind's moral development comes through the expressionism of the Voice in the closing scene of *The Green Pastures*. Connelly has made it the cutting edge of his play. In doing so, he has transcended the light sketches of Bradford's *Ol' Man Adam* and the first impressions of the heavenly fish fry of the early scenes of *The Green Pastures*.

Perhaps one uncomfortable fascination in the apocrypha of this play lies in the divine *anagnorisis*. For while theatergoers are accustomed to finding recognition scenes in their best-known plays, this one is unique. King Lear's confession in his speech in acts 3 and 4, when he learns that his own daughters, Regan and Goneril, are ungrateful and cruel; or when Hamlet learns "there is special providence in the fall of a sparrow"; or Othello's tardy understanding of himself as "one that loved not wisely, but too well"; or yet Macbeth's coming to know his purpose has been frustrated and his deed has been ironic—all of these are standard tragic heroes in the theater whose painful knowledge toward the end of the experience that is the plot of these dramas is understandable to us. But who has thought of God as a tragic hero? Yet Connelly's God, in our final glimpse of Him, has experienced a revelation about His own nature. Even as has been the case with Lear, Othello, Macbeth, and Hamlet—all their kin in the canons of the drama—God's plan has been frustrated. To the shock of the audience, He sees and knows and accepts His limitations. Even as God, the dramatic event is novel. It is fascinating. It brings discomfort. The dramatized thought is a sharp contrast to the familiar —even in the colloquial and folksy God that country, Southern Negroes create from the Hebrew Scriptures. This concept troubles the apparent security of men. No wonder they tarried at the final curtain to see what else Connelly's God had to say about Reality.

The Green Pastures does not reflect correctly and faithfully black Americans at worship. It begins, however, at a point in time and in imagination—the point at which Mr. Deshee tries to teach his Sunday school class. That undertaking, itself, is a task that requires some admissions that no one knows the answers to some of the questions the young ask and flights of the imagination—spoken or not—taken by one who undertakes to teach and one who tries to understand the ways of God. Its profundity of thought about mankind in ancient times and in the America of the 1930s gave the play its popularity in the theater. The figure of God, on whom the entire question of the play's theology lies, rests with the acting ability of one who will play "De Lawd." For in incapable, pseudo-sophisticated, urbane hands it would be a worthless burelsque that would insult the sensibilities of practicing Christians—white or black—and orthodox Jews. Sensitive, ingenious playwright and sensitive, ingenious actor playing "De Lawd" came together in *The Green Pastures* to make a play that might not ever be called great, but that contains elements of greatness that remain high accomplishments of the theater.

Brooks Atkinson, the foremost drama critic at the time of the popularity of *The Green Pastures*, wrote well about the making of the play:

> Although simple Southern Negroes were the characters in *The Green Pastures*, the story they told and their responses to it became universal. Their willingness to believe made them the perfect instruments through which a glorious story was spoken. And *The Green Pastures* contributed one exalting idea to the Bible legend. It showed the Lord—the mighty man with awful powers—learning something humbling from the children of the earth. He learned that mercy comes from suffering.[24]

Forty years after *The Green Pastures* reached Broadway, Connelly reflected on why he wrote it. "I tried to echo Brad [Roark Bradford] as much as I could, so I used a lot of lines straight out of his book," he wrote. Brad, he felt, was writing pretty much for the joy of the separate scenes themselves. He had not given much thought, for instance, to the fact that the God in his book was a white granddaddy-colonel sort of figure. The black God was his own idea, Connelly reminds himself and his readers. "You had to think of the Old Testament as it would be looked at by the ingenious, uninformed Negroes, especially the illiterate, underprivileged field hands of the Deep South," he added. But he had one more serious reason for writing the play, he goes on to explain—one that might have actually transcended all of the others written here: "Once I got into it, I wanted to find, as I wrote, some reason for the rejection of conventional liturgy that was spreading through my generation. We were all becoming agnostics. I wasn't profound enough, in my own mind, to be able to recognize what I see now—that we simply wanted conscious escapes from tradition." More than the sentimentality that has been considered a basic fault in the play, the rise of religious nihilism in America and in Western Europe and the plethora of sermons and lectures on whether God was, indeed, dead, Connelly made a play that was a soothing balm for a nation grown fearful for its future and questioning about its value system. Thomas Cripps attacks it for social document that reflects the loss of innocence white America felt with the economic distress and its attendant social upheaval during the Great Depression.[25] Perhaps so, but to relegate *The Green Pastures* to so cynical an allegory without giving at least some reference to the redeeming features of the play is not to give a balanced story of Connelly's creation of the script and Harrison's making it a live organism on the stage.

NOTES

1. John L. Phillips, "Before the Color Fades: *Green Pastures* Revisited," *American Heritage*, 21 (February 1970):28.

2. Marc Connelly, *Voices Offstage: A Book of Memoirs* (New York: Holt, Rinehart & Winston, 1968), p. 74.

3. Ibid.

4. "The Play," *New York Evening Post*, 27 February 1930, p. 6.

5. Ibid.

6. William Bolitho, "*The Green Pastures*," *New York World*, 1 March 1930, p. 6.

7. "The Living God," *Saturday Review of Literature*, 19 April 1930, p. 941.

8. Ibid.

9. The study guide, *Marc Connelly*, The Green Pastures (New York: Monarch Press, 1966), pp. 20-21.

10. I am indebted to a summary in Joseph T. Shipley's *Guide to Great Plays* (Washington, D.C.: Public Affairs Press, 1956), pp. 296-97, for this note.

11. See William Smith, *Bible Dictionary* (New York: Pyramids Publications, 1975), p. 196, for this definition.

12. See Gustav Davidson, *A Dictionary of Angels* (New York: Free Press, 1967), p. 117.

13. Heywood Broun, "It Seems to Heywood Broun," *The Nation*, December 1930, p. 982.

14. Brooks Atkinson, "Sketch-book to Miracle Play," *New York Times*, 8 June 1930, sec. 9, p. 1.

15. John Hutchens, "The Black Miracle," *Theatre Arts*, May 1930, p. 369.

16. Salem Tutt Whitney, "Timely Topics," *Chicago Defender*, 8 February 1930, sec. 2, p. 6.

17. Ibid.

18. Theophilus Lewis, "Harlem Sketchbook," *New York Amsterdam News*, 8 October 1930, p. 11.

19. Marc Connelly, *The Green Pastures* (New York: Farrar & Rinehart, 1929), p. 143.

20. Ibid., pp. 155-56.

21. Richard Watts, Jr., "Sight and Sound," *New York Herald Tribune*, 5 March 1930, p. 7.

22. Connelly, *Green Pastures*, pp. 165-67.

23. Ibid., p. 173.

24. Brooks Atkinson, *Broadway* (New York: Macmillan, 1970), p. 239.

25. Thomas Cripps, *The Green Pastures* (Madison: University of Wisconsin Press, 1979), p. 12.

4

THE STAGING
OF THE PLAY

Marc Connelly had completed his play. He had satisfied himself that he had listened carefully to the dialect he was using as language. He knew the play would contain many scenes and moments of pageantry. The work had met his conceptual expectation. Once the dramatic blueprint was clear in his mind, he saw that his narrative would "concern man's ancient, intensive search for his own soul," as he wrote in his memoirs.[1] His theatrical document would show that as the American black slave embraced Christianity, he had, at the same time, made a valiant attempt to find divinity within himself. Thus, Connelly could congratulate himself for having found what he called "rich promise in the vision of Negroes uprooted from their African culture, ties broken with animistic theology, looking with hope and reverence to Jehovah and Christ." And he vowed that his play would try to interpret a spiritual phase of the Old Testament—the search of God for man, and man's search for God. He had committed himself to, as he wrote, "eschew all temptations to be funny for fun's sake." He kept himself aware of using Bradford's sketches that were "bright with Southern Negro field hand's innocence," but he had also been careful to avoid imposing any element of humor that would be racially offensive.

These high purposes placed the script beyond the pale of practicality for Broadway producers. When he received the six bound copies from the typing bureau, he sent them to managers who had indicated some interest in reading any play he might write. After all, he had already achieved some success in the theater. Connelly recalled that Dorothy Parker, who had transcribed the Exodus scene for him, said she cried while typing it. He felt proud of what he had written. Inasmuch as he had never had an agent before, he was more than a little surprised when all six of the copies came back accompanied by notes that were not at all heartening. Philip Moeller, reading it for the Theatre Guild—one of the organizations Connelly had expected to respond favorably—found it "outrageously sacrilegious." Arthur Hopkins, busy and successful producer with whom Connelly's friend Robert Edmond Jones had worked on several productions, was the only one who offered encouragement. "I liked it," Connelly said Hopkins told him on the telephone, "and I've read it twice. If I knew how it could be produced, I think I'd do it." Within a period of three weeks, every producer he had approached refused to back the play. "On the first of December I did not share the common woe of anticipating Christmas," Connelly recalled. No one seemed willing to wager that the play would ever be produced. Its subject matter was taboo; its requirements in sets and costumes and size of house for stage were lavish; and the Depression had hit the nation.

Connelly met Rowland Stebbins quite by chance. George Kaufman, who had collaborated with Connelly in writing several stage plays, was a friend of Stebbins. They played bridge together frequently at the Cavendish Club. One day when they were in the midst of a game, Stebbins asked Kaufman whether he had any uncommitted play scripts. He did not, but he said Marc Connelly, a friend of his, had one that seemed promising despite many rejections. The next day, as the story goes, Stebbins' business manager arrived at Connelly's apartment to pick up a script. Two days later the two men met. Stebbins began their conversation with his enthusiastic announcement that he would produce the play as soon as it could be put on the stage. When Connelly told him that one producer had told him the author and the backer of such a play might go to jail for temerity, Stebbins was still undeterred. His only concern was that the play would not appear sacrilegious. "Of course, there are bigots everywhere," he told Connelly, "and I can imagine some of them wanting to burn us at the stake. I can see those with political pressure running us out of Philadelphia, Boston, and other cities on the rail." Right then and there, the two of them agreed there would be no out-of-town tryouts. The play would open forthright in New York. From the beginning, Rowland Stebbins was taking more than the traditional producer's role.

Stebbins, a native New Yorker, was the son of Charles H. Stebbins and a grandson of the late Henry G. Stebbins, three times president of the New York Stock Exchange. He had studied engineering at Columbia University and at Union College, graduating in 1904. Three years later he abandoned engineering and acquired membership in the New York

Stock Exchange. He was a general partner in the De Coppet and Doremus firm, a family enterprise, from 1917 to 1929. From that time until his death in 1946, he was a special partner. In 1930 he transferred his exchange seat to his cousin, J. Randolph Grymes, Jr. He had disposed of his personal wealth of blue-chip stocks at the moment of their greatest value, before the financial boom crashed. Before 1929 Stebbins had several times helped to finance plays. But in that year he settled down to the theater as his principal active business. His first venture was *Merry Andrew*, which opened at the Henry Miller Theatre in New York on January 21, 1920. It failed, as did his second show, *Maggie the Magnificent*, which was produced in the fall of that year at the Cort Theatre. Within the next several years Stebbins produced some fifteen plays, including a staging of Shakespeare's *Antony and Cleopatra*, starring Tallulah Bankhead. He also sponsored the Players' revival of *Uncle Tom's Cabin*, which toured with Otis Skinner in the title role, and *The Pursuit of Happiness*, which ran in New York for forty-eight weeks, played in London, and was also a movie. It was perhaps his most successful venture in the theater, excluding *The Green Pastures*. With so resourceful a producer and new friend, Connelly's new play was on the road to reaching the stage and thousands of Americans in hundreds of theaters and auditoriums throughout the nation.

The week after the meeting between Stebbins and Connelly was frenetic. Robert Edmond Jones was free and eager to develop the rough sketches he had already made for the sets and costumes. Stebbins, who was part of the local musical community, knew Hall Johnson and his work with choirs. So Johnson was engaged to make the vocal arrangements and to conduct the singing of the chorus. He would use his already-famous choir. Miriam Doyle of Stebbins' staff would supervise the costumes that would be made from Jones' designs. Finding an appropriate theater was a challenging task. It would have to have a stage large enough to accommodate the heavy load of scenery and, particularly, to house the two treadmills Jones had planned as people-movers for the cast in the many scenes. Fortunately, Actor's Equity had already adopted a rule that permitted musicals to rehearse for five weeks rather than the traditional four. Nevertheless, Connelly had to appear before Equity Council in person to request the one-week extension. With a five-week rehearsal schedule possible, the play could open February 26, 1930, provided work started immediately. According to the provisions of the Dramatists' Guild contract, the final authority on the casting of plays rested with the author. As a rule, he and the director chose the performers. The relationship between Stebbins and Connelly was exceedingly cordial in this case, however. There was little chance that either would run the risk of disturbing the harmony that the men, who were strangers to each other until just a few days earlier, had achieved.

The uncommon genius of several persons accounts for the making of the record-breaking aesthetic and financial success in the theater that was *The Green Pastures*. As we have seen, Rowland Stebbins was Connelly's "angel." His friend Robert Edmond Jones was ready and willing to play his role as artist-designer. Stebbins had selected Hall Johnson to take care of the music. Richard B. Harrison was yet to be found to carry the text and the sets from the footlights to the audience as the principal actor of the unique experiment in the theater.

Jones and Connelly were friends. Both were regular "members" of the Algonquin Roundtable. Jones was one of the brightest lights in the developing profession of set design. He sought to create settings that would project more fully than had been the convention of the playwright's thought. Departing from the old realism of Davis Belasco, he drew on the imagination, color, and lighting to enhance the play visually. In his "manifesto" about the role of the designer in the theater, he wrote: "The designer creates an environment in which all noble emotions are possible." He believed the scenery was most important to the play. For, as he wrote, "when the curtain rises, it is the scenery that sets the key of the play; the setting is not a background; it is an environment."[2] This vision of the theater served Connelly's new play well. From its first scene, the audience has to understand that the dramatic action will emerge from the environment of the minds of the young children in Mr. Deshee's Sunday school class. That environment—mental and fanciful, not literal—permeated the play. How one perceives it determines the response to the drama. It was indispensable for seeming not to make fun of the religion of the people the play described.

Jones was an artist. His mother, a concert pianist, had taught him to play the violin in childhood. When he came from his New Hampshire home to enter Harvard, he became interested in a wider range of artistic studies than music. And he developed his ability in drawing and sketching. On graduation from Harvard College in 1910, he remained there for two school years as an instructor in the Fine Arts Department. There he became interested in theater set designing. For a time he worked as a costume artist for a New York firm.

Early in 1912, Jones went to Europe with high hopes of studying with Gordon Craig in his school of theatrical arts in Florence. Craig totally rebuffed Jones. Moving on to Germany, the young man studied at and worked in Max Reinhardt's Deutsches Theatre for a year. When he returned to New York, he became associated with, in the winter of 1914, a group of young freethinkers who met often in Greenwich Village to discuss art and politics. They organized themselves into the Washington Square Players, which was the precursor of the Theatre Guild. Together with the Liberal Club, they met often in the MacDougal Street Bookstore, which was located on the ground floor in a brownstone building.

Laurence Langner, Max Eastman and his wife, Crystal, and Albert Boni had been classmates at Harvard. Jones one day suggested the group should make its own theater for a new American thrust in drama. They organized the Bandbox Theatre on Fifty-seventh Street. That was before the Provincetown Players were organized. Jones mounted *Suppressed Desire* for the new group on an improvised stage with makeshift scenery in Hutchins Hapgood's house on Cape Cod. This experiment was probably one of his first, and it led to the long professional relationship between Jones and Eugene O'Neill, the new playwright who was attracting attention with his new focus in some Freudian trends in playwriting.

Jones designed the sets for Anatole France's *The Man Who Married a Dumb Wife*, which opened in January 1915 at the Wallack Theatre in New York. That production established his reputation as an artist-designer. Influenced by him, stage designing developed to the point that persons following that craft achieved importance equal to that of the director. Arthur Hopkins saw the setting of France's play and immediately engaged Jones. Their first production as a team was *The Devil's Garden*, also appearing in 1915 and remaining praiseworthy for its innovations until today. During the next five years Jones worked with Hopkins in making scenes for seventeen plays, two ballets, and five masques. He had directed the three Ridgely Torrence one-act plays of Negro life in 1917. In 1921 he began working with Eugene O'Neill when Hopkins produced *The Hairy Ape*. In successive years Jones was the principal designer for O'Neill's *Anna Christie, Desire Under the Elms, Mourning Becomes Electra, Ah Wilderness!, The Iceman Cometh*, and other works. During this same time he designed sets and costumes for other ballets and operas, including productions for the Metropolitan. Easily he was the most talented property among the rising art of artist-designers in the theater. One sees readily how fortunate it was for Connelly to secure Jones' interest in *The Green Pastures* and how well suited the play was for Jones' vision of the theater. With Stebbins' unflagging support and the finance the extravagant settings would require for his unusual script, Connelly had in place one of the requisites for success with his new play. Jones' role was more than that of mere set designer for the play, notwithstanding the importance of that art in the theater. He was totally compatible with Connelly's theatrical imagination, which sought to transform the basic dramatization of some loose sketches into a cohesive concept and to execute it as theater. Some important insight into what would come of this collaboration can be inferred from Jones' statement about this approach to the theater:

What precisely is it, then, that we can find inside a theatre that we cannot find inside a picture gallery or a concert hall or

> a church? A show. We go to the theatre to see a show. A show
> of what? A show of human life: life like our own. But with a
> difference. We can see life like our own on any street corner—
> hurried, disorganized, fragmentary, incomplete, eternally
> "ever-not-quite," as William James expressed it. But in the
> theatre we see this same disorganized fragmentary life of ours
> somehow organized and made continuous, flowing together in
> one strong current.[3]

Jones saw the opportunity to exercise his rich anticipation of the
theatrical potential for the artist in the theater through his designs of sets
and costumes for the human fantasy Connelly had written on paper.
Fantasy it was that still was intended to portray the imaginings of a
people who the playwright believed took their religion seriously. The
potential was expansive for Jones and for Connelly. Nothing quite like
this opportunity had ever happened to either of them before. *The Green
Pastures* could hardly avoid becoming an artistic success. If only
producer and director could find the human beings to execute their
concept.

The music had to match the intensity and aesthetic dimensions of the
script and the settings and the costumes. Even as Connelly's drama on
paper had been an emanation of the black American's creation of his
own rendering of the basic incidents in the Old Testament books of
Genesis and Exodus, the music that was organic to the play would also
have to be a clear artifact of those people. In fact, its relationship to the
essence of the play was even more significant than Connelly's script or
Jones' sets. Theirs were the products of their imaginings. The spirituals
Connelly had chosen to integrate into the dramatic script were live art
forms, already existing and steadily held in the hands of the people who
created and used them. What, then, was the state of the art of using the
Negro spirituals in the theater? That question must have emerged in the
minds of the creators of the new play.

The musical comedy that had replaced vaudeville and minstrels as a
principal black American art form had become "a bit worn," as James
Weldon Johnson expressed it in 1927. The new genre contained slight
dramatic plots, richly embellished with song and dance, not unlike the
material of the stage performances that preceded them. They were
vaudeville and minstrel in a new key, albeit the songs were often
composed by highly competent black musicians who used their conser-
vatory education for popular fare that would get a hearing before the
footlights. Some variations had come along. Paul Green had used the
Negro spiritual in his prizewinning *In Abraham's Bosom*. But that was not
a dominant feature. Singing spirituals establishes the character of
Abraham McCranie, the principal character in Green's play. And while

Dorothy and Du Bose Heyward's *Porgy* also does not rely on singing spirituals for its drama, the closing scene of the first act—that in which all of Serena's neighbors on Catfish Row in Charleston, South Carolina, gather in her cottage for the traditional wake for her murdered husband—makes intense use of the songs. The play becomes a religious frenzy by the time the final curtain falls. Spirituals had come to replace "coon songs" and light romances in drama about Negroes that reached the commercial stage. John Lovell writes in his *Black Song: The Forge and the Flame* that American dramatists and other playwrights had used spirituals thousands of times to make theater.[4] Connelly never recorded any observations that would indicate his particular awareness of these practices. But he could hardly have avoided knowing about those that reached Broadway. Certainly he was personally familiar with *In Abraham's Bosom* and *Porgy*. He did write about wanting to use Negro folk songs to provide cohesion for the eighteen scenes he planned to use for the dramatic action of his play. He must have been familiar, too, with the international controversy that raged between Sean O'Casey and William Butler Yeats about O'Casey's expressionism in his play *The Silver Tassie* in 1927. Harry Heegan, the cripple in that play who has been driven from elemental man in his hometown to sniveling paraplegic as a result of his injuries in World War I, sings "Swing Low, Sweet Chariot" as he comes face to face with his total impotence and rejection by his former lover. This invention is O'Casey's way of relegating Heegan to utter helplessness, as well as of making a statement about the helplessness of the American slaves whose lot in the plantation society paralleled Heegan's.[5] Lovell might be hard pressed to come up with "thousands of examples" of spirituals used in twentieth-century drama, but more illustrations could be shown. Nevertheless, the popularity of Afro-American religious folk music on the stage in the 1930s did contribute significantly to the success of *The Green Pastures* on the stage.

Connelly might not have known the history of *Heaven Bound*, a morality play-type pageant that was common in black churches. That art form was said to have been first performed by the choir of the Big Bethel African Methodist Episcopal Church in Atlanta in January 1930, one month before *The Green Pastures* opened at the Mansfield Theatre. The pageant became so popular that it was produced annually in the Atlanta church well into the 1960s.[6] Mrs. Lula Byrd Jones, a member of the church then working as a spotter in the Excelsior Laundry, said she had overheard while at work about a pageant performed somewhere in Florida. Mrs. Nellie Lindley Davis, a member of the faculty of Clark College in Atlanta, wrote the narration. The lyrics from familiar hymns and spirituals provided the context for the dramatic action. The spoken parts and the action were ad-libbed. The principal set was the front of the church, decorated to represent the gates of heaven. For two weeks, be-

ginning January 3, 1939, the choir performed the pageant in the Atlanta
Theatre, located downtown on Exchange Place. The Atlanta unit of the
Federal Theatre, under the Works Progress Administration, sponsored
the production. By November 1963 the pageant had been performed 644
times. It was a feature during the World Ecumenical Conference in
Atlanta in 1931. From time to time the choir of Big Bethel Church
traveled to neighboring cities to perform *Heaven Bound*. But eventually
the church restricted performances to the home sanctuary because
members felt the religious quality of the play was threatened by outside
productions.

The pageant is a communal creation that has evolved into a stable
form, as Redding S. Suggs, Jr., describes it. Variations occurred regularly
in black churches. It is comparable to the morality plays of medieval
Europe, strikingly similar to the medieval liturgical drama. It has no discernible connection with any other dramatic tradition. Instead, it seems
to have been a new birth sprung from black religious life in the United
States. Suggs considers it a native "expression, now conventionally
preserved, meant to be performed rather than read, featuring music and
pantomime keyed to the lyrics of hymns and spirituals. There is no
dialogue, only the solemn pronouncements of the Narrator."[7]

Its main attraction is the ubiquitous Devil, who tempts mortals
marching down the church aisle on this journey toward heaven. His role
is vigorous. One reviewer wrote: "His leaping, his grimacing and his
posturing were so convincing that when, at times, he flopped himself
down in a vacant seat in the audience for a breather, people around him
shrieked and fled in terror."[8] In the end the Devil is slain, appropriately,
by a Soldier in the army of the Lord.

Suggs, folklorist, wrote of the pageant as folk art. He might not have
been aware of the rather common practice of drama in the black church
that is an Afro-American tradition, in which the church is, and has been,
the "comprehensive institution" in the black community: it is the temple
of worship, the theater, the concert hall, the entertainment center, the
meeting auditorium, the benevolent society, and the port of communal
safety for black Americans long excluded from the social and cultural
institutions commonly available to white Americans. Drama takes place
there. Moreover, the nature of the practice of Christianity among black
Americans provides dimensions of artistic expression that are indigenous
to that community alone. These facts about the experience of living
black in America are too numerous and too well known and well docu-
mented to be argued here. Had Suggs known his subject better, he might
have realized that Big Bethel Church in Atlanta simply institutionalized a
religious practice that was common in the culture. Gertrude Mathews
Shelby captured something of the widespread practice of the art form
Suggs describes in another setting far less sophisticated than Big Bethel
in Atlanta:

Sunday go-to-meeting clothes on a Monday night in a negro
[sic] church deep in the singing South, at Brunswick on the
Georgia coast. A sea of rolling eyes, the lustre of dark skins,
an air of intense anticipation; the place is packed for the treat
excitement of the season, *Heaven-Bound Soldiers*, a miracle
play conceived in the manner of the Middle Ages but acted
and directed by negroes [sic] for negroes [sic], the first of
record.[9]

Claiming this presentation is the first of record is questionable but
unimportant. One does marvel, though, at the comparison between the
description in the two reports. In both, the church is converted for the
occasion into a theater. Distantly, a choir breaks forth, in Shelby's
account, singing "When the Saints Go Marching In." In Brunswick the
saints have already made it to heaven. And they are all women, with the
exception of the impressive-looking male carrying the great book and
wearing gold-rimmed spectacles. He is St. Peter. The congregation joins
in the singing. Religion, deeply felt, begins to take hold. In this morality
play, St. Peter has the sole speaking part. He describes the Penitent
Sinner who travels toward heaven with eyes fastened on the gathering of
saints who have already arrived there. The Devil taunts the Penitent
Sinner, tries to tempt her with gifts, "offers her the world." She evades
him and the pitchfork. Other travelers follow the same pattern. The
theme of the pageant is simple: the struggle of human beings to choose
between God and the Devil. In this case, authorship of the piece is
attributed to a Negro postman in Atlanta, where the play was said to
have been first performed in lieu of a revival. All the dramatic episodes
are built on spirituals. The coquettish courtesan who yields to the Devil's
temptation changes her mind and tries to reject him at the very gates of
hell. She throws her eyes imploringly on the saints in their heaven. But
they are unforgiving. St. Peter shuts her out when she rushes to the gates
of heaven. The choir and the congregation sing, "Too late . . . Too late."
An old woman carrying a heavy load on her head brings forth the strains of
"There Is Rest for the Weary." The Rich Man fails to enter heaven
because, in the ethic of the approved saints, "You Must Have That Pure
Religion." "I Shall Not Be Moved," "Let the Light from the Lighthouse
Shine on Me," "Get on Board, Littl' Chillun," "Roll, Jordan, Roll," all
come in their turn as communal participation in song that enforces the
slight dramatic content of the pageant. Each performance must be
freehand.

When copies of these examples of folk religious drama created by and
performed for and among black Americans have moved from the
churches to the professional stage, they have seldom been successful.
Pearly Gates, a spiritual morality play by Frederick Hall, a native
Atlantan who was supervising music in public, black schools in Jackson,

Mississippi, came to the Shubert Theatre in Chicago in September 1931 ostensibly to challenge the popularity *The Green Pastures* was enjoying. After the venture failed, *Variety* reported, "this play, so-called, was rushed into the Shubert House before anybody knew anything about its hopes, aims, or nature."[10] Notices to the press claimed the company was brought into the Loop theater because no available church could hold the anticipated patrons. Not more than 150 persons attended any one of the few performances that went on stage before *Pearly Gates* closed. Rumors abounded that promoters hoped to gain for *Pearly Gates* a large part of the audience that otherwise would be buying tickets for *The Green Pastures*, due to open in Chicago at the Lincoln Theatre on Labor Day.

Subtitled "A Musical Morality Play Based Upon the Negro Spiritual Depicting the Negro's Conception of the Journey from Earth to Heaven," *Variety*'s review concluded that *Pearly Gates* was a "rendition by a competent enough group of Negroes of the fine spirituals, shaping up on the stage as a concert, however, and not as a play. It is revivalist in intent." There are two acts. The first is set in a camp meeting with a chorus of thirty persons singing the spirituals. The second act shows these same persons—saints, sinners, and preachers—trying to travel to heaven. The musical failed. In addition to its disappointment as theater, it created a crisis for the performers, who seemed to have thought they had a contract with J. J. Shubert. They threatened to sue the impresario. The matter was settled when, after *Pearly Gates* was pulled out of the Shubert after remaining on the board for a week, the performers were quietly returned to Atlanta by bus.[11]

The Green Pastures came to Broadway and played before thousands of Americans out of a milieu filled with black choirs that performed in their churches and in concert. Semiprofessional groups of singers sprang up with the advent of national radio networks. As is commonly known, black Americans had sung their folk music for whites since slavery. Schools started by whites for black people often made their money for support from their singing choirs. The Fisk Jubilee Singers are the best known of these groups, although the choirs of Hampton Institute and Tuskegee Institute were famous in the United States and in Europe. Throughout the years, and continuing in some groups until today, college choirs among black institutions go on fund-raising tours each spring. With the decline of the musical revue, which followed the minstrel on the theater stage for black entertainers, the professional choirs brought an innovation into the stage art for blacks.

Connelly had initially planned "to hold the play together by having Negro melodies sung during the many scene changes."[12] Music was to be incidental to the dramatic action. When he met Bradford to discuss his ideas for the drama, Connelly's thoughts changed. As he learned more about the southern Negro and about the personal religion of which he intended to write a successful stage production, he realized that music in the black church was integral to the culture he proposed to represent. "Rise, Shine, and Give God the Glory," the song the angelic choir sings at the fish fry in an opening scene in *The Green Pastures*, and most of the other music came into the drama as a result of the discussions he held with Mrs. Hubbard in Bradford's home on Jackson Square. Connelly decided that spirituals would become an integral part of *The Green Pastures*. Indeed, they became essential to its success. They were, theoretically, the "curtain" that permitted the many scenes of the play to be set. But they were more. Their text and tone and timbre carried the impact of the drama as well as did the dramatic action.

So significant a component of the drama required a delicate balancing between authentic rendition of folk music and a choral sound appropriate for the theater. Mrs. Hubbard's collection of songs helped Connelly to choose those he would use. The other matter of having them sung by voices that could execute the delicate balancing assignment required a unique musical skill. The musical arrangements would have to reflect a quality that was at once simple, folksy, and theatrical. Spontaneity must appear to come from singers who were musically intelligent and stage-experienced enough to give *The Green Pastures* the combination of rendition of the Bible stories that remained essentially those Bradford wrote in *Ol' Man Adam an' His Chillun* and Connelly's aesthetic vision that guided him in using the Bradford stories as merely the story line base for theater. It must avoid burlesque; it must be recognizable; it must mirror the playwright's respect for the culture that was providing him a vehicle for his most ambitious undertaking; and it must cover up Connelly's lack of full familiarity with his subject.

The spirituals in *The Green Pastures* were sung in the following order: "Rise, Shine, and Give God the Glory," "When the Saints Go Marching In," "Certainly Lawd," "So High You Can't Get Over It," "Bright Mansions Above," "Turn You 'Round," "Run, Sinner, Run," "You Better Mind," "Dere's No Hiding Place," "Feastin' Table," "I Want to Be Ready," "De Ol' Ark's A-Movin'," "A City Called Heaven," "My Lord's A-Writing All De Time," "Go Down, Moses," "Mary, Don't You Weep," "I'm No Ways Tired," "Joshua Fit De Battle of Jericho," "Cain't Stay Away," "Death's Gwinter Lay His Cold Icy Hands on Me," "A Blind Man Stood on De Road and Cried," "March On," and "Hallelujah, King Jesus." The last one of these was written by Hall Johnson especially for the finale of the drama.

Anyone familiar with the religious music of the Afro-American culture recognizes these titles. They are regularly sung in church services; they are an artistic expression; and they are welded to the experience of slavery in the United States. They are, indeed, the artifacts of American black people. They are folk art. They are utilitarian, in that they are in common use in the black community, and they are known to whites who find in them a kind of primitive charm. They are, essentially, "a decoration upon a decoration." For they are a particular people's distillation of their unique association with the Christian religion they had been taught by their slaveholders. Because the titles and lyrics of the spirituals were based on the Old and New Testament images, personalities, and tales, the spirituals formed communication between the primary group out of which the art form came and the larger society with which they lived daily.

This interrelationship of the use of the Negro spiritual brought about the concertizing black choir, singing this art form in the music halls of the world. Individual singers used it as their one most significant avenue to the distinction between entertainer and artist. Roland Hayes, the internationally famous tenor in the 1930s, and Marian Anderson, the equally famous contralto, are two of the most notable examples.

The professional choirs came a little later than the soloists. Although Miss Anderson and Mr. Hayes used the usual variety of operatic arias, art songs, and folk songs in their programs, they also included spirituals. Miss Anderson became associated with singing "He's Got the Whole World in His Hands." Roland Hayes captivated audiences with his "Were You There When They Crucified My Lord?" Eva Jessye and Hall Johnson were leaders among the choral directors for semiprofessional performers. Miss Jessye, the daughter of black slaves, came to New York at an early age and, in the 1920s, organized a chorus that usually numbered from ten to fourteen mixed voices. Recalling her early days in New York, Miss Jessye said, "Back then, audiences expected black performers to sing nothing but 'Swanee River.' "[13] Her task in securing profitable engagements for her singers was especially difficult. Their first break on Broadway was singing in theaters as a warm-up to films. She formed the Original Dixie Jubilee Singers, which eventually gained a reputation for its rich sound. The choir played the Major Bowes Family Radio Hour for a year, and in 1927, Miss Jessye formed the group that bore her name—the Eva Jessye Choir—for nearly half a century. In 1929 she scored the music and directed the choir for King Vidor's film *Hallelujah*. Two years later the National Broadcasting Company aired her epic folk oratorio, *Paradise Lost and Regained*. In 1934 she was choral director for Virgil Thompson's *Four Saints in Three Acts*. Her "The Life of Christ in Negro Spirituals" follows the pattern of *Heaven-Bound* and anticipates *The Green Pastures*' use of folk music as an integral part of stage drama. Also in 1934, George Gershwin chose her to direct the chorus for his opera *Porgy and Bess*. Particularly because she was a personal friend of Richard B. Harrison, having taught with him in a small black college in Oklahoma, Miss Jessye was a candidate for the position of music director of *The Green Pastures*. There were other choirs like hers, but Hall Johnson's was the most prominent. He secured the appointment as music director and scored the arrangements, and trained and directed the singers.

The Green Pastures could hardly have become the American theatrical success it was without the musical genius of Hall Johnson (Francis Hall Johnson). Born March 12, 1888, in Athens, Georgia, the son of an African Methodist Episcopal church preacher, Johnson studied piano and violin at an early age. When his talent clearly outdistanced teachers in his hometown, his parents sent him to Knox Institute in Knoxville, Tennessee (now Knoxville College). Later he studied at Atlanta University, and at Allen University in Columbia, South Carolina, for three years—from 1905 to 1908—while his father was president of that church-related institution. Johnson studied music at the University of Pennsylvania, where he was awarded a bachelor of arts degree in 1910. When he moved to New York City, he studied with Percy Goetshius at the Juilliard School of Music. By 1914 he had become a regular performer with organizations that popularized Afro-American music. He played in James Reese Europe's troupe which toured with Irene and Vernon Castle, and with Will Marion Cook's New York Syncopated Orchestra. During these years he also conducted his own music studio, played local concerts, and worked with theater pit orchestras. His most notable engagement in this part of his career was with Eubie Blake's *Shuffle Along* in 1921. Two years later Johnson organized his own Negro String Quartet, in which he played the viola. Although his formal study of music was restricted to composition and instrumental music, Johnson was to make his greatest accomplishments in choral music. Musicologists credit him with playing a large part in the preservation of the Negro spiritual. His appreciation for the art form originated, no doubt, in his early childhood through hearing the songs sung in his father's churches and in the neighborhoods in which he lived as a youth. His musical education, together with his inherent love for Afro-American music, caused him to specialize in the spiritual as choral music. Beginning in 1925 with eight mixed voices, he created a living laboratory for performance of the spiritual. The Hall Johnson Choir made its formal debut in February 1926, at the Pythian Temple in Harlem, and sang again at Town Hall in March of the same year. Soon the choir had built a strong reputation on the concert stage and in the rapidly developing medium of radio. It began making recordings for Victor RCA the same year *The Green Pastures* opened on Broadway. Johnson was official music director of *The Green Pastures* throughout its New York run. In 1933 his *Run Littl' Chillun* reached Broadway and gained acclaim as a folk opera that was set in the black church. Even while Johnson's choir sang on Broadway in *The Green*

Pastures, another of his choruses performed concerts. When Johnson died in 1970, he was, without doubt, the best-known black choral conductor and arranger of all times.

He found his professional role in building and maintaining respect for the Negro spiritual. Some thirty years after *The Green Pastures* left the stage, Johnson wrote about his purposes in organizing the choir: "Its principal aim was not entertainment." Johnson continued:

> We wanted to show how the American Negro slaves—in 250 years of constant practice, self-developed under pressure but equipped with their inborn sense of rhythm and drama (plus their new *religion*) created, propagated and illuminated an art form which was, and still is *unique* in the world of music. The slaves named them "spirituals" to distinguish them from their worldly, "everyday" songs. Also their music style of performance was very special. It cannot be accurately noted but must be studied by imitation.[14]

Marian Anderson wrote a tribute to Johnson on the occasion of his accidental death as the result of a fire in his New York apartment. She called him a "unique genius"; for although he invented no new harmonies, designed no new forms, originated no new melodic styles, discovered no new rhythmic principles, he was yet "able to fashion a whole new world of music in his own image."[15] She spoke of his guiding her to a true interpretation of folk songs she had known from childhood. "Gently he prodded, corrected, refined, and indeed taught me subtleties of rhythm, of diction and of phrasing that deepened, broadened, and altered the character of the songs I was to sing." She continued that Johnson heard things in a special way and could not rest until everybody heard them that way. She felt that was how the sound Johnson alone heard as a youth became the sound of later generations. And that, she wrote, was how he was able "to take the diamond-in-the-rough that was the spiritual of his youth and shape it, fashion it, and polish it into the transcendent musical instrument it became in his hands." These were the skills he performed, paticularly, with the chorus in *The Green Pastures* and in his own *Run Littl' Chillun,* Miss Anderson wrote.

Evelyn Burwell was assistant director of the choir. It was made up of seven sopranos, five altos, four baritones, and five bassos.

Ulysses Chambers, a tenor and a newspaper columnist writing on show business, followed Hall Johnson as director of the choir in *The Green Pastures* when the company went on tour. Chambers, who furthered his reputation by making the arrangements for the chorus and training the singers for the second season of Lew Leslie's *Blackbirds,* was a native of Baltimore. He studied at Morgan College in Baltimore and had studied privately at prestigious Peabody Institute. He earned the bachelor of music degree in 1921 from Teachers' College of Columbia University. In addition to serving as supervisor of music for black schools in Baltimore, he had taught at Dunbar High School in Washington, D.C., and supervised public school music in St. Louis. He performed as tenor soloist, pianist, and organist. He played theater organs at the Lafayette Theatre in Newark, New Jersey, and at the Royal Theatre in Chicago. He had sung as soloist in several prominent churches, including St. Luke's Cathedral, Trinity Parish, and the Chapel of the Incarnation in New York City, as well as at the First Presbyterian Church of Southhampton, Long Island. He had given organ concerts in several cities throughout the United States.[16]

The Green Pastures brought to the American public on its performance stages a complex, but unified, American creation. Connelly's vision, as he saw it, of primitive, black Americans caught in the act of exploring the mysteries and the delicacies of the religion of their slave masters was wedded to Hall Johnson's passionate love for the Negro spiritual and his genius for rendering that sentiment into choral direction. These two ingenious elements combined with Richard B. Harrison's inherent respect for the artifacts of his own religious heritage to create the most successful pageant of its time. These qualities brought thousands of Americans into the theater to see *The Green Pastures*.

Olin Downes, esteemed music critic of the *New York Times*, paid a tribute to the music of the drama when he wrote during the first year of the New York performances:

> Those who like to ponder profoundly on questions of the forms and future of opera might well reflect upon the felicity with which the Hall Johnson Negro Choir welded together with the drama of "The Green Pastures." This is not grand opera or opera-comique, or a thing that fits into any classified operatic form. Nevertheless, in more than a superficial fashion the singing of the spirituals imparts to the play something of the nature of the music drama. Indeed, it is impossible, at least on the part of one who listens with the musical consideration habitually in mind to conceive of "The Green Pastures" without the very characteristic and impassioned singing which binds the episodes together and completes the emotion at the place where the action stops. If it is true that the manuscript play was refused by more than one manager before it saw the stage, the fact is easy to explain. It can be added that only half its effect could be realized without the sound of the spirituals in the mind of the reader.[17]

The statement is clear and fervent testimony to the strength of the spirituals as sung by the Hall Johnson Choir and their indispensable role in making the play intelligible. Whether he intended to do so or not, Connelly had struck it rich by signing on Hall Johnson to provide the singing that became a nonpareil for the theater of his play. Notwithstanding the popularity of black choirs at the time, Johnson's was an exceptional group. Its role in *The Green Pastures* was more than a concert; however, the spirituals did far more than divide the scenes of the dramatic action. They sustained the sense and mood of the script. Moreover, they took the audience into realms of emotional satisfaction that could not have been reached by any other part of the elaborate production. And they produced, before larger audiences than he could ever have reached in any other way, the purposes Johnson had in mind for the Negro spiritual when he first formed his choir.

The sets were impressively constructed. As Jones had said, they caught the attention of the audience as soon as the curtain was lifted. And they set the tone of the play. In this case the sets made the difficult transition between imagined religion and its enactment by human beings on earth. The music was provided for. Hall Johnson was the nation's best authority on presenting the Negro spiritual. His arrangements would correlate well with Jones' artistry in the visual art of stage design. Now human action in the form of speaking and human movement—the third and perhaps most important element of the evolving play—needed to come on line. American audiences knew Robert Edmond Jones' work. Merely knowing he was working with Connelly gave some measure of validity to the play long before anyone saw any part of it on the stage. But the actors were a more serious problem. In fact, that dimension was an enigma. No known black man could be speculated about for the role of "De Lawd." That was God on the stage in a nation that took its religion seriously even if it considered its black people who came across the footlights entertainers rather than actors. The dilemma was more than academic. Judicious choice of a cast was the essential element in staging *The Green Pastures*. Broadway knew little, if anything, about those who were eventually chosen. That is, not before opening night. After the first few performances, the nation knew the principal characters well. Richard B. Harrison was the principal force in energizing the script, the settings, and the music.

How Harrison came to the stage of the Mansfield Theatre that February night in 1930 and carved a niche in theatrical history is, indeed, a story of one of nature's triumphs. And it represents a strong nuance of that rich living tapestry that is America. Harrison's mother and father—IsaBella Benton and Thomas Harrison—were among unnumbered black American slaves who escaped from Southern plantations to freedom. Many who moved across the borders from the South into non-slave states never felt secure as long as they remained in the continental United States. Fugitive slave laws made their freedom precarious. Accordingly, many who stole away from their slaveholders pushed north into Canada. There a law enacted in 1783 declared that any Negro or Indian slave who entered the Province of Upper Canada was declared free. Southern Ontario, in particular, became a new frontier for black Americans fleeing slavery. Slaves were welcome in Canada at the time. They bought land and voted in elections in their new Canadian home. Perhaps between fifty and sixty thousand fugitive slaves settled in that portion of the Dominion between 1830 and 1861.

Little is known of Thomas Harrison other than he had been a slave on the Bullock plantation near Lexington, Kentucky. He fled North from that place after seeing two of his brothers sold down the river into the Deep South. More is known about Harrison's wife, IsaBella, who was the personal maid-slave girl for the elegant ladies of the famous Chouteau family of St. Louis. As their maidservant, she accompanied the Chouteaus to the theater and the opera. She spoke fluent French and was said to have known little English. The family's patriarch was Auguste Chouteau, one of the founders of St. Louis, who was born in New Orleans in 1750 and helped Pierre Laclède Liguest develop St. Louis. His family's wealth and influence occupy a great deal of the history of St. Louis. Apparently, IsaBella, a mulatto, was a favored slave in the household. She escaped from the Chouteau estate, however, and traveled the Underground Railroad by way of East St. Louis, Springfield, Chicago, and Detroit to London, Ontario. There she met Thomas Harrison. They were married in 1854. Negroes of London became interested in establishing a black colony in Haiti. The Harrisons joined the enterprise. The plan failed, and they returned to London. Mrs. Harrison is said to have insisted on the luxury of seeing Edwin Booth play Richard III as the couple passed through New York en route to London. She was pregnant with her fourth child. That child was to become "De Lawd." According to legend, he was named Richard in honor of Shakespeare's famous character. When this child was born, his mother was reported to have said to friends, "I shall name him Richard, and I pray he will be a man of much service and credit to all of us."[18] The mother's wish was noble but unlikely to come true. The large family was extremely poor.

Harrison liked to recall that among the odd jobs he held in boyhood, the one he liked best was selling newspapers in front of the local theater in London. There he could chat with the actors, whose tales about their work and travels intrigued him. When he had the money to do so, he bought gallery tickets to watch the performances. He referred to those days around the theater as his dramatic training. When he was nine years old and a student at the Wellington Street School, Harrison won a contest prize for reciting a poem called "Little by Little." Some of his hometown acquaintances recalled that young Harrison developed his interest in acting by gathering children in the Wellington Street neighborhood into an old barn near the family home. There he reenacted scenes from plays he had seen at the local theaters. He quickly gained a reputation as a "born impersonator." When the family moved from London, Ontario, to Detroit, Harrison—then sixteen years old—began to study drama and elocution. Because his father died soon after the family came to the United States to live, Harrison had to work at odd jobs. He and his brothers had no specific skills, so they worked at whatever odd jobs became available. Hotel work was one kind of employment black boys could perform rather easily. Richard worked at the old Russell House Hotel in Detroit and enrolled in the Training School of Dramatic Art. Later he studied privately with Edward Weitzel, drama editor of the *Detroit Free Press*, who had been, at some time, associated with the Henry Irving Dramatic School of London, England.

While Harrison was working as a bellhop in Detroit, a guest at a hotel gave him a copy of *Richard III*, which he studied until he knew many of the passages by heart. When he could afford tickets to the theater, he was fortunate enough to see such actors as Edwin Booth, Henry Irving, Lawrence Barrett, Sarah Bernhardt, and Louis James perform. As he became older, the youth followed the path of many other young black men. He found employment as a dining car waiter. First on the Chicago and Alton Railroad and then on the Chicago, Milwaukee, and St. Paul line, he worked several years in the Chicago area. After a few years he started working for the Santa Fe Railroad, where he made the acquaintance of A. G. Wells, one of the line's officials. Wells became impressed with Harrison's dramatic ability in reading and recitation and spoke to his wife of the youth's talents. Mrs. Wells put Harrison in touch with L. E. Behymer, a California impresario, who took the young man under his wing and arranged his first dramatic reading. That was in 1891. The checkered career was launched, interspersed with working for various railroad lines. His repertoire consisted of fifty separate recitations, including the Dunbar poems, and portions of three Shakespeare plays. His engagements as a reader took him into the South and Midwest in the United States, and eventually into Mexico. In the Chicago area, Richard B. Harrison gained the significant friendship of Paul Laurence Dunbar, the Ohio-born black poet whose poetry was attracting the attention of the American public.

Dunbar's career was young and far from financially remunerative. Like many artists, both black and white, he decided to go to Chicago and seek employment at the World's Columbian Exposition, which was opening in the spring of 1893. He had written an ode in honor of the event and believed he might find there a new audience for his works. He proposed to make his living selling his poetry and reciting it to groups of persons who would pay for his services. Arriving in Chicago three weeks before the official opening of the Exposition, Dunbar stayed with his brother and his family, who were living in the city. First, he got a job as a waiter in a downtown hotel, much like the one he held after graduating from high school in his native Dayton, Ohio, and which he was performing when he first started to write and publish his poems. Dunbar then worked as a caretaker in a washroom until Wendell Phillips Dabney, one of his newfound friends, introduced him to Joseph Douglass, the grandson of Frederick Douglass. Douglass had been unable to secure a position with the United States concession, but he was in charge of the Haitian exhibit. He had been United States minister to Haiti. From their meeting, Dunbar secured the job as Douglass' assistant in the Haitian exhibit. The position paid little money, but it fostered close association among the young black artists who had come to Chicago to try their fortunes at the Fair. Dunbar had published his first collection of poetry, *Oak and Ivy*.

Colored American Day at the Fair—hastily arranged for August 25, 1933—featured many of the black artists who had assembled in Chicago with a hope of participating in some way in the Exposition. Will Marion Cook and Joseph Douglass played violin selections. The noted baritone Harry T. Burleigh sang. Dunbar read a poem he had written especially for the occasion. The black tenor Sidney Woodward sang excerpts from the opera *Uncle Tom's Cabin*, and the elocutionist Hallie Q. Brown read the poem "The Black Regiment." Harrison was present. After the Fair, Dunbar and Harrison formed a mutual-aid pact. Harrison read Dunbar's most popular poems from a platform while the poet moved about the crowds trying to sell copies of *Oak and Ivy*. Their friendship grew, and the two men established a home together in Chicago. Cook introduced Harrison to Gertrude Janet Washington of Chicago, who was the first black graduate of Chicago Musical College. They were married January 1, 1905. Dunbar was best man at the wedding. The Harrisons' first child was named Laurence Gilbert Harrison in honor of the black poet and friends of his parents. Although Harrison and Dunbar soon sought different paths for their lives, they were associated together on occasion until the poet's untimely death in 1906. Dunbar is best known as a poet; however, he also wrote fiction and tried his hand at playwriting. Two of his efforts were written at the request of Harrison, who referred to them some thirty years later in this manner:

The play he (Dunbar) wrote for me was called *Robert Herrick* around the life of the English poet of that name. It is on the order of the old English Robin Hood plays, and I do not think the theme is quite strong enough to make an appeal at that time. It was in prose and beautifully written, but it is a light, airy theme, without what seems to be essential to present day fancies. In other words, he had no sex appeal, and I am afraid at my age I could not put it in if it had. There were three acts. He wrote it about 1899. . . . He wrote a little play, also for me, called "Winter Roses." A little love theme where an old man was urged by his son to see his sweetheart, with the usual results. He sent her some flowers for Christmas, and he called them winter roses.[19]

From 1892 to 1896, Harrison worked under the sponsorship of the Great Western Lyceum Bureau of California. Engagements came occasionally, but he continued working as a waiter or a porter on the railroads that ran between Chicago and the West Coast. At one time he was a clerk in the audit department of the Pullman Company in Chicago and served for another period as a mail clerk for the Santa Fe Railroad in Los Angeles. In those years, toward the close of the century, Harrison endeared himself to the Chicago Southside. He gained confidence and a strong following in that part of town. Among them he had astounded an audience that packed the basement of Quinn Chapel African Methodist Episcopal Church, then located at Twenty-fourth Street and Wabash Avenue, a year before the World's Fair. He was equally popular with performances at Olivet Baptist Church and Bethel African Methodist Episcopal Church. His first performance in a theater was at the old Peking at Twenty-seventh and State streets, the first black-owned theater in the United States. From there he went on to appear at the Grand Theatre at Thirty-first and State streets. His standard repertoire included passages from *Macbeth, Julius Caesar, The Merchant of Venice,* and, particularly, Dunbar's "Little Brown Baby." Other selections included poems by Edgar Allen Poe and Rudyard Kipling. Clearly, he could not support his family on proceeds from his recitals. But he was making a reputation as a dramatic reader forty years after he met Dunbar at the World's Fair in Chicago. This time a *Chicago Daily News* columnist, writing about Negro Day, August 11, 1933, called Harrison "the most admired Negro alive" as a result of his role in *The Green Pastures.*[20] When *The Green Pastures* cast arrived in Chicago for its first road tour in 1931, old-timers on the Southside considered Harrison one of theirs. They had helped him become a national celebrity who had taught them to appreciate the poetry and drama he read. Most black performers of the time were performing in vaudeville acts.

His success on the reading platform convinced Harrison that there was an interest in developing dramatic performances among black churches and schools. Speaking of those days later, he recalled: "As I traveled and lived in the houses of various friends, it was astonishing to see the material among young people who were eager for this training, and I felt that our religious and educational institutions should provide it for them."[21] In the early years of the twentieth century, Harrison taught English and speech at Flipper-Key College, a small African Methodist Episcopal church school in Oklahoma. Bert Williams, Jim Europe, Jesse Shipp, and Lester Walton were among the black men associated with entertainment who first brought him to New York with a view toward his joining the commercial theater. In September 1914 they persuaded Harrison to come to New York to furnish the feature attraction in the Autumn Exposition they were planning for the Old Manhattan Casino. Harrison was promised fifteen dollars for the first appearance. Promoters wondered whether New Yorkers would respond favorably to an obscure country schoolteacher who recited Shakespeare. The image was not compatible with their perceptions of the new black variety shows, but their fears proved unfounded, for audiences warmly accepted Harrison's work. He was so pleased with the reception that he was not concerned when he learned he could not get paid even the fifteen dollars offered. He often referred to this experience as one of the happiest nights of his life. It was probably a reason for his deciding to move East and divide his time between reading on a lyceum circuit in New York and working with black schools and colleges on a part-time basis. He used Haines Institute in Augusta, Georgia, largely as his headquarters during this period. Lucy Craft Laney, founder and principal of that school, which was partially supported by the Presbyterian Church in the United States, provided Harrison a basis for operation. He could teach there, direct dramatic productions, and assist Haines in its ever-necessary fund drives. And he could fill recital engagements as they came along.

Harrison's next jaunt into popular entertainment on the stage came in 1922, primarily as a result of his previous association with Dunbar, Cook, and Burleigh at the Columbia exposition in Chicago in 1893. Cook's son, Mercer Cook, recalled that incident some twenty years later:

Rehearsals were in progress down at the old Clef Club on 53rd Street. Every afternoon, Paul Robeson, Carl White, the inimitable Tom Fletcher, Taylor Gordon, the unforgettable "Bass" Foster, the late Hartwell Cook, and a few others whose names I no longer remember, would practice vocal numbers. Sidney Bechet, Ralph "Shrimp" Jones, Henry Saparo, Duke Ellington's Broh, the late Julian Arthur, an unknown young man named Fletcher Henderson, and about twenty odd musicians would be working on such current favorites as "Tiger Rag" and "When Hearts Are Young," as well as more difficult selections like Brahms' *Hungarian Dance* (Number five) and Dvorak's *Bohemian Dances*. Georgette Harvey, the Rivera Sisters, and a young dancer, Bessie de Sessaure, provided the feminine relief. Richard B. Harrison attended these daily meetings, but never rehearsed. I still failed to see how he and "Tiger Rag" were going to compete on the same program.[22]

The show opened at Gibson's Theatre in Philadelphia. It was well received. Paul Robeson had to sing three encores of J. Rosamond Johnson's *Li'l Gal*. Georgette Harvey made a hit singing "Eli, Eli" and "Love Sends a Little Gift of Roses." Harrison seemed out of place with the denizens of the Jazz Age on the program. When his turn came to perform, he recited Dunbar's "Little Brown Baby." By the end of the first stanza, Cook wrote, "he had convinced his listeners—and how they were listening!—that there actually was a baby on the stage." As encores, he recited "The Shooting of Dan McGrew" and "The Face on the Barroom Floor" and became the feature attraction of the show. Al Jolson and other successful show people attended performances of the extravaganza, but it failed financially. Harrison had to assist his colleagues by lending them carfare back to New York. These two brief flirtations with New York theater, including his taking a role in Frank Wilson's *Pa Williams Gal*, a melodrama written and produced by one of the several black figures in show business at the time, quite possibly brought Harrison to Marc Connelly's attention when the playwright was casting for *The Green Pastures*.

During the summer of 1922, Harrison went to North Carolina, primarily to recover from a "nervous breakdown." There he met James B. Dudley, president of the Agricultural and Technical College at Greensboro. Warmouth T. Gibbs, a president emeritus of that institution, who was dean of its College of Education at that time, describes in part the experience that led eventually to the phenomenal success of Marc Connelly's *The Green Pastures*:

> Mr. Harrison gave a concert at A. and T., and it was then that he and President Dudley first met and agreed on a plan to have him return to the college at the end of his concert season to teach elocution and dramatics in the A. and T. College summer school. He readily admitted that his teaching salary was small, nevertheless, it was definite and certain, which had not been the case on concert tours. Mr. Harrison's students in the summer school were regular public school teachers who attended summer school to seek new and more effective ways of teaching students. They were especially interested in his ability as an elocutionist and would become so thrilled with his instruction that they frequently engaged him to give concerts at their schools during the ensuing regular term. In this way he was able to present the type of concert before the type of audience which he had hoped for but seldom was able to get under the old commission plan.[23]

Harrison first joined the college summer school faculty there in 1923 and continued his association each year until 1930, at which time he accepted the role in *The Green Pastures*. He was not a member of the regular college faculty. During the school year he resumed his reading performances around the country. The college has always given strong recognition to Harrison's work there during those several summers. The principal auditorium on the campus is named Richard B. Harrison Auditorium, and the dramatic group of the institution bears his name. His summer courses opened with seventeen teachers in attendance. When he left A. and T. to take the role of "De Lawd," about two hundred persons were enrolling in the courses or the cast of the plays Harrison presented. Many persons have commented on Harrison's reluctance to accept the role in *The Green Pastures* when it was first offered to him. It is commonly thought he liked his work at A. and T. and wanted to continue teaching there in the summer school. A deeply religious man, Harrison balked at playing God on the stage. He feared that audiences would consider the role sacrilegious. And he simply did not relish trying his hand at so demanding a task to be undertaken in his sixty-fifth year. From among the many interviews he gave concerning his reluctance to accept the part when it was offered, the following excerpt is representative of Harrison's comments on the matter:

> When Marc Connelly asked that I read the text, I was not at all impressed. "Is you been baptized? . . . Yes, sah, Lawd. . . . On with the fish fry." . . . I just couldn't see it, and returned the play to Mr. Connelly, who insisted that I keep it. There was no hurry, he said, and to read it at my leisure, but each time I had the same feeling. . . . Then one day Mr. Connelly asked if I wouldn't drop in to rehearsal just to "help out," and I consented. One night I was laughing over those opening lines with some friends of mine, the telephone rang. Mr. Connelly was reminding me of my promise. I said, "Yes, I'll be at rehearsal at eleven in the morning, and I'm going to stick with you until the end." . . . My friends said I was trembling as I replaced the telephone. I cannot tell you what brought about that sudden reversal of my former decision.[24]

Connelly's version of this part of the casting story is somewhat different from Harrison's. The playwright had little assurance that he would find the multitude of actors his play required. Stebbins insisted on participating in interviewing prospective performers. He had hoped that the mere announcement that a play with an all-Negro cast of nearly one hundred persons was about to go into rehearsal would produce a host of prospective actors. However, they rather quickly exhausted the list of theatrical persons they knew. Wesley Hill, the actor they knew best because of his impressive role as Jake in Du Bose Heyward's *Porgy*, was signed to play the angel Gabriel. Within a few days, dozens of other actors, some of proven accomplishment, had been secured. Filling the role of "De Lawd" presented the most serious problem. Connelly and Stebbins realized that the success or failure of the play depended on their casting for the role. So they canvassed all of their friends for candidates for the part, and they moved up to Harlem to interview continuously at the Lafayette Theatre. Somehow they had believed hundreds of blacks in Harlem could be found to play in the drama. But they had specific qualifications for the principal character. He had to be physically big, have a dignified and noble bearing, and a voice that was rich with authority and capable of thunderous wrath. They had tried several times to entice the Reverend Adam Clayton Powell, Sr., pastor of the prestigious Abyssinian Baptist Church in Harlem and the best-known pulpiteer amng black clergy, to consider the part. He had the physical characteristics. And he liked the play. But he declined to leave the pulpit for the stage. Connelly tells about the day he and Stebbins made one more trek to Harlem to interview prospective actors for the part:

> When we arrived at the agency, the agent had a scattering of new faces for us to see. Desperately we tried to picture one as improving with voice lessons, another at least a little bit taller with shoe lifts, this one's scanty hair covered with a wig, or padding on a tall, scarecrow-like figure. When the last one had been thanked for coming, Rowland and I were wordless, silently plumbing new ocean-like depths of depression. Then the casting agent came in from the outer office. "I've got an old fellow here I just heard about the other day. He's not an actor, but he'd done some reading in schools and certainly looks like what we're after."[25]

The old gentleman was shown in. Connelly remembered the incident forty years later and compared the appearance to a line in the play *Here Are Ladies*, in which James Stephen says, "God came down the street like a man and a half." For in the dingy little office, "Richard Berry Harrison appeared with similar dimensions." There was the physical size, the leonine gray hair, the face that "had managed to weather sixty-five years of struggle and disheartenment." That face, Connelly wrote, was "maturedly serene because of the dauntless inner strength of the gentle being who wore it."

Harrison spoke with his "voice like a cello's" and said he had heard they were looking for actors, and that he had been told he might be right for the part. And Connelly continued:

Mr. Harrison agreed to read the play that night. The next morning he telephoned that he had read the play. He had found himself agreeing that a great many Negroes interpreted the Bible the way the people in the play did. He was doubtful of his qualifications to play De Lawd. It was true, he said, that in Negro schools about the country he had read scenes from Shakespeare's plays and recited the poems of Paul Laurence Dunbar who he told us had been best man at his wedding. He also questioned the ability to learn to speak in the dialect of the deep South because his speech was acquired in Montreal where he had been born. As a religious grandson of slaves who had fled from Alabama to Canada by way of the Underground Railroad, he had a final and much more serious question that must be answered. "I know you weren't trying to make fun of my people when you wrote the play, Mr. Connelly, but I wouldn't like to do something that might make Negroes feel I'd let them down. I just don't know what to do."[26]

After he learned Harrison was a member of the Episcopal Church, Stebbins asked his personal and close friend Herbert Shipman, the Suffragan Bishop of New York, to talk to Harrison. After their conversation, which lasted longer than two hours, Connelly received the telephone call Harrison had promised. They agreed to sign the contract for the play. Literally forty-eight hours before they were scheduled to begin reading the drama in preliminary rehearsal, Connelly wrote that he and Stebbins "came as close to uttering a prayer as a couple of agnostics could." Quite aside from his reservations about the propriety of performing the role of God on stage, Harrison considered Connelly's play foreign to the kind of work he had done on stage all his life. He had recited the Dunbar poems as a staple of his repertoire, but he was not a comic actor. This impressive dignity, in demeanor and diction, qualified him eminently for the role. He could bring the complex dimensions playing "De Lawd" would require from anyone who undertook the part.

Copious reviews attest to Harrison's unique qualifications for carrying the major meaning of *The Green Pastures*. He *made* the play. His task was made more difficult than that undertaken previously by any other black American in the theater. The role represented the end of major successes achieved by white playwrights writing black drama. And he carried the complex transition from the vaudeville tradition into another form of theater. Moreover, he was working in the delicate area of religious representation in the theater. One taking on the role would have to satisfy the "New Negro" concept that permeated the art, society, and politics of the post-World War I era. At the same time he would seek to bring success to a play using hundreds of black actors and singers in the throes of the Great Depression.

William Fields, a commercial publicist, sent out an announcement that *The Green Pastures*, a play with an all-Negro cast, was about to go into rehearsal no later than December 29, 1929. The opening would take place February 26, 1930. When he and Stebbins went uptown to Harlem to seek out actors for a play they would bring to the Broadway stage within five weeks, they believed their task would be routine. Many years later Connelly wrote that while there were no official statistics to prove it, people said Harlem's population included "ten thousand actors and actresses, dancers, and other entertainers." He apparently believed this myth that infuriated black Americans. Two weeks after the play opened at the Mansfield, James "Billboard" Jackson, a Harlem publicist and musician, wrote scathingly about the tone of reviews of the drama:

> Another Drama with a colored cast has been launched on Broadway: and again we have the spectacle of a producing manager being presented in interviews in the daily press as a diligent searcher through all the byways for Negroes capable of depicting the parts called for by their scripts. . . . The (pernicious) habit of depriving Negro talent of any recognition of its past achievement, any benefit of its experience, or of the utilization of the history of the individual artist, seems to be a fixed policy with the producers and the press. It grudgingly admits inherent acting ability, but denies the existence of training or professional poise. This prevents performers from acquiring reputations and keeps the salaries down.[27]

Unlike Connelly, Jackson did know black actors and their experiences with the theater. He wrote that the persons chosen for *The Green Pastures* had not been discovered "in kitchens and other out of the way places," as the press claimed, but that their names "sound like a Who's Who or the membership of the Equity Florence Mills' Memorial, Dressing Room Club and Clef Club all in one." His column, addressed to black readers of a Harlem black weekly newspaper, hardly changed the myth. Connelly gives the same impression in his memoirs. Although he might not have known much about the Harlem theatre movement that flowered in the 1920s, until it was temporarily halted by the Depression, or about the Ethiopian Theatre Group of W.E.B. Du Bois' Krigwa Players, Connelly fell heir to the best of the old-time vaudeville personalities and of those who played the musicals and revues that replaced the minstrels. And he stood to benefit from the experiences actors had gained on the legitimate stage playing the few parts for black actors in the commercial theater. The number was not large, but they furnished the large cast. They were not those few names most Broadway producers knew from the few plays that had been put on stage during the earlier "cultural paternalism" period. Those who played strong supporting roles, as well as atmosphere players, had to be contacted. Their estrangement from the mainline of agency representation becomes clear when one realizes how Connelly and Stebbins went about looking for a cast.

Their primary contact was Bernard Burt, a former manager of the old Lafayette Theatre, who, together with John Carey and Malcolm Frazier, operated the Colored Independent Theatrical Agency on 132nd Street. Burt was white, Carey and Frazier were black. They also owned the Nest, a nightclub in the same building with the agency. During his visits to Harlem, Connelly learned about the "Tree of Hope" that stood in front of the Lafayette Theatre on Seventh Avenue. "It was an ordinary plane tree," he wrote, and the bark was practically worn off. According to legend among the actors, one who touched the trunk of the tree and prayed for work would be lucky. That bit of lore must have seemed particularly attractive to Connelly. It fitted well with his view of the black American's religious practices, a view that was the dramatic action of his new play. Jules Bledsoe, Charles Gilpin, Rose McClendon, and Paul Robeson—the best-known black actors—are noticeably absent from the cast of supporting characters who took to *The Green Pastures* stage with Richard B. Harrison. James Weldon Johnson notes that "at least twenty parts in which the acting is of high merit could be singled out."[28] And he judged that the play could hardly be mentioned without giving attention to the work of Wesley Hill, Daniel Haynes, Tutt Whitney, and Charles H. Moore. Roles for black actors were so scarce that few persons could make a living in the theater. Whitney, who was also a columnist for the *Pittsburgh Courier*, wrote about the impact of the opening of *The Green Pastures* on the employment of black actors:

> If there has been a plethora of one thing this past winter it has been a superabundance of the unemployed. The scarcity of work laid a heavy pressure upon actors. There was no bread-line in evidence, but every time an actor secured a week's work there was a line of landlords, landladies and creditors waiting to relieve the actor of his salary.[29]

Some of the ninety-six actors and singers had been members of the Lafayette Players, the first black stock company in the United States. It arose out of the history and development of two theaters in Harlem—the Lafayette and the Lincoln.[30] The Lincoln opened on Christmas Eve of 1908 as a "storefront" experimental theater with 297 seats. Its fare of regular vaudeville and motion pictures made the Lincoln one of the most popular playhouses in the United States. The Lafayette was built in 1912.

Bill "Bojangles" Robinson was the one who was said to have planted the "Tree of Hope" outside the theater. Both houses featured "tab" shows as fillers between vaudeville acts and silent movies. These skits of fifteen to twenty minutes were the forerunners of the full-length plays that brought "straight drama" into vogue in Harlem.

The first full-length drama performed at the Lincoln was *The Girl of the Fort*, a five-act drama written by Billie Burke. It opened November 14, 1915. From this inauspicious beginning, the Anita Bush Stock Company, later called the Lafayette Players when the bulk of their activity moved to the Lafayette Theatre, came the most important theatrical tradition in Harlem. The Bush Company made its debut December 27, 1915, with *Across the Footlights*. Cyril V. Briggs, a popular politician and journalist in Harlem, wrote drama and sports news for the *Amsterdam News*, beginning with a review of the Billie Burke play. Lester A. Walton, a member of the staff of the *New York Age*, wrote drama reviews and announcements for his paper, and he also became involved in supplying musical and vaudeville shows in the Lafayette from 1914 until 1916. He was part owner of the theater at one time. He and Briggs initiated drama reviews in black newspapers and, in doing so, fostered the growth of a viable black theater in Harlem. Charles Gilpin, who made Eugene O'Neill famous with his portrayals of the leading role in *The Emperor Jones*, was an early member of the Players. Others included Dooley Wilson, who later was known for his role in motion pictures such as *Of Mice and Men*, *Cabin in the Sky*, and *Casablanca*, and Clarence Muse, Inez Clough, and Abbie Mitchell, to name only a few of the most popular personalities.

Connelly offered one of the first contracts to Wesley Hill, a veteran of some forty years in show business. Born in Baltimore, he had begun his career in the theater as a dancer and a bit player in the medicine and "Tom" shows. He had played the role of a Kickapoo Indian and had barked to provide sound effects for the hound dogs in the old comedy circuits. Moving to a long career on the dramatic stage, he had appeared in such sturdy dramas as *In Old Kentucky* and *Slavery Days*, and he was famous in vaudeville before the reign of the fabled Bert Williams and had parts in the musical revue *Running Wild* and *Shuffle Along*. Before joining the cast of *The Green Pastures*, Hill had completed a successful run as Jake, the fishing boat captain, in Du Bose Heyward's *Porgy*. He played Gabriel in the Connelly play and became a favorite among audiences for his opening line, "Gangway for de Lawd God Almighty," which critics called the most arresting announcement on the American stage. Photographers liked to catch whoever played that part in the impish gesture of fingering the large horn that would signal the end of the world and the Lord's good-natured chiding that the imperial trumpeter should wait just a little longer before signaling the eternal damnation of the sinful race of men who had grieved God by their incontinent behavior.

Hill played the role for nearly twelve months of the first New York run. In December 1930 he was struck down by a taxicab as he walked toward his home from the Florence Mills Theatrical Association offices after a performance at the Mansfield. He was pronounced dead on arrival at Sydenham Hospital. Hundreds of mourners attended his funeral at St. Mark's Methodist Church in Harlem on Sunday afternoon, December 13, 1930. Daniel Haynes, who played Adam and Hezdrel on stage, read the obituary. Members of the Hall Johnson Choir sang. Honorary pallbearers included prominent members of the cast.[31] Brooks Atkinson wrote about Wesley's death: "Every newspaper mourned his journey to the greenest pasture of all, and every one in town understood why."[32]

Charles Winter Wood, Richard B. Harrison's longtime friend, was his understudy throughout the five years of the play's first successful runs. One year younger than Harrison, Wood was born in Nashville, Tennessee, the son of a Methodist preacher who moved his family to Chicago when Charles was nine. He first met Harrison when both were in their teens and working at odd jobs in Chicago. They shared an interest in the drama. Through the intercession of Charles L. Hutchison, president of the Corn Exchange Bank in Chicago, Wood was admitted to Beloit College in Wisconsin. Hutchison had heard the youth reciting Shakespeare as he shined shoes in the Loop. Plymouth Congregational Church in the city contributed to the cost of his college education. At Beloit, Wood majored in the classics. There he also represented the college in a state declamation contest for which William Jennings Bryan was a judge. After receiving his bachelor's degree at Beloit, Wood earned a master's degree at Columbia University in New York City on a Rockefeller Scholarship and returned to Chicago to pursue a bachelor of divinity degree at the University of Chicago.[33] Immediately before joining the cast of *The Green Pastures*, Wood worked as a librarian and drama teacher at Tuskegee Institute in Alabama. He played the part of Abraham in addition to understudying Harrison's role as "De Lawd." The two men were together in a dressing room when Harrison collapsed from physical exhaustion just before he was to go on stage on March 3, 1935. Previously, Wood had never appeared in the principal role. Several times he had come close, once when Harrison's taxicab was wrecked en route to the theater. The star was unhurt, and although the curtain was delayed for half an hour, "De Lawd" played as usual that night.

Wood bore a strong resemblance to Harrison, although he had to have his short black hair powdered to resemble the star's long, silky white locks so familiar in any photograph of the actor.

The role of Noah was played by Salem Tutt Whitney, who was born in Logansport, Indiana, shortly after the close of the Civil War. He was one of twelve children of a small-town preacher. Whitney began his career in 1894 with the Puggsley Brothers Tennessee Warblers as a bass singer. Within the next decade he performed with several touring companies and their shows, including Black Patti's Troubadours, Eph Williams' "Silas Green from New Orleans," and Sherman H. Dudley's "Smart Set." In 1908 he and his brother, J. Homer Tutt, organized the Smarter Set Company, which became one of the most successful of the black touring companies. They produced fifteen musicals, including *Mayor of Newtown, George Washington Bullion Abroad,* and *Darkest Americans.* Their most successful production was the popular jazz operetta *Bamboula.*

Salem also wrote poetry. He published a slight volume of his poems titled *Mellow Musings.* His best-known play, *Mammy's Journey,* was set in a jim crow railroad car. For more than twenty years Whitney wrote columns for black weekly newspapers. His "Seen and Heard While Passing" appeared in the *Indianapolis Freeman* and his "Timely Topics" was carried in the *Chicago Defender* during the entire time that Whitney played in *The Green Pastures.* These columns proved some of the most reliable and comprehensive information available on black theatrical activities in the 1920s and 1930s. He died in 1934, having been hospitalized while on tour with the drama in New Orleans the year before. He was often quoted as saying, "I'd rather be 'Noah' in 'Green Pastures' than mayor of Harlem."

A contemporary of Whitney's, Jesse A. Shipp, was known as the dean of black theatrical personalities since the passing of Sam Lucas. At some time he played Archangel, Abraham, and Noah. Shipp had been a member of Bert Williams and George Wasker's company of vaudeville troupers. Like Whitney, he wrote books for many musical comedies, including *The Policy Player,* with music by Will Marion Cook and featuring Williams and Walker. In rapid succession, his shows appeared in the early years of the twentieth century in black theaters in Harlem, Chicago, and Washington and on the several theatrical circuits. The most successful of them included *The Sons of Ham* (1900), *In Dahomey* (1902), *In Abyssinia* (1905), *In Bandanna Land* (1907), and *Mr. Lode of Kal* (1909). Shipp retired from his active career in the theater in 1917 but returned to perform in *The Green Pastures.* At the time of the opening of the drama, he had been in show business for forty years. Born in Cincinnati, he began his career there singing in a quartet in white churches. He first went on the popular stage with the Eureka Minstrel and worked with the Primrose and West show, which was composed of forty white and thirty black entertainers. After the demise of the popular Walker and Williams troupe, Shipp went to Chicago to produce stock theater for the Pekin Theatre. He continued his association with vaudeville. His son, Jesse Shipp, Jr., founded the Shipp Association in Harlem, a booking agency. Salem Tutt Whitney once wrote that Shipp had "won the right to be the esteemed dean of the Colored Theatrical profession." He continued: "Mr. Shipp is now playing the role of the 'Archangel' in 'Green

Pastures.' He goes to heaven every night and every Wednesday and Thursday afternoon. That is some compensation for a life of notable achievement."[34]

The Green Pastures opens with the Sunday school scene, in which Mr. Deshee, the kindly and patient rural black preacher, is reading from Genesis to young children in his congregation. He establishes the state of the universe before the creation of the world as it is told in the Old Testament. His interpolations set the scene for the fantasies that make up the principal body of the eighteen scenes of the pageant. Called the "old man" among the Lafayette Players, Charles H. Moore, who played the part of Mr. Deshee, had been a schoolteacher in the South before taking on a career in the theater. He, no doubt, understood well the nature of the vivid imagination of children who pondered the dramatic stories of the Old Testament and fashioned them in their minds as the preacher went about his duty as Sunday school teacher. Moreover, Moore understood well the contemporary theater. Like others taking principal parts in *The Green Pastures*, he had been part of the touring companies of the Williams and Walker troupe. Moore joined the Lafayette Players in the early 1920s. From time to time he served as director for units that performed on the Theater Owners' Booking Association circuit. When the Players left New York to establish themselves in the new Lincoln Theatre in Los Angeles in 1928, Moore remained in the East. His most important dramatic role before joining the Connelly drama had been the central character in Frank Wilson's *Meek Moses*, which enjoyed a reasonably successful run in the theater in 1928. He also played in both the stage and screen versions of *Porgy*.[35]

Adam opens the Old Testament stories that make up the dramatic action of *The Green Pastures*. Hezdrel, a creation of Connelly's imagination, concludes it. Both roles are brief. In the Garden of Eden scene, Connelly omits the snake as the tempter of Eve in order to show, from the beginning of the action, his concern with how God deals with evil in the world rather than how evil comes into the world. Hezdrel carried the full impact of the progressive development of God as a power oriented more toward mercy than toward justice. Playing both these roles requires uncommon talent. Daniel Haynes played both well. Unlike most of the other principal actors in the drama, he had no experience with vaudeville. Atlanta-born and college-educated, he came to New York to pursue graduate study in theology. He soon dropped that pursuit and became actively interested in singing and acting. He joined the Art Students' League of New York and achieved some distinction among his peers as an amateur painter and served as a soloist in a church choir in Jersey City. For a living, he worked as a clerk in a Harlem phonographic recording concern.

Haynes came first to the professional stage as understudy to Charles

Gilpin, who was scheduled to star in *The Bottom of the Cup*. When Gilpin was unable to open the play because of illness, Haynes took the principal role. That same year Haynes appeared in Miller and Lyles' musical comedy *Rang Tang*, which showed at the Majestic Theater. After the close of *The Green Pastures* and its first five-year run, Haynes became a motion picture personality, starring in such films as King Vidor's epochal *Hallelujah!* and *The Last Mile*.[36]

In his weekly column after the opening of *The Green Pastures*, Salem Tutt Whitney wrote about all of the black actors who were included in the cast. He knew them personally. He wrote that the production had "added another page to the history of Colored actors" and that it had "given an impetus to Colored theatrical business and benefits not only to those immediately identified with the show, but to the entire Colored theatrical profession."[37]

Harrison did not come out of the theatrical tradition that had been common to most of the supporting cast. They knew him, however. For during the many years he had performed as an elocutionist throughout the United States, his path had crossed those of most black actors and musicians. This bank of talent did not rise spontaneously the moment Connelly and Stebbins walked into Burt's little theatrical agency in Harlem. *The Green Pastures* on the stage was a distillation of the experiences and aspirations of black Americans in the theater. That quality made the performance unique.

Difficult as finding a producer and choosing a cast for the play had been, Connelly's problems did not end with accomplishing these goals. It was difficult to rent space in the Broadway area to rehearse plays with Negro actors; so great was the prejudice against them. Connelly reports that every stage except one was denied to him. The one he found was the tiny Belmont Theatre on Forty-eighth Street just off Times Square. Its stage was far too small for the cast of some one hundred actors and singers. When Bryant Hall, on Sixth Avenue opposite Bryant Park, became available, he moved the rehearsals there. Built as a luxurious mid-nineteenth-century collection of several floors of elegant assembly rooms, Bryant Hall had deteriorated by the late twenties into what Connelly described as "a dilapidated warren" for performers in every branch of professional entertainment. Especially for those operating on tight budgets. It was hardly a respectable stable for the birthplace of the drama that would become the "Prince" of the American theater for its age, for

> day and night through thin walls call the noise bedlam of musical comedy choruses, jazz bands, and other groups rehearsing. Floors sagged under the pounding feet of dancers and acrobats. The pungent smells of disinfectants failed to

subdue the building's permanent odor of decay. Wintry gusts jostled drafty windows. The clanking steam radiators did not provide as much heat as the bodies of the hall's tenants.[38]

Yet the cast was cheerful. Many of them guarded themselves against optimism because they knew only too well the tenuousness of the theater business and the too many times that a planned production never moved from rehearsal hall to the commercial stage.

Harrison's inexperience as an actor proved less troublesome than Connelly had at first thought it would be. He had to learn the mechanics of movements and especially how to act while walking on the complex treadmill that three ingenious engineers had contrived in order to execute those parts of the sets that called for movement in dramatic action of hundreds of members of the cast. Harrison was apprehensive about learning the long lines of his part of the script in the less-than-five-week rehearsal period. His fears were eased when Connelly promised him at least three prompters instead of the customary one. (In the early days of rehearsals, during a conference between Connelly and Stebbins, the two men disagreed seriously over whether to retain in the script the "Little David" scene that dramatized the biblical fight between David, the shepherd boy, and the giant Goliath. For reasons Connelly does not fully explain—other than that he had decided this element did not fit the tone of the rest of the work—he convinced Stebbins to eliminate it. This piece was published separately later as a dramatic sketch in *Cosmopolitan* magazine and was produced several times by puppeteers in the United States and in Canada.)

Aside from the problems of casting and production and technical staging—complex and challenging as they were—Connelly worried about another series of problems that he could not solve by technical or artistic experience in the theater. He had no way of knowing how two acknowledged agnostics—Connelly and Stebbins—could accurately anticipate how the Christian church in America would react to this play on religion. Rumors floated in that certain fundamentalist protestant ministers were set to attack the work as sacrilege. As late as forty-eight hours before the opening, Connelly uttered a prayer of thanks, as he wrote about it, that matters had gone well to that point. They knew, however, that several Southern newspapers had already warned that they would take to their editorial pages to scream their indignation for what they considered intemperate use of the Bible, and especially for what they knew must be the forthcoming burlesque of the sacred Scriptures placed in the hands of black singers and actors. On the morning of the premiere, Miriam Doyle, wardrobe mistress, and some of her corps of tailors and seamstresses found in the secondhand clothing store on Seventh Avenue the perfect black frock coat for Harrison to wear as "De Lawd." Danny Murphy,

one of the property men, also found that same afternoon a handsomely
bound copy of *A History of Ireland*, which proved to be a perfect book
cover for the Sunday school teacher to use for the passages he would
read to his class of children.

Equally serious was the concern over how black Americans, flush
with the vigor of the "New Negro" philosophy and ethos, would react to
this portrayal of their race in a folk idiom of language and behavior that,
though perhaps historically accurate as fantastic theater, might offend
the sensitivities of those who sought hard to find rapprochement among
white and black Americans. The principal black periodicals—the newspapers that were circulated throughout the nation in areas in which
black people lived—and the house organs of the National Association for
the Advancement of Colored People and the National Urban League de-
manded respect, even if to a tentative degree, from the most sophisticated white authors and entrepreneurs. Stebbins and Connelly sought
advice on how best to at least let leading black personalities in Harlem
know what the play would contain. So they invited Walter F. White,
author of two strong propagandistic novels against lynching, and secretary of the NAACP, to attend one of the rehearsals. How seriously
producer and playwright viewed securing the tacit approval, or at least
to diminish the possibility of outright hostility toward the play, is shown
in their having relaxed their strict locked-door policy against outsiders
during rehearsals to invite White to sit in. In writing about this incident
in an article he published three years into the New York run of *The Green
Pastures*, White wrote:

> I have been invited to sit in on rehearsals and have been reluc-
> tant to do so, for I had known Marc Connelly only as the
> author of shrewdly satirical plays such as *Beggar on Horse-
> back*, *Dulcy*, *To the Ladies*, and *The Wisdom Tooth*. After
> offering various excuses, I finally went to the theater one
> bitingly cold Sunday afternoon early in February, 1930. The
> theater was cold and drafty, there were no costumes or sets,
> the cast had reached that stage of rehearsing hated by mana-
> gers and stage directors where pristine excitement had died
> down and the actors are looking ahead to the far-off opening
> night more or less as children do to the coming of Christmas.
> But for Marc Connelly there was no Santa Claus a long way
> off—for him Christmas was already here. His bald head glis-
> tening in the footlights, he dashed about, giving a word of
> advice here, of encouragement or approval there, of instruc-
> tion to this one or that. Between times he told in vivid
> snatches of description of the sets Robert Edmond Jones had

designed, of the costumes then in the making. And above all else there was a tenderness and respect in the relations between Mr. Connelly and Mr. Harrison that was not of the theater. It was as though the simplicity of the play and its characters had also filled the author and leading player of *The Green Pastures*.[39]

Connelly apparently told White at some time during that period before the play opened its first New York run that he had been searching for a long time for "something tangible in belief in a world of scoffing, of skepticism, and of doubt of everything and everybody." Time and time again, Connelly claimed, he had believed his search ended only to find himself mistaken until he had by chance read Roark Bradford's *Ol' Man Adam an' His Chillun*. He found in these sketches, Connelly told White, that Bradford had been content simply to serve as amanuesis in recording what he had heard from the lips of Negroes living in his native Louisiana. Clearly, Connelly had embellished the Bradford works, and he had done so by going to see and hear for himself the material another man had recorded but that he would make into theater. This indication of a sincerity of purpose seemed to satisfy White's skepticism about Connelly's purposes. And, to a large extent, observing the relationship between Connelly and Harrison—particularly the respect with which the playwright and director handled the venerable Richard B. Harrison—led the NAACP to reserve its judgment about the play until it reached the stage.

Prepared as best he could be for his revolutionary forage into so complex a spectacle as his play about black folk, played by black actors to the accompaniment of black music sung by black singers—all performed primarily for the delectation of white audiences—Connelly approached the stage premiere of *The Green Pastures*.

With the cast in place and in one of the shortest periods of rehearsal given to a major production that became an instant success on Broadway, *The Green Pastures* was ready for the opening on the date Connelly and Stebbins had set. The names of the entire cast follow.

CAST OF CHARACTERS

(in order of their appearance)

Mr. Deshee	Charles H. Moore
Myrtle	Alicia Escamilla
First Boy	Jazzlips Richardson, Jr.
Second	Howard Washington

Third Boy .... Reginald Blythwood
Randolph .... Joe Byrd
A Cook .... Frances Smith
Custard Maker.. Homer Tutt
First Mammy Angel .... Anna Mae Fritz
A Stout Angel.. Josephine Byrd
A Slender Angel .... Edna Thrower
Archangel.. J. A. Shipp
Gabriel... Wesley Hill
The Lord .... Richard B. Harrison
Choir Leader .... McKinley Reeves
Adam.. Daniel L. Haynes
Eve... Inez Richardson Wilson
Cain.. Lou Vernon
Cain's Girl... Dorothy Randolph
Zeba .... Edna M. Harris
Cain the Sixth .... James Fuller
Boy Gambler... Louis Kelsey
First Gambler .... Collington Hayes
Second Gambler... Ivan Sharp
Voice in Shanty... Josephine Byrd
Noah .... Tutt Whitney
Noah's Wife.. Susie Sutton
Shem.. Milton J. Williams
First Woman... Dinks Thomas
Second Woman ....Anna Mae Fritz
Third Woman .... Geneva Blythwood
First Man .... Emory Richardson
Flatfoot.. Freddie Archibald
Ham.. J. Homer Tutt
Japheth.. Stanleigh Morrell
First Cleaner... Josephine Byrd
Second Cleaner... Florence Fields
Abraham.. J. A. Shipp
Isaac.. Charles H. Moore
Jacob .... Edgar Burks
Moses .... Alonzo Fenderson
Ziporah.. Mercedes Gilbert
Aaron .... McKinley Reeves
A Candidate Magician .... Reginald Fenderson
Pharaoh .... George Randol
The General... Walt McClane
First Wizard .... Emory Richardson

Head Magician .... Arthur Porter
Joshua... Stanleigh Morrell
First Scout... Ivan Sharp
Master of Ceremonies .... Billy Cumby
King of Babylon... Jay Mondaaye
Prophet.. Ivan Sharp
High Priest .... J. Homer Tutt
The King's Favorites .... Leona Winkler
Florence Lee
Constance Van Dyke
Mary Ella Hart
Inez Persand
Officer .... Emory Richardson
Hezdrel .... Daniel L. Haynes
Another Officer .... Stanleigh Morrell

The Children

Philistine Bumgardner, Margery Bumgardner, Fredia Long-
shaw, Wilbur Cohen, Jr., Verdon Perdue, Ruby Davis, Will-
may Davis, Margerette Thrower, Viola Lewis

Angels and Townspeople

Amy Escamilla, Elsie Byrd, Benveneta Washington, Thula
Oritz, Ruth Carl, Geneva Blythwood

Babylonia Band

Carl Shorter, Earl Bowie, Thomas Russell, Richard Henderson

The Choir
Evelyn Burwell, Assistant Director

Sopranos: Bertha Wright, Geraldine Gooding, Marie War-
ren, Mattie Harris, Elsie Thompson, Massie Pat-
terson, Marguerite Avery
Altos: Ruthena Matson, Leona Avery, Mrs. Willie Mays,
Viola Mickens, Charlotte Junius
Tenors: John Warner, Joe Loomis, Walter Hilliard, Harold
Foster, Adolph Henderson, William McFarland,
McKinley Reeves, Arthur Porter
Baritones: Marc D'Albert, Gerome Addison, Walter Whit-
field, D. K. Williams
Bassos : Lester Holland, Cecil McNair, Tom Lee, Walter
Meadows, Frank Horace

NOTES

1. Marc Connelly, *Voices Offstage: A Book of Memoirs* (New York: Holt, Rinehart & Winston, 1968), p. 147.

2. *The Dramatic Imagination: Reflections and Speculations on the Art of the Theatre* (New York: Theatre Art Books, 1941), pp. 24-25.

3. Robert Edmond Jones, "The Artist's Approach to the Theatre," *Theatre Arts*, September 1928, p. 630.

4. John Lovell, *Black Song: The Forge and the Flame* (New York: Macmillan, 1972), pp. 522-23.

5. In his notes to the play, Sean O'Casey wrote: "Perhaps a more suitable Spiritual than 'Sweet Chariot' would be chosen for Harry to sing. For instance, 'Keep Inchin' Along,' or 'Keep Me from Sinking Down.' " O'Casey, *Collected Plays*, 4 vols. (London: Macmillan), 1949, 2:3.

6. See Redding S. Suggs, Jr., "Heaven Bound," *Southern Folklore Quarterly*, 27 (December 1963):249-66, and "Diabolical Doings in Atlanta," *Life*, 26 January 1953, pp. 55-58.

7. Suggs, "Heaven Bound," p. 250.

8. "Diabolical Doings in Atlanta," p. 55.

9. "Heaven-bound Soldiers," *Theatre Arts Monthly*, October 1931, p. 855.

10. " 'Pearly Gates' Fails," *Variety*, 8 September 1931, p. 107.

11. See "Actors Worked Before Asking About the Pay," *Chicago Defender*, 10 October 1931, p. 7.

12. Connelly, *Memoirs*, p. 149.

13. "Daughter of Ex-Slaves Who Made Good on Broadway Recalls Life," *New York Times*, 7 October 1979, p. 76; "Whatever Happened to Eva Jessye?" *Ebony*, May 1974, p. 162.

14. Eileen Southern, ed., "Notes on the Negro Spiritual," *Readings in Black American Music* (New York: W. W. Norton, 1971), p. 272.

15. "Hall Johnson, 1888-1970," *New York Times*, 24 May 1970, sec. 2, p. 17.

16. Maud Cuny-Hare, *Negro Musicians and Their Music* (Washington, D.C.: Associated Publishers, 1936), p. 12.

17. "Future Opera: Negro Choir in 'The Green Pastures,' " *New York Times*, 29 June 1930, sec. 8, p. 3.

18. This anecdote is taken from Alyve L. Jeter, " 'De Lawd' on Broadway," *The Crisis*, April 1931, p. 118.

19. This reference appears in a letter of Harrison's to Benjamin Brawley, dated 30 September 1933. It is in the Harrison Papers in the Moreland Spingarn Research Center at Howard University in Washington, D.C.

20. "The Theatre to Get Place of Honor," *New York Age*, 5 August 1933, p. 6.

21. Jeter, " 'De Lawd' on Broadway," p. 118.

22. " 'De Lawd' and Jazz—An Incident in the Life of Richard B. Harrison," *The Crisis*, April 1940, p. 114.

23. *History of A. and T. College* (Dubuque, Ia.: William C. Brown Co., 1966), p. 84.

24. Hazel McDaniel Teabeau, "Daniel L. Haynes, Distinguished Catholic Actor: A Glimpse of Him and Richard B. Harrison," *Interracial Review*, May 1932, p. 79.

25. Connelly, *Memoirs*, pp. 169-70.

26. Ibid.

27. "Another Producing Manager Discovers Negro Talent," *New York Amsterdam News*, 3 March 1930, sec. 1, p. 8.

28. James Weldon Johnson, *Black Manhattan* (New York: Atheneum, 1969), p. 220.

29. "Line Up," *New York Amsterdam News*, 16 April 1930, sec. 1, p. 11.

30. I am indebted to one source for the history of the Lafayette Players—Sister Mary Frances Thompson, "The Lafayette Players: The First Professional Black Stock Company in America" (Ph.D. dissertation, University of Michigan, 1972).

31. See "Gabriel of Stage Killed by Auto," *New York Times*, 11 December 1930, p. 23; "Theatrical Profession Pays Tribute to Charles Wesley Hill," *New York Age*, 20 December 1930, sec. 8, p. 7.

32. "They Are Still Green," *New York Times*, 1 March 1931, sec. 8, p. 1.

33. See J. Shirley Shadrack, "Charles Winter Wood, or From Bootblack to Professor," *Colored American Magazine*, 5 (September 1902):345-48; Lester A. Walton, "Negro Players Star in New Success," *New York World*, 9 March 1930, p. 16.

34. See "The Life of Jesse A. Shipp, Actor, Playwright, Thinker," *Abbott's Monthly*, October 1931, pp. 20-22, 60-62.

35. See Thompson, "Lafayette Players," pp. 252-53; *Chicago Defender*, 1 November 1926, p. 8; *California Eagle*, 18 December 1931, p. 10.

36. See Lindsay Patterson, ed., *Anthology of the American Negro in the Theatre: A Critical Approach* (New York: Dodd, Mead & Co., 1936), pp. 172-73; Teabeau, *Daniel L. Haynes*, p. 79.

37. "The Green Pastures," *Chicago Defender*, 8 March 1930, sec. 2, p. 7.

38. Walter White, "Negro in American Drama," *English Journal* (College Edition), 24 (March 1935):185.

39. Ibid., p. 186.

Richard B. Harrison as "De Lawd." Courtesy of the Moorland-Springarn Research Center, Howard University.

5

THE FIRST NEW YORK RUN

Rehearsals for *The Green Pastures* began December 29, 1929, and the curtain went up on the premiere February 26, 1930. The Great Depression had already fallen upon the nation with the stock market crash the previous October. But theaters on Broadway had not been seriously affected. George Bernard Shaw's *The Apple Cart*, the play the Theater Guild chose to produce instead of *The Green Pastures*, was playing at the Martin Beck Theater. Reviewers praised it highly and predicted it would be the major dramatic success of the season. *Outlook* magazine published a list of other plays that would probably succeed most easily of those opening in 1930. Among them were *Strictly Dishonorable*, *Berkeley Square*, *Fifty Million Frenchmen*, *Sons o' Guns*, *Michael and Mary*, *Death Takes a Holiday*, *Strike up the Band*, *Street Scene*, *Journey's End*, and *The Infinite Shoeblack*. Amid announcements for all of these promising productions and reviews of those already playing, a small notice appeared in the *New York Times* about the opening of *The Green Pastures*. Critics, theatergoers, and Broadway wits were curious about the Connelly play. They knew it had gone the rounds of prospective producers, and all of them, including the cooperatives of actors and groups that would normally champion experimentation in the theater, were reluctant to put it on the stage. Their apprehensions were understandable. Another Negro play was unthinkable. Certainly, one that, as rumor had it, placed a Negro God on the stage. If such a drama should ever see the glare of footlights on Broadway, most knowledgeable people would have thought it would be a burlesque, at best. Connelly, best known as a satirist and solid member of the sophisticated Algonquin Roundtable, probably would make for the stage a racy and clever story about Negro religion. Such a work might last a few weeks for the delectation of Americans who were beginning to worry about the worsening economy. Black actors hoped the play would bring them a new significance. Jobs were scarce for them, and they had never worked on Broadway in large numbers. So they rushed to rehearsals and held their hopes high. Never before had so many black actors and singers been employed in a single stage endeavor. The eve of the opening of *The Green Pastures*, therefore, was a particularly hopeful time for them. For all the mystery about Connelly's play, it did create curiosity and excitement in the theatrical world.

With Rowland Stebbins as producer-financier and Robert Edmond Jones as set and costume designer, Marc Connelly's most ambitious effort had a chance to succeed. But no one was sure. There had been no out-of-town performances and no previous reviews. According to rumors, rehearsals had been held behind locked doors. The press knew little about the play other than what Connelly told them. Critics had to wait and see what experienced hands would think of Connelly's folly. What they did know, however, fascinated them. The debonair playwright always exhibited a pioneering spirit, and some thought he would surprise Broadway. Heywood Broun wrote that it was "interesting to find that the great white public on Broadway will manifest enthusiasm about the play dealing with Negro life and acted by a cast composed wholly of Negroes." Such a play, he felt, would seem to be "a reproach against public taste," inasmuch as the rich literary field of Negro life was practically closed to native actors.[1] Torrence, O'Neill, Green, and the Heywards had exploited that subject about as much as the public would stand to see in first-class theaters. At least that was the prevailing judgment. Conventional wisdom held that the Negro was a low-comedy figure at best. How, then, could a play about Negro religion—and especially one that put God on the stage—be anything but low comedy? Connelly seemed to enjoy the mystery he had created, even as he fretted about the outcome of his endeavor.

"When the curtain rose on that crucial night I stood in the rear of the Mansfield so attentive to the play's technical operation that I had no time for playwright's jitters," Connelly wrote in his recollection of the premiere of what would become his major contribution to American theatrical history.[2] He had worried over the massive and complex forty-foot treadmills that would move the hundred or so characters across the stage in the Exodus scene. He was particularly anxious about the difficulties Harrison had experienced in dress rehearsals in trying to walk, stop, and speak on the treadmill. He had instructed the children in the

Sunday school scene at the play's opening not to speak or move should the audience laugh when the curtain went up on the scene. They obeyed him completely. As the laughter that had come died down and the scene faded on cue, from the darkness came the burst of the magnificent sounds of the Hall Johnson Choir singing the first of the spirituals that would be used throughout the drama. "I held my breath as Mr. Harrison made his first entrance," Connelly wrote. More than a thousand first-nighters sat expectantly before him as Wesley Hill, in the beautiful purple and gold vestments Jones had designed for Gabriel, silenced the children at the heavenly fish fry with those often-to-be-repeated words: "Gangway! Gangway for de Lawd God Jehovah." Harrison, who had worried over whether those very words would demean the drama and would make burlesque of the religious lore of this people, silently entered at that moment, went to the center of the stage, and calmly greeted the angels and the cherubs. "From the moment he began, he had the audience in his pocket," Connelly remembered happily. And the audience, including the host of drama critics in the theater, agreed with him. The trick of putting a black God on the stage turned into fortune as Richard B. Harrison's talent at acting, dignity, rich voice, and gentle, endearing humor flooded over the auditorium and balcony. With what he called "incredible smoothness," Connelly saw one scene follow the other. The play was going well. When he went backstage at the end of Part One to congratulate the crew and the cast, he found Harrison completely at ease and happy with the audience's response. Connelly apparently never realized that Harrison had, for more than forty years, been faced with the precarious challenge of pleasing audiences. But none was nearly so large as the one he faced that night, and perhaps none was so critical. The sixty-five-year-old actor, who had heretofore been unknown and untried by the commercial theater and its audiences and critics, had achieved a personal triumph. At the same time he had secured Connelly and Stebbins' investment and had, to a large extent, rescued the legitimate theater from the hiatus the motion picture and the Depression were leading it toward.

At the play's end the applause was overwhelming. Suddenly, Connelly remembered he had not laid out and rehearsed the curtain calls during the frenetic hours leading up to the premiere. He rushed on stage as the final strains of the spiritual "Hallelujah, King Jesus" settled into the recesses of the theater and shouted to the cast, "Hold your positions." A dozen picture curtain calls were taken. Still the applause continued as the audience called for "De Lawd," Gabriel, Noah, Moses, and the other principal characters by name. Connelly directed each of them to come forth and take their bows on the stage apron. "I don't remember how many times I stood behind the curtain sending out Mr. Harrison and a score of the other members of the cast for personal accolades. I was

becoming numb with the immensity of the play's reception," Connelly
wrote, indicating by his description of that first night the excitement he
still felt some forty years after the event. The afternoon of the next day,
and before it was time to return to the theater, Connelly bought a cane
for Harrison to supplant the one he had used on the stage the night
before. On the silver handle he had engraved what he referred to as "a
feeble expression of my gratitude for having the privilege of having met a
truly great artist." Harrison carried that cane on stage throughout the five
years he played the role. The sentiment engraved on the cane was one of
the infrequent, direct commendations Connelly gave to the old actor.
Most often he and the critics sought, at first, to praise the play and its sets
and costumes without giving much attention to the actors. As time went
by, Harrison became, in his own right, the perceived star of the production. His name never appeared on the theater marquees as playing the
starring role until his seventieth birthday, during the performance in
Norfolk, Virginia. Why this was the case might be left to conjecture, but
it is a curious aspect of the story of Richard B. Harrison and *The Green
Pastures.*

The next morning, after the premiere, Brooks Atkinson, drama critic
for the *New York Times*, wrote that Connelly's play excelled as comedy,
fantasy, folklore, and religion.[3] He, who became the play's most continuous and most ardent supporter, wrote that it was a work of surpas-
sing beauty from almost any point of view. He called it a "divine comedy
of the modern theater," in which Connelly had lifted his fable of the
Lord walking the earth to those exalted heights where utter simplicity in
religious conception produced a play of great emotional depth and
spiritual exaltation. Atkinson saw on the stage that first night a drama
that enacted a transition from Negro comedy to universal drama by the
"effortless process of increasing emphasis upon enduring themes." He
saw at once the captivation of seeming incongruities—the angels at a fish
fry, the Lord in His office cautioning Gabriel not to blow his horn, Noah
blowing the steamboat whistle on the ark, elephants clamoring up the
gangplank—not struggling against one another, but all coming together
as magnificent strokes of imaginative comedy in satisfying theater. This
organic whole fascinated Atkinson. Hardly had the genial comedy of the
fish fry got underway, he wrote, before it became clear that the playwright had a universal purpose in mind. The Lord is the central figure
for that purpose, and His role is the graphic and the thematic vision of
what the play is about.

> Dressed in the formal garb of a parson, with his long coat and
> white tie, he is unpretentious. Even in his speech he is of
> humble origin. But straightaway you perceive that he is a

good man, the fusion of all the dumb, artless hopes of an ignorant people whose simple faith sustains them. He is a Lord
of infinite mercy.

This, to the critic, is "sympathetic comedy," this putting the Lord on
the stage in such simple terms that exalts *The Green Pastures* into drama
of great "pith and moment." In this kind of theater, one's imagination is
stimulated into a "transfiguring conception of sheer, universal goodness." That quality, Atkinson wrote, was Connelly's finest achievement
in the play. For in it one saw drama as collaboration: a harmony
achieved by the text, the setting that gives theme a "vaulting impetus,"
and the spirituals that are actually chorales between the scenes. The
overriding element of this harmony on the stage, as Atkinson saw it, was
Richard B. Harrison. His part carried the greatest responsibility in the
matrix. He made the audience believe in the play. "He is belief
incarnadine," and such things are truer than the Truth. With encomiums
of this type, Atkinson moved the attention of the public and the critics
from wonderment about Connelly's folly and from single-minded con-
centration on the technical aspects of the drama and placed them
securely on Richard B. Harrison as the critical attribute of the play.

Other drama critics praised *The Green Pastures* after the premiere.
Arthur Ruhl, writing in the *Herald Tribune* the next day, was not so
ecstatic as Atkinson. He recognized the unusual qualities of the play,
writing, "It was something quite out of the usual run, an entertainment
amusing, touching, and curiously impressive by turns."[4] Like Atkinson,
he praised the acting of Harrison, whose "fine voice and sound and
honest acting" contributed much to the impressiveness of the performance. And he mentioned Charles E. Moore, who played the role of Mr.
Deshee, the Sunday school teacher. These were the first wave of reviews. They were followed by many dozens of other evaluations
throughout the sixteen months that the play remained at the Mansfield
Theatre. But equally as important as the newspaper critics' comments on
the play were indications of approval that came early from the clergy
and from New York black intellectuals. Connelly had feared that these
two groups might react unfavorably to *The Green Pastures*: the clergy for
what they might have considered a low-comedy portrayal of the Sacred
Scriptures that are essential to the Christian religion; and the black intellectuals because the "plantation tradition" in American art that had
emphasized Negro dialect and stage stereotypes had been repudiated by
the "New Negro" concept of the post-World War I era. Both these
important voices from the American public came forward early to praise
the play, however. The Cardinal Newman Fund, representing powerful
Catholic laity and the priesthood, was the first of many groups that

called the Mansfield to arrange to purchase blocks of tickets for benefit performances of the play. W.E.B. Du Bois, editor of the NAACP's *The Crisis* magazine and by no means a verifier of what his colleague Walter F. White might have felt about the play, as reported in chapter four, would have been expected to speak directly and critically of any work in the theater that seemed to him to denigrate Negroes and his often stated aspirations for a native black American drama. In an editorial in his magazine, he raised the question of whether any work of art is "genial and satisfying" rather than whether it is a realistic picture or a caricature of black people. The difficulty in judging art lay in that white audiences, on the one hand, demand caricatures and farces and Negroes, on the other hand, either "cringe to the demand because [they] need the pay or bitterly condemn every Negro book or show that does not paint colored folk at their best," he argued. He praised *The Green Pastures* because in it Marc Connelly "has made an extraordinarily appealing and beautiful play based on the folk religion of Negroes." He could not agree with those who considered the play sacrilegious.[5] Because as a sociologist he had included the black church in America in his highly respected Atlanta University Studies in the early years of the century, Du Bois probably knew the purpose and practice of black Christianity in the United States better than almost any other American.

Lester A. Walton, black managing editor of the *New York Age*, the leading Harlem weekly newspaper, possessed unusual knowledge about the theater. He had written theatrical reviews of stage productions in Harlem for his paper and had been a theater manager. What he had to say about *The Green Pastures* is important in any survey of reactions to the first New York run. Noting the praise that was directed toward the production, Walton added knowledge about the cast, especially biographical facts about the lives and stage careers of Jesse Shipp, Charles Moore, S. Tutt Whitney, and Wesley Hill. He denied outright some flippant claims in the white press that many members of the cast were gathered up from maids and cooks in Manhattan. If they were working in those jobs, it was because they could not find employment in the theater playing roles for which they were fully qualified, he declared.[6] Theophilus Lewis, drama critic of Harlem's other black weekly, *Amsterdam News*, wrote that the success of the play provides a lesson for every Negro businessman. Recalling *Variety*'s comment that the new play was an interesting novelty and possibly a thing of unique beauty whose author probably would be praised more than he would be paid, and Connelly's pilgrimage through offices of New York financiers seeking a producer for the play, Lewis notes that Stebbins did not agree to finance the play because he thought his judgment of its commercial potential was greater than that of others who had rejected it. Rather, he saw in backing it "an opportunity to add to the world's store of beauty."[7] When

Stebbins saw that Connelly had "created something fine," he decided it should not "languish in obscurity." Lewis' chief purpose in mentioning Stebbins, however, was to chide black businessmen in Harlem who were hesitant to back plays written by Negroes for production in Harlem theaters. Only Lewis wrote about the cost of the production of *The Green Pastures* at this early stage of its life. In addition to the cast of almost a hundred actors and the musicians and a score of persons needed for business and stage management, there was also the expensive treadmill and the lighting apparatus. Lewis estimated the cost of sixty thousand dollars for taking the play into the Mansfield. Given the economic scare over the stock market crash, one can understand the hesitancy among potential producers to invest in the play, together with their concern about the feasibility of success for an all-black drama.

Once the play had settled in for its lengthy New York run and the preliminary reviews had been written, digested, and reacted to, critics and other observers of the American scene found *The Green Pastures* a momentous religious experience for a nation struggling desperately with the ravages of the Great Depression, the rise of fascism in Europe, the puzzling tide of nihilism raging throughout Western civilization, and a general search for spiritual meaning. This unworldly drama of faith with the flight from the doldrums of reality that Atkinson had praised it for taking would enjoy 640 performances in New York City and five tours throughout most of the nation. Somehow the drama's force sparked in audiences, in drama critics, and in theologians an expression of a balm sufficient for the longings of the times—one that integrated a search for God with a palpable melding of sophisticated, philosophical questions with already-existing folk answers. The marvel lay in the unexpected source of the antidote. Connelly had written that the unique rapport between the play and the national personality grew out of "something of the background a majority of the American people experienced in living with their puritan and essentially religious forebearers, together with a knowledge of and a kindly sympathy for the Southern Negro and his religious faith." Later revisionist critics would interpret Connelly's attitude to reflect what they called the sentimentality over "lost innocence" and of disappearing rural, primitive folklore that could not survive longer than the life of the play on the American stage.[8]

As would be expected, the question of whether Connelly or Roark Bradford should garner the greater praise for the play arose. Joseph Wood Krutch would give the praise to neither. The greater glory, he wrote, should go to the "anonymous geniuses who composed the spirituals upon which the whole is based."[9] Connelly and all of the cast and the musicians had simply cooperated with great skill and delicacy with the folk consciousness and the art form it produced. For they seem, one and all, to have been gifted with a remarkable imaginative insight into the mood of the materials at hand. But neither Bradford, Connelly, nor any other white man could possibly have invented a mythology as rich and simple and satisfying as that which Negroes evolved when they made over the heroes of the Old Testament into their own images. He called "the corpus of these spirituals" the finest expression of the religious emotion achieved anywhere since the seventeenth century. Admittedly, anthropologists and other cultural scholars had recognized the unique character of the songs, but *The Green Pastures*, alone, had translated the spirituals into a pictorial form that represents imagery and ideology as the basis for an epic drama in the course of which a black God creates a world, saves a Noah, and leads the black children of Israel out of their Egyptian bondage. Obviously, Krutch knew nothing of the tradition of the dramatization of the spirituals in the black church, or of the pageants the black American enacted of the lives and actions of the ancient Hebrews, or of the black preacher's stock portrayal of the "Suffering Servant" image of Jesus Christ. Like others, Krutch marvels that theater using such folk material as this was not grotesque at its worst and quaintly charming at its best. Krutch's comments here sound like James Weldon Johnson's poem *O Black and Unknown Bard*, that is, a paean to the genius of the black American slave, who, in his "Darkness," still "came to know" the power and beauty of the minstrel's lyre and "sang a race from wood and stone to Christ." Krutch intended his analysis of the play and his fulsome praise of the spiritual-making slave to be high compliments, but they brought fire from the first of many black Americans who would reject Connelly's material and purpose in *The Green Pastures*. Mary Burrill wrote to *The Nation* that Krutch's ecstatic review, which praises the play for having achieved "this Negro version of Christian mythology," compelled her to write about Connelly's work as a representation of the Negro's religious belief, not as a play. It "no more represents the untutored Negro's conception of God and heaven than it represents a Chinese's ideal of Confucianism," she wrote. And she continued:

> Those of us who are bound by ties of blood, who have lived in the South, and who therefore truly know the Negro, realize that when the Negro whom Mr. Connelly represents visualizes God, he visualizes Him not as a kindly preacher of his own race but as an anemic-looking *white* gentleman with golden beard and flowing hair, garbed in a long nightshirt with bishop sleeves! In other words, the unlettered Negro pictures his Heavenly Father in terms of the cheap chromo representations of God that are hawked by gimlet-eyed white peddlers through the Negro quarters of the South. To such Negroes not only God but the cherubs are also white. I know

of a Negro preacher who almost disrupted his congregation by ordering for his remodeled church stained-glass windows showing black cherubs.[10]

Ms. Burrill related the Negro's concept of God and heaven to his social life on earth. He would not want to take the handicap of his daily life into his heaven, she argued. Instead, he looked on death as the greater emancipator that would lead him into a heaven in which he "will blossom out in all that this world holds dear—fair faces, golden hair; where the toil of life will be forgotten in endless hours of ease."[11] No one could gainsay her complaint. She was an authority on something Bradford and Connelly merely found "quaint" and good material for publication and for the stage. No other records show that the press critics raised any of the questions Ms. Burrill presented in her letter.

Nearly a month after the premiere, Alison Smith, drama critic for the *New York World*, wrote that adding praise to what had already been written and said about *The Green Pastures* was "much like rising to say a few kind words about the sunset."[12] Never in his memory had accolades for a play and its first-night performance been so unanimous. But one group had not been heard from, he wrote. That was the audiences—the "house," which cannot fail to have its effect on the production considered solely from the showman's standards. He had sat with murder in his heart and heard the agonized lines of *The Waltz of the Dogs* greeted with delighted chuckles from a Greenwich Village slumming party. And he had watched the most touching scenes of *The Cherry Orchard* "done to death by restless shuffles," and he remembered the lady who decided to explain the plot through the singing of the love duet in *Tristan and Isolde*. All these incidents remained etched in his memory of phenomenal annoyances in the theater brought on by thoughtless members of audiences. But for himself, one who had hung wistfully about *The Green Pastures* since its opening and found his steps leading sometimes involuntarily and almost mysteriously to the Mansfield each evening the theater was showing, he had to report nothing but perfect understanding of the play by the audiences. Night after night they reacted to the varying moods of the play with the "subtlety of a well-trained orchestra," Smith wrote. This collaboration between those playing and those played on is an event in the theater, he felt. He applied it to his experience with *The Green Pastures*:

> The first test comes with the entrance of the Lord in the midst of the fish fry. Up to that time the house has been given up to the increasing crescendo of laughter that greets each detail: the solemnity of the celestial cooks, the touching absurdity of the tiniest cherub, the purple and gold winged glory of the

Angel Gabriel. Suddenly, however, as this same Gabriel an-
nounces above the jubilant murmurs of fish fry hilarity,
"Gangway for de Lawd God Jehovah," the laughter stops
with the abruptness of a pause in a symphony. The silence
that follows the appearance of the Lord's homely, majestic
figure is breathtaking in its intensity, and it obtains through
his fatherly catechism ("Has you been baptized?" "Certainly,
Lord.") until, with the final assurance that his children have
been baptized, have been redeemed and do bow down mighty
low, the Lord utters the benign order, "Let de fish fry
proceed." And with this hilarity breaks out again in the audience as it does on the stage, with much the same quality of
childlike and innocent gayety.

From the beginning to the end, Smith observed, the audience gives
faithful reaction to the nuances of the play and follows it from the first
scene to the glorious burst of the finale. He had never seen an audience
more reluctant to leave the theater at the last curtain, he adds. This
uncommon attentiveness to what is going on before the footlights is an
impressive tribute to the universality of the theme; for through that
element the play can make so varied a mass of people as a theater
audience behave as one body. These reactions could not have been better
if Connelly had directed them himself, Smith concludes.

Like Smith, Atkinson returned to the Mansfield often to see the play
that had delighted him at its opening. Two weeks into the run he was
even more favorably impressed than he had been the first night. Now he
spoke of the play as a work of "ethereal beauty and of compassionate
comedy without precedent," especially after the "peccadillos here and
there" have been conceded and the "dogmatizing about religion" has
been conceded. Unaware of how prophetic his words would prove to be,
Atkinson predicted *The Green Pastures* would stand in the history of the
contemporary theater along with stalwarts like *Abraham Lincoln, What
Price Glory?, The Dybbuk, Strange Interlude,* and *Journey's End.* Indeed, it
was finer than these, for "it lives in the sunlight air of the imagination
where an author must be in the truest sense a creator carving images out
of his dreams."[13] Such a theatrical method is fortuitous for American
theater, Atkinson told his readers, as the play provides welcome relief
from the emphasis on practicality and reality that playwrights had lately
thought of as the proper and safest way to subdue audiences. Connelly
does not subdue, nor does he try to do so. He captivates his audiences by
the magic of the theater and illuminates an infinity of far-off things. He
leads his audiences into the unique halls of imagination, and in doing so,
they must distinguish between fact and impression in order to fully
appreciate *The Green Pastures.* Thus, like Du Bois, Atkinson defends the

play as theater. It is art, not propaganda. The fact is simple. The playwright has stated it in the program. He told everybody he was attempting to present certain aspects of a living religion in terms of its believers who had adapted the Bible, the treasure house of their faith, to the consistencies of their everyday lives. And he had done just that. He had moved the Bradford sketches from "hardly more than sophisticated travesty" into fragments of faith that stand as evidence of belief and aspiration. What Connelly had done with the raw material—the fact—is what Atkinson called "sympathetic comedy" in an earlier review. In such a genre of the theater, the playwright can be extravagantly comic without betraying his characters or breaking faith with his theme. That quality and characteristic of this art separated the minstrel tradition and the lore of the old black preacher from magic in the theater. This distinction is the basis for sympathetic comedy. And the audience finds itself moving between those polarities of the comic. One is conservative and comfortable; the other is new and bewildering. Atkinson judged that audiences were rapt in attention because they realized they were in the presence of a new cultural artifact being performed before their eyes. That was the elevation of the folk art from riotous low comedy to something not yet named but essentially and demonstrably different from the ribald jokes and denigrating stereotypes of the black stage idiom. Yet the folkway in a new key is discernible. Its language provides a glossary for understanding what Connelly was doing to American culture. He might not have articulated his purposes in quite the same words as Atkinson. But critic and creative artists of what is being analyzed are hardly expected to perform the same functions for the public. One makes the product and the other reacts to it.

Atkinson was the first critic to recognize this transformation, and he was the first to recognize that *The Green Pastures* would be little more than a tender oddity if it did not introduce the Lord as its principal character and gradually work out the Negro fantasy into universal drama that would be a modern miracle play. That role would, of necessity, move the work from what could be blasphemous audacity into religious exaltation. Seen through the eyes of those whose belief in Him transcends every fact of experience or every quirk of theological speculation, He is the divinty of an overwhelming faith. In the beginning, He is the Negro's God, conceived in terms of the kindly black Sunday school teacher in a frock coat and a white tie. That is the image the teacher relates to his students. He says he thinks God is something like old Mr. Dubois, a wonderful preacher at New Hope Chapel over in East Gretna. By extension, the Lord is the black preacher. When that person creates the earth and Adam and appoints Moses custodian to lead His chosen people out of Egypt to the Land of Canaan; when He cherishes and ministers unto and chastises the whole earth, a new concept of authority and of basic theology has been created on the stage. Theology is not an abstraction now. It is the direct relationship between God and Man. By play's end, through nobility of character, the Lord has become the ruler of all people. He is the apogee of all religious faith. Atkinson believed Connelly created a miracle on the stage, which, after all, is what the theater is supposed to do. He had done so like the Lord of the early portions of the play, who so readily "ra'red back" and passed a miracle, first by representing the Lord in utterly simple terms as a good man, lovable, wise, and compassionate; second, by showing how fervently everyone from angels to mortals to flowers of the fields revere Him. To find that God, later in the play, grieving over the calamities attending the human race He has created and while walking the earth as a natural man; to find Him repenting that He ever made man; to find Him moving from a Lord of moderate wrath and vengeance to one of infinite mercy—all these sharp turns in the character of the Lord require an uncommonly talented actor. Richard B. Harrison played that role with what Atkinson called "humble grandeur." This review by Atkinson marked a turn in direction for the critics' comments from the play as technical marvel to "De Lawd" as the centerpiece. Without knowing he was doing so, Connelly had depicted the black preacher at his best in the play. That sonorous, sagacious artist with words and gesture was the living religious symbol among black people in the United States. His sermons ranged from the creation of the world to the death and resurrection of Jesus Christ, much as did the plot of Connelly's play. And histrionic sermons, sometimes observing the broad outlines of the Scriptures, were punctuated in performance by the singing of his people, even as Connelly's "De Lawd" and His words and actions were buttressed by the singing of the choir. Theater in the thousands of little black churches in America came to fruition in the Mansfield by making concrete the flights of the imagination that many a black member of the church saw in what he would have called his "mind's eye" as he contemplated his personal relationship with God. Few other than black Americans would recognize the sophisticated rendition of this folk reality in the raiments of costume designers and enacted on a physical stage that moved men and God around even as the folk imagination moved Him. Few men of the theater could fully understand and explain to others what they saw on the stage. It mystified them with its beauty and grandeur, but it was not part of their collective folk experience.

As others quibbled over whether Roark Bradford or Marc Connelly should have the greater honor for the success of *The Green Pastures*, Francis R. Bellamy observed that Connelly had done the precise thing that distinguishes the genuine dramatist from the mere adapter. He had been fired by the idea behind the Bradford book and had accepted the broad outlines of the Negro's imaginative picture of biblical history and of the Lord Himself as Bradford had presented it, but from this source material he had built a play with a coherent story of its own. And it proved to be full of moving moments as well as joyous entertainment. It is a plain, humble story of the Lord and His troubles and grief over man, His pet creation and an "onery, disappointing critter from the beginning." As for whether it is sacrilegious, Bellamy challenged any one reading his review to go into the Mansfield "as soon as possible and see if you can keep your eyes dry over the effort of this endlessly patient, plain, good Lord, who so suspiciously resembles the old colored preacher."[14] Watch Him trying to run the universe from His little office in heaven, trying to get one bit of comfort, one grain of love and obedience in return from His ungrateful favorite child, he continued with his challenge. And then reflect on the question of whether the play is sacrilegious. The key to the drama, Bellamy contended, lies in the truth that the Lord is no abstraction in the play. This is the familiar Lord, who actually makes the weather a little hotter or "a mite cooler" and who sits in Noah's humble cabin and gives that rare man a ten-cent "segar" as a preliminary act to confiding to Noah His plans for a flood. The God on the stage takes the form of a man as He fulfills His promises to Moses in Egypt and, in sight of the walls of Jericho, takes him to heaven, where life is one long, magnificent fish fry through eternity.

In the theater such a Lord is viewed through a mist of laughter and tears that cannot hide His utter goodness, His patience, His compassion. For here is a good man whose stature reaches to heaven itself. Such a portrayal, to Bellamy, is *religion*. And had Bellamy known the role the black preacher played in America every Sunday, as has already been pointed out alongside Krutch's comments, he would have realized that Connelly's God on the stage was compatible with that black preacher's God in the pulpit, as the preacher constantly told his story of God's compassion and patience toward men. That, to the preacher, was the essential lesson of his religion, even as Bellamy suggests it is the essence of *any* religion. Bellamy continues by insisting that the play brings a theatergoer back to his own childish Sunday school picture of the Bible. Thus, the black religious experience becomes universal and certified as a human religious expression rather than a detached primitive black man's entertaining misconception of God and the meaning of religion.

When a newspaper editor in Asheville, North Carolina, wrote to question how New York critics could rave over a play that undertook the impossible task of staging a drama like *The Green Pastures* without having it become shockingly sacrilegious, Richard Watts, Jr., went back to see the play three weeks after its opening in order to determine for himself whether its favorable reception issued primarily from its uniqueness. He concluded that while nothing even faintly resembling it had ever made an appearance in the national drama, Connelly's play did not depend on its novelty for its virtue. On the contrary, he wrote, at least some of the appeal and national dramatic event lies in other essentially stable considerations. In its own right, this dramatization of the Old Testament, as it might filter through the mind of some pious Negro preacher, is "so eloquent and beautiful and inexpressibly touching, so reverent and so tender, so richly humorous, and so incomparably poignant that its magnificence seems indisputable," he concluded.[15] He was willing to grant that time might prove the play is not great; yet, he maintained, "there is greatness in it." Perhaps the most amazing thing about the play, he continued, is that its author should be a white man, a sophisticated New Yorker, hitherto distinguished chiefly as a wit and a satirist. Yet there is nothing "smart or brittle or merely quaint" in the play.

By this time during the first year of its run, critics had written enough about the scenery and the uniqueness of the play for Broadway. And they had taken due recognition of the extraordinary acting talent and demeanor of Richard B. Harrison, perhaps the only actor in America who could have played the part of "De Lawd." Edward A. Steiner, who was among those who related *The Green Pastures* specifically to the religious Christianity of Grinnell College in Iowa and a regular contributor to *Christian Century* magazine, was traveling in Europe in the summer of 1930. Part of his reason for being there was to see the Passion Play that had been performed in the Bavarian village of Oberammergau every ten years since 1634 in commemoration of and appreciation for the villagers' rescue from a devastating plague suffered the previous year. Oberammergau, as the play was commonly called, dramatized the portions of the life of Jesus Christ that led to his trial before Pontius Pilate, his crucifixion, and his resurrection. By 1930 serious Christian scholars questioned whether the impact of the Passion Play had remained unsullied. Oberammergau had been commercialized. Places of accommodation had been overpriced, and visitors there who had previously looked on attending the play as a major religious experience in their lives were becoming disillusioned with the conventional image of the village and the play. Within that context, Steiner wrote that Marc Connelly's Broadway play had, in a sense, supplanted the Bavarian Passion Play as a true and heartfelt representation of the basic Christian experience of the Judeo-Christian tradition. He wrote that he had gone to Oberammergau expecting to see God and he saw a good show there. On Broadway, at the Mansfield, he went to see a show and saw God. The nihilism at Oberammergau and Oswald Spengler's dire prophecy of the decay of Western civilization rapidly being fulfilled and the dying of a great, simple religion as the triumph of materialism arising to take its place terrified Steiner. But in *The Green Pastures* he had glimpses of the new world to come, "not through Broadway Jews or Gentiles, but through simple people, a new, chosen race, a race still in the making or as yet unborn." This drama that he considered the "Passion Play of the New Day" was an American creation that retrieved Christian religion and prophesied a hopeful new national life.[16]

While Steiner saw *The Green Pastures* as a Passion Play without Jesus, who has not come yet, Stark Young, son of the South and drama editor for the *New Republic*, criticized the play because it was not Jesus-centered. "Negroes have Jesus at the center of their religion and close to their warm, childish hearts," he contended. And within the "plantation school" tradition at its patronizing worst, he went on to explain that to the Negro there is a God, the Devil, and the Blessed Jesus. The need for saints and a virgin to intervene between them and a stern judge and a magical Satan is not felt, he wrote. Their idea of the Father in heaven makes the complex hierarchy of saints and a Trinity unnecessary. Yet, to him, Connelly, Bradford, and Harrison had cooperated to present on the stage a figure of God "with His kindness, His tricks, His patience, pleasures and human troubles and ups and downs," making for the theater a remarkable interpretation of the whole soul of the people in the play. Thus, *The Green Pastures*, in his judgment, presented in the finest sense a creation of an idea in dramatic form.

These observations are not essentially different from those expressed by many other critics who had written numerous times before Young on the accomplishments shown on the stage in the Mansfield. But for all of his serious attempts to explain a play about people he wants his readers to understand he grew up around and could qualify to interpret in the creative art of writing theatrical criticism, Young regrets that the cast is not black enough. Too many mulattos, he thought, is not a realistic spectacle.

Stark Young seemed to have forgotten that in the Louisiana of Mr. Deshee's Sunday school class, basic setting of the play's rising phantasmagoria, the complexion of Negroes covers most of the spectrum of color. After all, he was born and reared in nearby Mississippi, where the skin color was strikingly similar to that of Negroes in Louisiana. Further, he fails to understand the dramatic logic he touches on when he seeks to assign appropriate use of the spiritual in the Negro's "soul":

> At the moment, for example, when the Lawd sits in his chair surrounded by the heavenly hosts, and the idea springs into his mind of his own necessity for suffering, the spiritual is sung—quite rightly—about Jesus; but it sounds too like a choir, in the first place—which is true of most of the singing throughout the evening—and in second place, it bursts out with all the appropriate comment of an oratorio finale. There are many spirituals with Jesus as the theme, and a simple effect of these

> Negroes bursting into one of them, childlike, appropos only
> by the round-about course of the heart, emotionally appropri-
> ate but not so obviously, would be far truer to the racial
> material and much more disarming and moving.

Had Stark Young been able to undergo a "willing suspension" about
his, to him, valid and informed knowledge about the Southern Negroes
among whom he had been, as he said, brought up, he might have known
that the range of spirituals is wide. Some category fits almost any
occasion. Those identified with Jesus as the Suffering Servant might have
pleased Mr. Young better than those about the triumph of an idea and
the cosmic reaction to it and its acceptance. But Hall Johnson, the choir-
master of the production, probably knew more about Negro spirituals
than anyone in the nation at the time. If he failed to accept Johnson's
"Hallelujah, King Jesus" as an appropriate musical expression for the
crucial point in the development of a theory of God from the magic
Overseer into Hosea's God of mercy and justice, Young was the loser.
One joyous and triumphant spiritual seems as appropriate at this point in
the play—its finale, by the way—as "The Hallelujah Chorus" seems in its
place in Handel's *Messiah*. Both anticipate the grandeur and elevation of
the coming of Christ, not the full knowledge of his suffering that follows
later in the development of Christian theology. For Mr. Young to
complain that some pliant spiritual about Jesus should come at this point
in the play is the same as to say "Surely He Hath Borne Our Griefs"
should come at the close of the Christmas portion of *The Messiah*.

In the denouement of the theological development of God in *The Green
Pastures*, the Lord sits in heaven. Gabriel at His side asks, "What are you
thinking about, Lord?"

God: 'Bout somethin' de boy tol' me. Somethin' about Hosea, and
           himself. How dey foun' somethin'.
Gabriel: What, Lawd?
God: Mercy. [*A pause.*] Through *sufferin'*, he said.
Gabriel: Yes, Lawd.
God: I'm tryin' to find it, too. It's awful impo'tant. It's awful
           impo'tant to all de people on my earth. Did he mean dat even
           God must suffer?[17]

Then "De Lawd" looks out and sees men compelling the Son of Man to
carry the cross up a high hill. God rises and murmurs, "Yes," as if in
recognition. The appropriateness of the "oratorio finale"-sounding
spiritual speaks for itself. It becomes the ultimate expressionism of the
drama. And, as Steiner has told his readers, it is the Passion Play without
Jesus Christ, who has not come yet.

That final scene confounded those critics who could not include the promise of the emergent Christian religion in the old black preacher's vision. The "Apocrypha" rendered by Connelly in the character of Hezdrel represents a Judas Maccabaeus incompatible with the strict simplicity the rest of the play projects. The childlike, patronizing, happy-go-lucky Negro of the "plantation school" in post-Civil War American literature and sociology fails at this point. The "charm" of Mr. Deshee as the prototype of the village God melds ingeniously into a universal religious paradigm of Negroes acting out ancient Hebrew folklore in their feeling for its content and meaning. Harrison and Connelly added dimensions to that age-old religious experience and brought to the stage more unity of the American psyche than most sophisticates could have imagined. They enacted a response to the question the nation did not know exactly how to ask itself but felt painfully. Through enactments of the "play people" of the American world—the stage religious Negro—the play literally vibrates with the most complex ironies of Christianity. Playing God gives way to the only essential question in a modern nation's continued practice of an ancient, alien religion. Is it evolutionary? *The Green Pastures* answers with a resounding yes. But the evolving nature of whoever and whatever is God to America emerges from the black God's almost painful but compelling willingness to understand that a sense of community among God, angels, and human beings comes through suffering. "De Lawd," at play's end, and anyone who holds the uneasy and unflagging responsibility for the universe, must learn what human beings already know. The awesome equalizer and pacifier is nothing less than the common experience of suffering.

The efficacy of Christianity, if it becomes the religion for the times, lies clearly in the meaning of Hosea's discomfort in "De Lawd's" heaven and in the farseeing Hezdrel, who teaches even God what it means to be human. God has never walked the earth as a natural man, notwithstanding the charade that takes up four-fifths of the play's action. But Hosea has come to heaven through the processes of earthly life and death. He has been a moral man and has understood humanity's dimensions. Throughout this *tour de force*, easily overlooked in the preponderance of singing and enjoying heaven, the play confirms the purity and validity of the human condition. That message provides an affirmation worlds away from the pessimism and emptiness of the world, even in the face of the 1930 Passion Play at Oberammergau. *The Green Pastures* presented night after night the dramatization of a shared religion and a vision through which both black and white Americans who realized their common bond in this experience could approach a social, moral, and philosophical coalition needed for the day. The artifacts of Hebrew folk stories, Negro spirituals, the dramaturgy of Marc Connelly with its superb stage sets, and the acting of the superb cast led by Richard B.

Harrison combined to provide the crucial thought-piece for a frightened and desperate 1930 America.

Variety reported the play a clear smash at the box office. The heavy demand for tickets continued from opening night well into the next season on Broadway. By March of the first year, after a run of less than a month, the prevailing top house prices were "kited to $10 and $12 a seat in the brokerages."[18] In May of that first year, the Pulitzer Prize Committee announced that *The Green Pastures* had been selected to receive its award for drama. As had been the case many other years, differences of opinion arose as to whether Connelly's play deserved the honor.

By midsummer Harrison had emerged as the centerpiece for *The Green Pastures*. Connelly complained mildly about the demands made on the actor's time and ordered the publicity office to restrict acceptance of invitations that came to Harrison to half-hour periods that would give the star at least an hour to rest before performance time. But the play's accomplishments could hardly be handled in the way management usually handles press conferences. Richard B. Harrison was Connelly's "find," but he was a broad and significant symbol of race pride to black Americans. Few of them could purchase tickets to see him perform at the Mansfield, but they related to him and clamored for his presence in their little theater groups, social gatherings, and churches. Stebbins and Connelly fully understood that Harrison was a principal advertisement for their play. Sermons preached in black and white local churches frequently included some reference to the play. The drama had proved a success aesthetically, financially, and socially.

At the time of the first anniversary of the opening, many reminiscences and evaluations came forth. The original cast was still intact with the exception of Wesley Hill, who had played Gabriel. He had been struck and killed by a taxicab one night after the performance. The 419th showing of the play had been witnessed by some 400,000 spectators. The march of the children of Israel on the treadmill had covered some 530 miles. On his sixty-sixth birthday Harrison had been honored by a party given by Stebbins. On March 22, 1931, he had been awarded the NAACP's coveted Spingarn Medal, established to be given to the black American who, in the estimation of a committee, had made the most important contribution to the edification of the Negro race during the year. The investiture took place at the Mansfield Theater before an audience of more than a thousand persons. W.E.B. Du Bois, who had been recipient of the medal in 1920, delivered the address, which he titled "Beside the Still Waters," and praised his longtime friend for bringing dignity to black American actors. The play was awarded the Pulitzer prize for drama during that same year. In addition to his many appearances in and around New York City, Harrison had lectured from time to time outside the city. Speaking on Race Relations Sunday, February 8, 1931, before the Ford Hall Forum in Boston, he reviewed the history of Negro contributions to American drama and the stage, recalling the historic efforts of the African Grove Theater in New York City in 1821 and the Krigwa little theater group, in his remarks. Richard B. Harrison and *The Green Pastures* had become synonymous with importance in the theater during that first New York run of the play.

Rumors persisted about a closing date. The management was struggling to decide whether to return to Broadway in late August after a summer vacation, to take the cast to Europe, or to embark on a national tour. After sixteen months the play was set to close June 27, 1931. Although ticket sales increased markedly during the last two weeks of the run, indicating that New York was ready to extend performances beyond the designated termination date, plans had been made final for moving the entire cast and sets to Chicago.

The last performance was an emotional night for the cast. In the year and a half that it had remained at the Mansfield Theater, *The Green Pastures* had gained praise from practically every source. It had kept the legitimate theater alive, literally, and had brought thousands of Americans and many visiting foreign dignitaries to see the spectacle at the time the nation was reeling from the pangs of economic disaster. That final night, ushers announced at 9 P.M. that no standing room was left. Harrison and Johnson, after the last curtain call, led the cast in singing "God Be with You Till We Meet Again." Roark Bradford was a guest at a party that night, as were major New York publishers, critics, and other celebrities, including Eleanor Roosevelt, Dorothy Parker, and Robert Benchley.

Connelly and his fantastic drama would return to New York after successful tours throughout a large part of the nation. And it would be received again with enthusiasm by the city in which it had first burst on an unsuspecting American public. When it returned, it had enhanced its status as a significant contribution to American theater.

NOTES

1. Heywood Broun, "It Seems to Heywood Broun," *The Nation*, 19 April 1930, p. 415.

2. Marc Connelly, *Voices Offstage: A Book of Memoirs* (Chicago: Holt, Rinehart & Winston, 1968), p. 186. All of these reminiscences by Connelly are taken from chapter 5 of his book entitled *The Green Pastures*.

3. Brooks Atkinson, "New Negro Drama of Sublime Beauty," *New York Times*, 27 February 1930, sec. 9, p. 26.

4. Arthur Ruhl, "The Theater," *New York Herald Tribune*, 27 February 1930, p. 14.

5. W.E.B. Du Bois, "*The Green Pastures*," an editorial, *The Crisis*, May 1930, p. 162.

6. Lester A. Walton, "Negro Players Star in New Success," *New York Age*, 16 March 1930, p. 6.

7. Theophilus Lewis, "The Harlem Sketchbook," *New York Amsterdam News*, 19 March 1930, p. 9.

8. This point of view is taken from Thomas Cripps in his introduction to his edition of the screenplay *The Green Pastures* (Madison: University of Wisconsin Press, 1979), p. 12.

9. Joseph Wood Krutch, "Miracle," *The Nation*, 9 April 1930, p. 429.

10. These lines come from James Weldon Johnson's poem "The Black Mammy," which appeared in his *Fifty Years and Other Poems* (New York: Viking Press, 1917), p. 12. It is a poignant attack on lynching in the United States that was the target of the NAACP while Johnson was its Field Secretary.

11. Mary Burrill, *"The Green Pastures,"* letter to editor, *The Nation*, 21 May 1930, p. 600.

12. Alison Smith, "In the Order of Their Appearance: The Gallery and *Green Pastures*," *New York World*, 23 March 1931, p. 12.

13. "Green Pastures" review, *New York Times*, 9 March 1930, sec. 9, p. 1.

14. Francis R. Bellamy, "The Theater," *Outlook*, 12 March 1930, p. 429.

15. This incident and Richard Watts, Jr.'s response appear in "When the Lord Walked the Earth," in the Letters and Arts section, *Literary Digest*, 22 March 1930, pp. 20-21.

16. Edward A. Steiner, "The Fashion Play of 1930," *Christian Century*, 13 August 1930, pp. 983-84.

17. These lines come from scene 8 in *The Green Pastures*.

18. "32-Week Buy for 'Pastures'—Gyp Ring," *Variety*, 12 March 1930, p. 57.

6

"DE LAWD"
ON THE ROAD

During the summer of 1931, everybody knew *The Green Pastures* had
become a financial and artistic success. Predictions that it "somehow
failed to click," that it was probably an artistic success that gives little
promise of attaining commercial prosperity, had long since died. *Variety*
had "eaten crow" rather consistently. Its critics were among those who
predicted miserable failure for Connelly's folly. On the contrary, it had
run for one and one-half years on Broadway, and leading drama critics
had used superlatives to describe it. Brooks Atkinson had repeatedly
called it the "divine comedy of the modern theatre." Robert Garland had
named it a "divine comedy in black face." The *New York World* had
called it "one of the finest things that the theatre of our generation has
seen." *Time* magazine had declared it a "quasi-religious, semi-public
United States institution." It had made a star of Richard B. Harrison, but
that sterling actor had more than returned the compliment by delivering
649 performances without ever missing a first curtain. Yet *The Green
Pastures* could not remain in New York forever. Connelly and Stebbins
had far more grandiose plans than that. They had already arranged for
companies to play it in Western Europe, and the fast-developing motion
picture industry seemed to offer a unique opportunity for placing the
folk drama into a medium that would perpetuate it for decades. Radio
and motion pictures were becoming the mode of the day. Elaborate theaters in New York and throughout the nation were turning into picture-
show houses or remaining dark for months on end. The social theater of

Elmer Rice and Clifford Odets and Eva LeGalliene and all of the trendy
performances of the Group Theatre and Theatre Guild and the other departures from the usual fare of the commercial theater were changing
forever the face of Broadway as the entertainment capital of the world.
The expense of legitimate theater in the grand style was prohibitive and
becoming more so daily. *The Green Pastures* had been a good thing, and
its author and producer deserved a chance to make its returns extend for
as long a period as they could. The Depression had wracked the nation.
But Connelly's play prospered. Justifiably, its author and managers saw
in it a national mystique. Perhaps it was a United States institution. Only
on Broadway, though, thousands of persons came from outside New
York to witness it. But who knew whether it would draw audiences in
Philadelphia, Chicago, Boston, Washington, Baltimore? In the South and
the Midwest and on the West Coast? Stebbins had to know. While
rumors abounded that the drama would close soon at the Mansfield, he
and his associates worked furiously to find out whether the luxurious
show could possibly make a road tour. It had never played outside Manhattan. After several months of hard bargaining, the producers decided
to move the show to Chicago. If it fared well there, they would activate
tentative plans to move through the Midwest all the way to the Coast.
Chicago was the second largest city in the United States and Richard
Harrison still called it home, although he had not actually lived there
year-round for many years. Yet going there gave reasons for pause. The
city was good for no more than two-week runs for road companies. Even
Shuffle Along, the most successful show that could be even remotely
compared with *The Green Pastures*, closed there after two weeks. Yet
Chicago was the most logical of cities. The plan was made, and the tour
was set to begin Labor Day, 1931.

Salem Tutt Whitney, Noah in the play and a regular columnist for the
Chicago Defender, wrote about the cast's leave-taking from New York en
route to Chicago. He captured the special relationship Negroes felt with
the play. They had gone to the Mansfield to see it—some had—but generally speaking, *The Green Pastures* was to them a white folks' enterprise.
They knew Harrison and many of the other actors, but the play was
downtown theater. Harrison lived modestly in a room in the Harlem
135th Street YMCA when he was in town, and the elite among blacks
entertained him and some other members of the cast. They appeared in
lectures, readings, and small vocal ensembles in the fashionable
churches of Harlem. W.E.B. Du Bois invited the Harrisons to dinner.
The price of tickets to the theater was beyond the reach of most black
folk, and they were ambivalent in their perception of the play. The
theater, Broadway style, was something apart from the common folk.
They had related well to vaudeville and to the billings at the biggest
theaters in Harlem. Little theater groups were plentiful, but they were

the activities of the "arty." Hall Johnson was known to most of Harlem. Semiprofessional choirs were particularly popular. Many were breaking into the "concert" business, and some were performing on radio programs. The Harlem Renaissance had seen a new interest in the Negro spiritual. People were less self-conscious than they had been when they had come to think of spirituals as reminders of the hateful institution of slavery and of patronizing whites after slavery. The black tenor Roland Hayes had established certain spirituals as part of his repertoire as he sang throughout the United States and Western Europe. But, curiously, Hayes had ended his formal concerts with the mystical "Were You There When They Crucified My Lord?" perhaps the most subtle of the Negro spirituals. Singing them to end a program that had featured the most popular fare for recitals, French, English, and German art songs, gave a strange currency to the spirituals.

Musical comedies that had performed to large audiences at the Lafayette and Lincoln theaters in Harlem were a far cry from *The Green Pastures*. They were entirely secular, and although they could be called folk art, they were intended for Harlem's run-of-the-mill population. Little theater groups were the activity of the elite in Harlem, largely those persons who had gone to college and had transplanted campus drama onto Harlem. Yet all black people were proud of Richard B. Harrison and his accomplishments in the theater gained in *The Green Pastures*. They knew him well from his many years as a reader on the New York Council of Churches Lyceum. But there was a respectable distance between the play on the stage and the enthusiasm of the average Negro in New York for Harrison and his fellow players on the stage at the Mansfield. Theophilus Lewis, a respected drama critic among Harlem Negroes who wrote columns for the *New York Amsterdam News* and the *Messenger* magazine, felt the play was degrading and was sparing in his praise of it as theater.

Negroes were ambivalent about the play. But they came out in droves to see the cast off to Chicago. Whitney wrote about it:

> Left the Pennsylvania Station Wednesday morning, September 2, enroute to Chicago. Nine cars in all—three baggage cars, diners and sleepers made up the train. Not within my knowledge has any other Colored company traveled in such regal style. Mr. Stebbins did not count the expense when the comfort and enjoyment of the members of his company were in question.[1]

Whitney had worked in vaudeville and knew well the way black entertainers had traveled, and he could gauge the public's reaction to the cast's move out of New York. He wrote that relatives and friends had come to the station to bid good-bye and good luck. The occasion took on the appearance of a holiday excursion, he wrote. People were glad to be working, and their friends and relatives were glad for them. No one knew how the company would fare on the tour, but hopes were high. The nearly one hundred singers and actors had it made for at least a few weeks longer. The Depression would not affect them nearly so badly as they had once thought. The occasion was an appropriate one for celebration.

When the special train arrived at the railroad station in Chicago, "at first glance it looked as though the whole Southside was on hand to greet us," Whitney wrote. The press was there and hundreds of pictures were taken. Black people in Chicago took Harrison and the rest of the cast to their hearts. Nevertheless, the reception there was not quite like that in New York. Harrison was the magnet that drew black Chicago to the station. Whitney wrote that as the venerable old actor descended from the train that September day, "he was hugged and kissed, patted and mauled until it looked like we would have to apply police protection if there was to be enough of him left for the Chicago opening." His entire family was on hand. Another columnist wrote in the *Chicago Defender* that Mr. Harrison was coming home. "He knew life in Chicago, youth, happiness, joy, pleasure, misery, prayer."[2] Other journalists wrote constantly about the "miracle of the aged, unknown, black actor who came from obscurity to stardom in 'The Green Pastures.' " Chicago knew him. He was not obscure to them. Connelly and Stebbins were the beneficiaries of the uncommon talents of the man black Chicago called "Mr. Harrison." His role in promoting the play began there and continued throughout the rest of the five years that it toured the nation. Moving from New York to Chicago was a fortuitous decision. For the reception there, the steady stream of news about Harrison and the players that flowed from the pages of the *Defender* and its publisher's monthly magazine, *Abbott's Monthly*, established an element of public relations that supplemented Stebbins' news releases. It was not protracted. It came about naturally. It was based on black pride about the cast of a black play playing there.

Opening-night seats were sold out six weeks in advance. One reviewer wrote: "You don't know what a wonderful place a theatre can be until you become acquainted with 'The Green Pastures.' " Most wrote that nothing so appealing had come to town since *Ben Hur* had played there for thirty-two prosperous weeks a decade earlier. Chicago media persons acclaimed the drama before it arrived, and they often deviated from the regular advance publicity materials. Fanny Butcher, drama critic for the *Sunday Tribune*, called it "one of the great plays in the history of drama." For it not only dramatizes a whole religion and the psychology of a people, but it also places that religion and that people into a universal perspective of man's search for his God.[3] Twenty, fifty years ago such a play would have been impossible to get into the possession of the public, either for reading or looking or listening, she noted. It would have been considered sacrilegious. And it would have been called "light" even if the religious matter could have been overcome. In Chicago, though, the average theatergoer and those who rushed to bookstores to purchase the play and read it found it contained "more emotion-stirring religious appeal than most sermons."

Frank Young, writing in the *Chicago Tribune*, continued the media emphasis on black Chicago's reaction to Harrison. That element was important, for one must remember that in 1931, Chicago was essentially two distinct societies—one black and one white. White Chicago—or a large part of it—went to the theater and became enraptured with Harrison night after night as he impersonated the Lord on the stage at the Illinois Theatre. At another end of the Harrison mystique, sensitive journalists saw a heartwarming beginning of the institutionalizing of a stage play and its chief actor. One piece in the press indicates the degree to which Harrison, aside from his role as "De Lawd," was a folk hero in Chicago:

> Out on Indiana Avenue there is a modest two-room house which is the home of Richard B. Harrison. Each morning groups of school children went their way in front of 5943 and point to the place as "where the Lawd lives" and each noon they pass enroute home to lunch hoping to see "the Lawd" in person as he oftimes sits in the rocking chair on the veranda.[4]

There were children and grandchildren of former neighbors who considered the Harrisons their friends. The Old Settlers Club called the aged actor one of its own. It was made up of Negroes who had lived in Chicago for thirty years or more. Almost all of them had migrated there from the Deep South in search of broader social and economic opportunities. Even if none of them went to see *The Green Pastures* in the theater, young and old Southside Negroes made their contribution to the success of the play's first appearance outside New York. The churches, the Eighth Illinois National Guard Regiment, neighborhood schools, little theater groups—all played their part in honoring Harrison and bringing attention to Connelly's new play. Many Negroes traveled to Chicago to see it and came away with a sense of pride that helped make the national tours possible. Those persons living in Missouri, Arkansas, Tennessee, and farther South feared the play would never appear in their towns. And even if it did, they would never be sure they could buy tickets and see it. Their influence—though probably never acknowledged by Stebbins and Connelly—was not inconsequential. Undoubtedly, the Chicago run made it clear that *The Green Pastures* could engage in the interest and commercial support of a nation that hungered for the opportunity to see

Richard B. Harrison and his fellow cast members perform Marc Connelly's new play. It played for sixteen weeks in Chicago. The reception far exceeded all expectations and motivated Stebbins to undertake a transcontinental tour.

It opened in St. Louis the week of February 29, 1932, with the announcement that the engagement would continue for two weeks at the American Theatre. The series of performances would loop across the prairie and over the Rockies to Seattle and then down the Pacific Coast to San Francisco and Los Angeles. It would play the larger cities and towns and exclude those locations in which few Negroes lived or little interest could be found in the play. The plan was extravagant and required costs that seemed incompatible with the anticipated revenue. Money had never been a primary concern of Stebbins in the entire enterprise. It still was not. He counted on long rounds in Los Angeles and San Francisco to make up for the expense of carrying the nine-car train through so large a part of the nation. And he counted on the tour to give the play a national life that was unprecedented in American road show theater history. He was not disappointed. For with its five-week run in Los Angeles and four weeks in San Francisco, *The Green Pastures* reached the zenith of its career as theater of the American culture that was, indeed, recognized as a reflection of either the actual life or the fancied imaginings of thousands of Americans. Equally important, it penetrated into the nation's own deep-seated feelings about its black and white racial composition. Communities had to decide what to say about the play, how they would arrange audience seating, and how reviewers would write about it, as well as how they would accommodate its cast.

The life story of the American performances of *The Green Pastures* as it traveled throughout the length and breadth of the United States, and of Richard B. Harrison's life in the principal role of Connelly's masterpiece, requires close study of the reviews, audience reactions, and the critical interrelationships between the cast and the black and white people in the towns in which it played.

St. Louis was a particularly interesting case. Going there represented a calculated risk for Stebbins. That border city was as strictly segregated as Atlanta, Georgia. But it was not considered "Deep South." Its long heritage of patronizing and spawning the fine arts left no doubt that audiences would come to see the play. Its reputation had preceded it, and St. Louis anticipated its arrival. Stebbins refurbished the press notices he had used for Chicago and geared them specifically for St. Louis. Roark Bradford received full credit for having "suggested" the play in his *Ol' Man Adam an' His Chillun*, and notices always made it clear that the cast was all-Negro. Harrison was not listed as the star, however. He did not receive that honor until his seventieth birthday anniversary and the beginning of the fifth national tour. His picture appeared on the billing and no one doubted that he was the star attraction. Stebbins delicately avoided offending a border city by calling a Negro a star. At the same time he exploited Southern sentimentality about black folklore. No one mentioned in reviews that Harrison's mother had been a slave in the household of one of St. Louis' most prominent slaveholders. Yet, as had been the case in Chicago, local black people took Harrison to their hearts. The leading black newspaper, the *St. Louis Argus*, gave wide coverage to the coming of the play and to social events surrounding the run there. One reporter wrote that he was impressed by the "wholesome simplicity" of the cast. For "although traveling in special trains and surrounded by glamour," they were "a humble and sincere lot" who displayed "no pompous or overpowering effort to startle or enrage the audience, no flaunting of famous stars or great names; no wisecracking, no spicy stories, no obvious effort to be funny or to engage in dramatic flights."[5] Harrison had performed often in St. Louis as a dramatic reader on the Federation of Churches circuit. Persons who knew him respected him as they did in New York and Chicago. Some of the reporter's comments must have been made in his reflection on the many black vaudeville performers who often played St. Louis in the days of high popularity for this form of entertainment. Too, because St. Louis was racially segregated in places of public accommodation, the cast lived among Negroes in their homes or in their segregated hotels and took their meals in black restaurants. Thus, black journalists found many social occasions to write about during the run. One was a luncheon sponsored by the Aldridge Players, named for the Afro-American tragedian. This affair was held in order "to give St. Louisians an opportunity of meeting the cast of 'The Green Pastures' in a social way." The program included brief selections sung by Major N. Clark Smith's local chorus, imitations of Bert Williams, and remarks by Mr. Harrison; W. C. Handy was there to tell the audience his inspiration for writing his "St. Louis Blues."[6]

The review of the opening performance that appeared in the *St. Louis Star* was impressionistic. Its writer concentrated on the play's effect on him and on the audience. He wrote about "a vision of the universe and the music of the spheres" that entranced the audience. The performance, he wrote, was "full of invincible magnetism with moments of rapture as well as moments of grotesque humor." The drama was "both one of the most original and one of the most superbly fine things of the modern theatre." Harrison was the principal conduit for these impressions. Through his role, the reporter wrote, he and the audience found the sincere projection of the play's mythology. Its melancholy as well as its exultant religious ecstasy were so well executed that "the comical aspects are magic in the theatre." The choir was another vehicle for this effect. For the spirituals were sung with "a lush, full-blown beauty," and the nearness of the singers to the audience only enhanced the magical effect of the music.[7]

Commentators seemed surprised by the way the audience listened "reverently at times" to the singing and the spoken lines. One began his review of the opening by admitting that "little more than has already been written needs to be said about the performance of Richard B. Harrison," who keeps the play, at all times, "a very lovely and entirely reverent drama." He was the first to observe that *The Green Pastures* is a religious drama only for those persons who believe in the Bible from cover to cover. Others had seemed slightly amused—and at the same time confused—by the quaint presentation of a "primitive" people's conceptions of God. Many in the audiences must have wondered whether there actually were people, though housed far on the other side of town, whose religion was so moving. The reviewer allowed, however, that the play is "good theatre and good entertainment for everyone and provided an entire evening of solid enjoyment without a moment of dullness, a rare combination in these days of unregenerate and uninteresting stage offerings."[8] In St. Louis the first indication began to emerge that *The Green Pastures* was operating as a social change agent outside the northern metropolitan cities of New York and Chicago. By the end of the first week in St. Louis, a feature story in the *St. Louis Globe-Democrat* reported:

> Not the least interesting of the many strange facts associated with the record-breaking career of "The Green Pastures" has been its influence on interracial solutions. The Commission on Race Relations of the Federal Council of Churches in America has reported that no circumstance since the civil war has done more to open the gate of opportunity to the Negro and to accord recognition to Negro talent.[9]

From St. Louis the company moved to Kansas City, Missouri, and to Joplin, Missouri, and headed northwest. Good audiences and favorable reviews followed them through performances in selected locations in Minnesota, Montana, and Wisconsin. By spring 1932 it had reached the Pacific Northwest. Seattle had been favorable. The appearance in Portland, Oregon, early in May was somewhat ironic. The management had feared that the newly opened Portland Auditorium was far too large a house for the moderate-sized audience expected. On the contrary, throughout the five-day engagement there, large audiences filled the hall. *Variety* called the appearance a "smash" that grossed some thirty-three thousand dollars for the five performances.

Although *The Green Pastures* had enjoyed enthusiastic receptions all along the path of its first national tour during the 1931-32 season, San Francisco represented a new triumph. It was by far the best setting for good houses since the show had left Chicago. Announcements had already been made that the tour would end in Los Angeles. Good showings in California would establish *The Green Pastures* as the truly national institution it was beginning to be called. West Coast audiences would be a significant indicator of what could happen to the play in the future. Southern California was accustomed to entertainment spectacles. How it responded to Connelly's unusual play for the theater held the secrets needed to be solved by both cast and management. Announcements in the *San Francisco Chronicle* reflected the importance of the run there. One referred to it as "the most talked of play and production of the last quarter century." After the initial announcement, the *Chronicle* kept its readers informed of reactions to the play and activities the cast members were involved in while they were in the Bay Area.

George C. Warren, a principal drama critic in the city, wrote the morning after the opening that a "goodly portion of San Francisco people became as a little child last night at the Columbia Theatre and sat at Marc Connelly's feet listening to Genesis and Exodus and the Prophets expound as the naive children of Africa understand them." It was an unusual experience in the theater, Warren continued. The play was thrilling by virtue of its tender beauty, exaltation, and its full, rich, warm, and wholesome humor. The mood was set in the prologue, the scene in Mr. Deshee's Sunday school class. Thereafter, spectators looked through the eyes of the Deshee children. But the play was not a preachment. It might have been a burlesque "but for the bigness of the idea, the tenderness and care with which it is staged and the fine quality of reverence displayed by Connelly in writing the play." That sensitivity and skill, together with Robert Edmond Jones' settings and the singing of the "Heavenly Choir" added to the delight the San Francisco opening-night audience saw in the play. But, as Warren saw it, "more than any other element in the performance, the dignified, benign, majestic figure of Richard B. Harrison gives it the splendor it undoubtedly possesses." His voice was "like music; his reading full of intelligence and beauty; his carriage venerable."[10]

Two weeks into its four-week run, Warren was as intrigued with the play as he had been after opening night. He wrote that San Francisco had seen it—at least many theatergoers there had by then—and like other communities, they had fallen captive to its charm, "its rugged beauty, its simple, reverent exposition of the first books of the Old Testament." Notwithstanding the reams of newspaper comment, magazine articles by the score, thousands of letters to individuals, and the spoken praise of those who had seen the play during its New York run or in Chicago or in other cities of the Midwest, it still astonished its first-night audiences.

Unlike most drama critics, Warren used Connelly's previous plays to illustrate him as a "highly civilized" writer. He exposes the follies of the movies in his adaptation of *Merton of the Movies*, excoriates the menace of the law courts and cast wealth in *Beggar on Horseback*, and revels in depicting the stupidity of the modern girl in *Duley*. He scorches Babbitry in *To the Ladies* and uses uncommon fantasy in *The Wisdom Tooth*. But in *The Green Pastures* he sets aside his criticism of the society of which he is a part. The thoroughly modern and polished playwright was, in the new play, becoming a naive, uneducated, primitive man, seeing from that angle the great story set forth in the books of Genesis and Exodus. His model had been the morality play, Warren observed, as many, many critics said before him. But Warren went beyond merely mentioning those generic titles of York and Coventry and Chester. He wrote that their naiveté of interpretation of contact with God and His miracles in a time when both man and God were simple is one and the same with Connelly's. For he uses the same quick movement of these fragmentary dramas and treats their sacred themes with simple reverence. Warren realized that Connelly must have studied these old guild dramas seriously before he set out on his work of bringing Roark Bradford's sketches of Negro life in Louisiana to the stage. Connelly never mentions in his public writing that he did any such thing, but Warren's point is well taken. Connelly did show in several statements that he deeply respected the historic tradition of the drama. That respect transcended Christianity as a religion. Connelly was a thoroughly educated man in the drama. Others who spoke of the quick movement in *The Green Pastures* seemed not to understand the relationship between Connelly's play and the miracle dramas. Both were characterized by fragments. Again and again, Warren reminds his readers that it is the Sunday school scene that sets the stage for the play. And, to him, it is the ideal for Connelly's unique treatment of the familiar stories. Thus, he has the viewpoint of those imaginative, untutored children and their naive shepherd.

So, *The Green Pastures* is a departure from the kind of play Connelly had written previously. And it is far more than a dramatization of the Bradford sketches, as Warren saw it. The play had the advantage of its author as director and the extraordinary fortune to have Robert Edmond Jones as set designer. Warren was the only reviewer at the time to point out that Jones' sets follow, in a way, the pageant wagons on which the medieval mysteries were presented. And the music is indispensable for executing Connelly's concept. Harrison, needless to say, brings Connelly to the audience. As God, He is the father watching over the happiness and welfare of His children, His own creations. He is, too, a God of wrath when He anesthetizes the wickedness of people He has loved so much. He is the ruler of the universe, its maker and its God at all times, but there is human tenderness and pity for the sinner and forgiveness for the repentant. This catalog of roles on the stage while playing "De Lawd" speaks for Warren's respect for Harrison's rich gift as an actor. Only a highly talented person could play such a multifaceted role.[11]

The drama would have remained longer than four weeks in San Francisco if a promotional deal had materialized. The Chamber of Commerce and a group of organizations with similar interests discussed at some length a "cent-a-mile" excursion into the city from outlying areas traveling over the Southern Pacific Railroad. Some confusion prevented the management and the business organizations from realizing this plan. Thus, after four highly successful weeks, *The Green Pastures* moved South to Los Angeles, the terminal stop on the long national tour.

Coming into town as Los Angeles was gearing up for the World Olympic games that would take place there later in the summer, *The Green Pastures* settled into the Biltmore Theatre on June 13, 1932. Somewhat as had been the case with Chicago, the opening and the run represented an additional personal triumph for Harrison. He was welcomed there by a delegation of old friends, headed by L. E. Behymer, who had been his adviser and business manager when Harrison took to the stage with one-night stands as an elocutionist. William F. Wells, vice-president of the Atchison, Topeka, and Santa Fe Railroad, who had been called Harrison's "discoverer," was not there for the reception. He had been transferred to the Chicago offices of the firm. People remembered that Wells had hired Harrison as his office boy and had arranged his first reading before a public group. That was the Friday Morning Club, whose scheduled speaker had to cancel his appearance one week, and Harrison went on in his place. Behymer was there and heard the elocutionist perform. He arranged an appearance before the Long Beach Women's Club, thus launching Harrison's commercial stage career in 1905. Shortly thereafter, Harrison went to Arkansas to take charge of a small, black, church-related school as its principal. But friends he had made in Los Angeles during those days that he worked for the railroad were on hand to greet him. Los Angeles was the home of many black actors and singers who had come West with dreams of breaking into motion pictures. Others were there as part of the revived Lafayette Theatre, which had been established in the new Lincoln Theatre on Central Avenue in the heart of the principal black residential district of the city.

As was the case with New York and Chicago—and indeed most large American cities—black churches were the quintessential institutions in Los Angeles. They were the concert halls, the mass meeting houses, the center of benevolence, the places of political forums, and the houses of worship. *The Green Pastures* touched this characteristic of the church. With white Protestant congregations, Harrison could be invited to share the pulpit with the pastor even in the Sunday morning worship. One or more singers from the "Heavenly Choir" could come along. The congregation felt it had exhibited Christian liberalism by inviting these black actors and singers into its church. But it was different with the black churches. Harrison seldom spoke from their pulpits because he was busy speaking to white congregations. Black churches, in their comprehensive role as their people's all-purpose organizations, presented members of the cast in recitals. In Los Angeles, for example, Ulysses Chambers, director of the "Heavenly Choir," who had replaced Hall Johnson for the national tour, played organ recitals the Sundays the show was in Los Angeles. He was on the list of the John Wanamaker Series. Quite appropriately, he played an organ recital in commodious Second Baptist Church, assisted by a contingent of members of the choir, who sang some selections from *The Green Pastures*. Charles Winter Wood, Harrison's understudy, who held a theological degree and had taught drama and English at Tuskegee Institute, delivered a lecture entitled "The Message of *The Green Pastures*" at the Hamilton Methodist Church in the Negro area. Jerome Addison, a baritone singer in the choir, assisted him with several solos. Salem Tutt Whitney, perhaps the best-known member of the cast for his long work with vaudeville and black musical dramas, was entertained by many who knew him in Los Angeles. A columnist for the *California Eagle*, the leading black weekly newspaper in Southern California, noted that twenty-five or thirty members of the company might appear on the concert stage. He realized that the company was "oversupplied with dramatic and musical talent." He wrote: "It seems a pity that two voices such as are possessed by Marguarite Avery and Nell Hunter can be used only in the aggregate of 28 choir singers." And he pointed out that "there are actors and actresses in the cast who ordinarily might be headline features were circumstances more favorable."[12] Others echoed Williams' statement with distinct bitterness as they realized that only an extravaganza like *The Green Pastures* could come along and offer sustained employment to black artists. These observations represent the basis for some of the resentment blacks felt about Connelly's drama and Stebbins' production of it. They were ambivalent in their feelings. Surely, they were proud of the attention the drama and its cast were receiving throughout the nation, but they realized the play was basically a white man's creation and that he and his associates were reaping the major benefits from its success.

When *The Green Pastures* moved into the Biltmore in Los Angeles, *Whistling in the Dark* was also opening in town. This was the first time two major New York stage attractions, with their New York casts, had played Los Angeles simultaneously. *The Green Pastures* topped with close to nineteen thousand dollars, at three dollars for the most expensive seats the first week. It was the first play to fill the balconies of the Biltmore in several years. Reviewers reported unusually large numbers of Negroes in attendance. The production planned to remain in Los Angeles for five weeks before going into vacation for the remainder of the summer. Despite the intense heat in mid-June, the turnout was large. When the company left town in late July, it had grossed more than eighty thousand dollars in the five weeks. These receipts were said to be the second highest legitimate gross of the year and unusually high for Los Angeles legitimate theater.

Isabel Morse Jones, the music critic for the *Los Angeles Times*, wrote about the music of the play: "For the musically conscious it becomes a revelation of the power of spirituals to convey the deepest emotions of the primitive man." When she attempts to analyze the lyrics and the music of these folk songs, she speaks of their titles "as a record of a dramatic faith and the agony of atonement." Using them, she concluded, Connelly has produced "something like a native opera." Further, she wrote about the "smooth transition from the melodic dialogue to the singing of the choir." Others had spoken of the relationship between the play and the old English medieval miracle plays, but Jones wrote about the relationship between the singing of the choir and the music of the old English madrigals and Russian choirs singing Slavic folk songs. And she added information about Rowland Stebbins that no other reports had mentioned. She wrote about his being the son of a musical conductor. His background in music, she claimed, caused him to see the possibility of using the spirituals alongside Connelly's own story of the genesis of the play. He rather consistently gave the impression that he had a vague idea about using spirituals as an integral part of the drama but did not know which ones to use until he visited Bradford in New Orleans and got the opportunity to visit black churches and to hear black folk singing. As has already been pointed out in this work, the playwright wrote in his memoirs that he learned about most of the spirituals from a black church pianist in New Orleans. Chances are he knew about Hall Johnson and some of the other choirs that were singing on the radio and in concert in the New York area at the time. Eva Jessye, one of those choir directors, insists that she was invited to submit arrangements of spirituals for the play, but that she lost out to Hall Johnson when the final arrangements were made. Whatever is the truth of the way Connelly came into contact with the Negro spirituals that make up so large a part of the effect of the play, Isabel Morse Jones is quite correct in her assessment of the music's role in making the play appealing. Unlike the sentimentalists who wrote about the singing as a return to some period of innocence in American life and in their own memory of their childhood in the South, Jones tried to comment on the cultural folk aesthetic in the songs. If she had had the opportunity to discuss them with Hall Johnson, she might have been aware of his prolific studies into the African and American cultural strains in the songs. He had made this study the focus of his work in musicology for many years. His choirs were his exhibits. They provided him demonstration laboratories for the highest artistic and social qualities in these songs. He was contemptuous of those singing groups that used them purely for burlesque purposes. Perhaps in later years, when Isabel Morse Jones got a chance to hear Johnson's folk drama *Run Littl' Chillun*, which is based solely on the theory and practice of black Christianity and its competition with the more pagan religion the slaves brought with them to the United States before they heard of Christianity, she understood more clearly what she was trying to express in this review. Even so, her observations move above the commonplace and repetition of her encomiums for the humor and reverence in the play. As a musician, she trained a different vision of the art form on the stage as she reviewed the performance.

By the time the Los Angeles engagement closed, Metro-Goldwyn-Mayer motion picture studios had offered to discuss filming *The Green Pastures*. Al Jolson had publicly expressed his interest in playing the role of "De Lawd." That would have been a travesty; Connelly did not take well to the idea. In the 1950s, Warner Brothers made a film that enjoyed moderate success. In July 1932 the cast performed for the thousandth time. It had played from coast to coast laterally and was by far the most financially successful musical drama in the commercial theater. And Richard B. Harrison had become largely a household name in the United States.

After Los Angeles the cast returned to Harlem. Harrison stopped off in Chicago to spend some time with his family there. Much of Harlem turned out at the 125th Street railroad station to greet the special train that carried the players eastward after a triumphant tour of the Far and Middle West. The media recapped the performance life of the play. It had gone on the road after the eighteen months in New York on Broadway and had played nineteen weeks in Chicago before twisting its way to the Pacific Coast, playing sometimes several days and sometimes one to five weeks in the principal towns and cities. It came with 1,023 performances to its credit to take a hard-earned vacation—the first since the opening on February 26, 1930. Neither Harrison nor Daniel I. Haynes (who played Adam) had missed a single performance since the play opened. A new Eve had come into the cast since it left New York. And there had been other changes of personnel, notably in the role of Gabriel. Charles Wesley Hill, the first Gabriel, was killed in an automobile accident in December 1930 before the company left on tour. His successor, Sam Davis, died in Indianapolis. The new Gabriel was Doe Doe Green. The homecoming was triumphant, as an account in the *New York Times* described it:

> The Negro players wore their bright raiment, broadest smiles and displayed wallets and bank books that attested to their

having found "green pastures," indeed. After showing in Boston the troup will go to Philadelphia and then venture into the Southland. They expect to break boxoffice records for another two seasons at least.[13]

Stebbins announced the Southern tour would open in Richmond, Virginia, October 2, and would move then into thirty-one towns and cities, and again going into the Southwest and Midwest but not to the Pacific Coast.

Variety had faithfully reported on the progress of the tour. Sometimes the gross receipts and the top ticket costs were also revealed. This biography of a play and its performers shows that Connelly's creation had found realization in a faithful and talented corps of actors and singers. They had acted out a permutation of the "darkey" entertainer on the theater stage. It had become an integral part of the dynamic aesthetic and social milieu of the turbulent 1930s. And it had contributed, no doubt, to the necessity Americans found in that decade of coming to grips with what they believed about themselves and the world in which they lived so perilous an existence.

Labor Day, 1932, *The Green Pastures* opened in Boston. It had toured the nation and had been well received everywhere it played. Because it had not been performed outside of New York City for the usual tryouts, each location had been a new experience. Boston might have been a place to test whether sophisticated Eastern cities would take well to a folk play about black Americans and their religion. Its population was largely Catholic and took its religion seriously. Boston audiences might be offended by the machinations of a black God and His errant children, or by the representation in human form of a half-Negro, half-Hebrew version of the Old Testament. However, Bostonians knew a great deal about the play. As a reviewer for the *Boston Evening Transcript* wrote: "They are acquainted by reputation with the 'Gangway for de Lawd.' They have heard about the fishfry. They are acquainted by reputation with the venerable Richard B. Harrison who plays the part of de Lord. Perhaps they may have heard him lecture."[14] It is a curious anomaly of the stage that too much familiarity with a play is a dangerous thing; this anomaly of the stage, rather than the possibility that Boston would take offense, was more likely to affect the Boston performances. Promoters in Boston feared that at that late date, September 1932, in a city so close to New York, the play might be unfairly regarded as a revival rather than as continuing entertainment, so they took steps to prevent such a problem. New costumes were prepared, and the scenery—though the same— was repainted. The players had been taking a well-deserved rest since the middle of July.

Along with attempts to bring vigor to a play that had been entirely across the continent before opening in Boston, other problems remained to be dealt with. Reporters noted that it was unusually hot even for a

Boston Labor Day. Enterprising members of the management took advantage of the heat to promote sagging interest in the play by distributing fans printed with one of "De Lawd's" lines from the play: "Let it be a little cooler." Despite these efforts, the performance was slow in gathering impetus. The response from the audience was "little better than mild." Perhaps the play's humor was becoming shopworn; no doubt the heat affected the actors and the singers. The role Connelly had written for "De Lawd" and Harrison's superb execution of it saved the production. As the reviewer wrote:

> As the playwright probed deeper into the perplexities of de Lawd, his perturbation and sorrow at the sins of the mankind that he had brought into being . . . took on breadth and color. . . . The humor was infused with understanding and . . . compassion. The performance like the material lifted noticeably. De Lawd . . . grew in stature and in dignity. His problem became the measure of humanity. The spirituals . . . took on a new meaning.[15]

As the less familiar Bible stories of Cain and Abel and Noah passed across the stage, God's little office, with its shabby furniture, became a familiar and restful place, not just something "different" and amusing. Gabriel, nervously fingering his shining trumpet, grew into a faithful and trusted friend. Even the solicitude of the angels as they dusted God's furniture is shared by the audience. This scene is not merely a caricature of the conventional heaven, according to the Boston reviewer, who used and demonstrated a special insight into the Boston performance of *The Green Pastures*. The special point of view was feasible because the play was getting something of a second hearing and viewing, one by a community well versed in artifacts of American literary heritage rather than one in which the audience waits with bated breath for the attraction of the century to come to its boring town. This unique vantage point lends credence to the *Boston Evening Transcript*'s drama critic's conclusion that no matter how often the play is seen, and no matter how many communities are waiting their turn to see it, the pleasures of the play are no longer new but are enduring. That substantive evaluation placed *The Green Pastures* high in the canons of American modern drama, a step considerably higher than that of a passing fad.

Another view of the relationship between Boston and *The Green Pastures* appears in the report of the correspondent from New England to the *Christian Century* magazine. That begins with the proposition that one would expect so largely Roman Catholic and "liberal" a location to give a cool reception, at best, to a play depicting native Negro faith in a God who appears in human form. In fact, one journalist had written that "it is difficult to comment (on the play) without offending someone" because the subject comes perilously close to the sacrilegious. The same reviewer continued by saying that the play teaches the principle that the "Almighty is wrathful when the people of Earth depart from rectitude, yet He is a God of mercy," a concept that drew no disagreement. In this respect, all critics in Boston conceded that they play contains unquestionable sincerity. Dr. Bernard Bell, a professor of comparative religion at Columbia University, rebuked those who, he said, missed the whole meaning of the play because they think "moderns have no religion." The professor went on to claim that *The Green Pastures* is the only American play worthy of the Greeks, for in it one sees the growth of a concept of deity into the conception that in the supreme Reality is compassion and creative suffering. The *Jewish Advocate* saw in Connelly's play a "mysterious spell" "De Lawd" exercises over man and found in the work a "glow that surpasses the lights which make it a pleasure," for there is a "message in its drawl that reaches the depths of the heart and proves the universality of the thought of God." Dr. William E. Gardner of Trinity Episcopal Church in Boston asked, "Why does the play draw packed houses?" Dr. William E. Gilroy, writing in the *Congregationalist*, criticized minor details of the dramaturgy but praised the staging of the Israelites marching through the wilderness as the finest he had seen. He liked it for its suggestion of "the intensity of the human quest," in addition to its spectacular nature.

After its run in Boston, *The Green Pastures* moved to Philadelphia. The booking was for seven weeks in the Forrest Theatre, opening December 29, 1932. The cast had been given off the week of December 18-25 for Christmas vacation. There critics wrote glowingly of the setting and the performance of the actors, as others had done scores of times. Harrison spoke to many groups of local citizens. He was invited by more than a hundred ministers—white and black—to appear in their pulpits. In one address to a group of Baptist ministers, he said that *Green Pastures* represents a living religion, and he told them some anecdotes about his entry into the commercial theater. He said he had previously avoided getting involved in black plays becuase they "generally rehearsed three months and played three nights, and seldom got paid."[16] Speaking before more than a hundred black Democratic leaders in Philadelphia as their guest of honor at one of their regular meetings, Harrison straddled the matter of partisan commitment by saying to his audience: "Whatever you are, be that thing 100%, whether it is Republican, Democratic, white, black or red." This overly cautious political position characterized his comments on political and social matters. It was in keeping with his attitude toward a highly inflammatory racial incident that would take place a few weeks later when he appeared in Washington.

He might very well have been acting with calculated prudence in these matters, for the drama was beginning its foray into those American cities with large black populations in which racial segregation in special and public life was the law and the practice of the land. He had dealt with it successfully in the cities of the lower Midwest. St. Louis and Kansas City and Oklahoma City had responded to him favorably, and his own real demeanor had seemed to smooth over potential incidents of racial discord. The public—white and black—looked to Harrison to issue the significant statements about black life in America. Blacks were proud of his unquestioned significance in the theater, but they were not entirely content with what the drama represented to them. These cities contained vocal politicians and professional people who were activists in social uplift organizations and in their own political organizations. Accommodating the preachers was fairly easy, although many of them were also political and social activists in their communities. But Harrison could talk to them about his role in the play and its spiritual dimensions. They wanted him to talk about what it felt like to play the part of "De Lawd." There was always just below the surface, though, the possibility that the miltant tone of local NAACP chapters and labor union leaders and the young "New Negro" would break forth into a rejection of the sentimental subject matter of *The Green Pastures.* Knowing about this feeling and sharing it to a large degree himself, as he had stated, was the basis of Harrison's ambivalence in taking the part when Connelly offered it to him. His was, indeed, an ironic human role. He could never have been brought onto the nation's theater stages other than in a vehicle like *The Green Pastures.* And although he enjoyed his role thoroughly, and he knew that, already past sixty-five years old, it was the last role he would play, the social relationships were always troubling. The management always had to work out delicate matters of seating arrangements for black and white members of an audience in places where the law required physical separation. Surely, so sensitive an artist as Harrison fretted over how he was perceived by other Negroes—and whites—in this matter.

Baltimore was one of those cities that would present necessity for special arrangement. Hotels and restaurants there—as in St. Louis and Kansas City and other cities they had played—did not accommodate black people. And theater audiences were segregated. Yet, as had been the case in other American cities, Baltimore took the staging of the play to its heart. One writer for the *Baltimore Sun* wrote a close-up portrait of Harrison and his personal reaction to his role. "Many a man in his life-time has wished he could play God for a few brief moments and set the world right, but not Harrison," he wrote. "He thinks of himself as preacher, teacher, or reader, but not as an actor."[17] Harrison told the critic that he spends his spare time reading, lecturing, and preaching sermons in churches, although he was not an ordained minister. During

his stay in Philadelphia, just before coming to Baltimore, he reported he
had occupied some church pulpit every Sunday. "I took a trio from the
choir with me and told the congregation the story of the coming of Jesus
as the Mr. Deshee of our play would have told it to his Sunday school
class," he explained. "And at the close of every sermon the audience
broke into applause, applause in the church, too." He was in his natural
habitat practicing the elocution that had become his life's work long
before Connelly signed him on as "De Lawd." But he was also advertising the play.

A reviewer for the *Baltimore Sun* wrote: "It would be a mistake to
approach this play with a theological chip on one's shoulder, or to
explain its long run and great popularity by the novelty of permitting the
Jehovah of the play to walk on stage in person." For the play is far more
than a burlesque or a shout. It would be easy to build up a case showing
that it is not even an accurate representation of the Southern Negro's
conception of the white man's heaven. To the critic it is "tremendously
moving and at the same time an extremely funny play." And that is
largely because its qualities transcend race and theological issues. Its
enduring appeal, instead, is based on the fact that it has throughout its
entire length the ability to arouse those simple, fundamental emotions
that have supplied material for the serio-comic dramatic spectacle that
has been going on since Adam's first entrance on that vast stage known
as the earth.[18] Moreover, it is an intensely human plan. In it "De Lawd"
is not so much the rationalization of a deity as the eternal Idealist. He is
the man who has walked alone in suffering and sorrow, the man who,
whatever his race or creed, has devoted his life to the welfare of humanity.

Critics had grown tired of trying to think up new words to describe the
play. Suffice it to say it was a magnificent spectacle in the theater. They
had praised Connelly's conception, Jones' designs, Hall Johnson's magnificent arrangements of the choir he had trained to sing the spirituals,
and Richard B. Harrison's carriage and delivery. More often now they
were beginning to write about the play as a living document about
humanism, in the general sense of the term. They were relating the
ancient and perhaps too-often-repeated Bible stories to twentieth-
century American life. They seldom wrote that the play was providing a
new key for American religious thought, but they talked about the
parameters of this phenomenon. *The Green Pastures* sounded like the
religion they had all heard about since childhood and had practiced in
some form or other as they went about their tasks in a higly civilized
society. But now they could think, in the quietude of a darkened theater,
of what the stories could mean in the real world. Somehow they moved
from the Sunday morning church pew and pulpit. Theatricality gave
them vitality. Men and women did not think of them as Hebrew folklore
rendered by black folk on a sophisticated stage before most civilized

people of American society. They saw themselves mirrored in a racial memory that moved from ancient Israel and its neighbors, to medieval England, to non-Christian Africa, and right into the theater in which the audience sat. Perhaps in ways that no one connected with the play ever anticipated, *The Green Pastures* was holding up a mirror to America, and the reflection was sobering. It was not a condemnation. Rather, it was an introspection and a sense of common thread that binds mankind. It was a miracle play in a new key. That seems to be the sense of the insightful reviews that characterized the play, particularly in its third year of performance. The scenes were the same; most of the characters were the same. The nation had grown wiser, or at least it was stretching itself for a wisdom that was sufficient for the Depression and its distressing uncertainties.

How the new awarenesses one felt on leaving the theater related to the day-to-day living in an America in which Negroes could "entertain" whites and some other Negroes on the stage met still another test as the drama moved on about its 1932-33 season's tour to Washington, D.C. There the social mores created a crisis for the management and for the actors—especially for Harrison. In Chicago and San Francisco and Los Angeles he had been lauded and entertained and revered by his black friends and neighbors and well-wishers. His performances night after night on the stages of the best playhouses of the nation were one thing and his relationship with black Americans among whom he had to live and eat and conduct his personal life off stage was a thing apart. In the cities and towns of the upper Midwest and Far West in which few black people lived, the cast found quite a different living environment for themselves during the time they were in town from that of the large cities in which many black people lived. That is simply an American phenomenon. But Washington was a unique setting. It was a small city, the nation's capital, and specifically Southern in its social orientation. Its inhabitants held no political clout as they did in Chicago, Philadelphia, or Los Angeles. They had no local government. But they did have pride and felt their society was far more advanced than Harlem's. They looked forward to the coming of *The Green Pastures* as enthusiastically as did any other city. Their Howard Theatre had grown up as a showcase for black theatrical talent. They were a proud and cultivated people. They took pride in Harrison, but they would be offended seriously by segregated seating for witnessing a totally black production. Many of them had seen it in New York or elsewhere. Its coming to Washington was a critical symbol to them. Not merely seeing the play, but also feeling it was a part of them. Their reaction to the arrangements for the production requires special notice in this stage biography of Harrison and *The Green Pastures*.

The two-week engagement was scheduled for the National Theatre, the principal theater in the city, which strictly forbade Negroes to attend any performance there. Washington was on the verge of the inauguration of

Franklin D. Roosevelt. Hopes for a new social climate were rampant among the black citizens. Washington was a seat of black American culture. Howard University, the capstone of black higher education, was located there, and it had recently installed its first black president. That incident, alone, spoke of a new day. For previously, practically all black colleges of any significance were headed by white representatives of the philanthropic organizations that sponsored them. Washingtonians spoke of their "positions" rather than jobs. Most worked for the federal government. The racially segregated public school system operated totally white and totally black schools, but most people considered the black high schools in the District of Columbia the best in the nation. Washington housed more educated, cultured Negroes in proportion to its population than any other city in the country. Further, in previous years, no color line had been drawn against Negroes attending the theaters. There was even a civil rights act designed to prevent discrimination in public places on account of race or color. Yet word came down that *The Green Pastures* would play to a white-only audience.

The scenario for confrontation began long before the cast arrived. Local daily newspapers announced that tickets would be sold only at the box office; no reservations would be accepted by telephone or mail. Negroes knew the meaning of that announcement. When the management stated publicly that the National Theatre had not changed its racial policy and that Negroes would not be permitted to enter the theater, a chain of events started. A committee of black ministers and representatives of the local NAACP chapter went to Baltimore, where the drama was showing, and petitioned the cast, through Harrison, to refuse to play the National unless the theater withdrew the insult to him and his race. Harrison and the cast, surprised at the request, raised questions: What of their art, their contracts, their livelihood? They were sorry—deeply pained at the insult to the race—but the show would go on. Black newspapers proudly denounced the National Theatre's policy. The local chapter of the NAACP addressed a letter to Connelly and Stebbins, requesting that the play should not appear at the National. The communication stated that prejudice against the management of the National had been so great that threats had been made against Harrison. They wrote that withdrawal of the play would signal "rebuke to the intolerance and prejudice in the capital of the country."[19] Stebbins answered that contracts with the management of the theater prevented cancellation of the presentation. He reasoned that the policy of the theater in excluding Negroes from the audience was a matter solely within the management's own province. He sent one of his representatives, Charles G. Stewart, to Washington to try to reach accommodation with aggrieved Negroes there. He returned to New York with the word that Harrison and the cast were eager to perform in Washington despite a few threats made by letter writers. However, Stewart had been able to arrange a special showing for Negroes at the National. The solution was not satisfactory to either side; Cochran, manager of the National, said every proposal for a workable answer had been rejected by the Negro group. Cochran complained that the majority of the Negroes insisted on nothing short of opening the National to them together with white patrons. He recognized that the protestors were trying to break down prevailing patterns of racial segregation in public activities in Washington.[20] "It has never been the policy of any first-class theater in Washington to admit Negroes, whose presence the white patrons will not tolerate," Cochran explained over and over.

Connelly made public a letter he wrote to the management of the National Theatre protesting the exclusion of Negroes from the performance scheduled to open one week in advance of the letter. It read, in part:

> Inasmuch as "The Green Pastures" has played to 1,500,000 persons, whites and Negroes, in all parts of the United States, none of whom has ever raised the question of Negro exclusion in the theatres in which it has appeared, we wish to protest against the reported exclusion of Negroes from the National Theatre. . . . While we are informed that there are no legal steps we can take which would confirm our disapproval of this exclusion on the part of the management of the National Theatre, we wish to state emphatically that, if this exclusion is proved to exist, no other plays with which we may be associated will play the National Theatre if we can prevent it.[21]

This action did little to assuage the indignation Negroes in Washington and elsewhere felt over the racial position taken by the National. Washington was practically as racially segregated as the southernmost cities and towns in the nation. Moreover, there was no political clout there. Washington was devoid of the usual elected local officials who could fight for equality of its people. One irate person made the ironical comment that if the president of Howard University or the black Recorder of Deeds wanted to go see *The Green Pastures*, he could not get into the National. And that, as was the practice, he would have to sit in the gallery of any other theater in the city that admitted black and white audiences. Rumor prevailed that the National employed "spotters" to report light-complexioned Negroes who might "pass" into the theater. If they were found, they were asked to leave. The coming of *The Green Pastures* brought to the surface the seething discontent over the theater's practice. This time Richard B. Harrison, the darling of the black elite, was coming to the city that considered itself the most cultivated community in the nation, but they could not see him perform.

Fraternal orders, clergy, educators, and journalists launched their attack. The *New York Age* denounced "this ruthless discrimination . . . ruthlessly practiced in the shadow of the Capitol—one that was not even as liberal as the large cities in Mississippi, Alabama, and Georgia where segregated seating was possible."[22] There Negroes could at least get into a theater by the rear entrance and sit in the gallery. When Roland Hayes, the world famous tenor whose successes were bringing pride to black Americans, sang in Atlanta and in Macon, Georgia, one side of the first floor was reserved for whites and the other for blacks. Victor Daly, writing in *The Crisis*, noted that Harrison's coming to Washington precipitated a crisis in race relations "that is of significance not only to colored people the world over, but to thousands of whites who have devoted their lives to the further advancement of oppressed, darker races."[23] An item in *Commonweal* magazine raised a curious question about the incident that its editors could not answer:

> The case of "The Green Pastures" has been curious from the first. It is a mystery play, in the medieval sense; it presents the Old Testament as the folklore of the American Negro without impairing (or so many devout people think) its character as revelations; its original cast are all Negroes. But besides these items, which merely mark the play as unusual, its history has been unusual. . . . What press reports say is happening in Washington is curious indeed. The National Association for the Advancement of Colored People has petitioned the authors to remove the play from the theatre there (which, incidentally, admits Negroes into the audience to view the original Negro cast only at special performances) though it is doing a thriving business, because it has called forth race prejudice and threats against the actors from some of the populace. And still the play goes on. Or should one say, "and therefore . . ."[24]

The issue was joined. Alarm and confusion reigned. Threats against Harrison's life reached him in Philadelphia. According to a New York newspaper, one of them read: "We'll take your black God [Richard Harrison in the play] so far there'll be no play."[25] Harrison lost face in the incident. Generally, black people thought that inasmuch as Stebbins would not require the theater to seat the audience without respect to color, it was Harrison's responsibilty to refuse to play there. The rest of the cast would follow him. Threats on his life were turned over to the police by the management of the National. When he arrived in Washington, Harrison was under heavy guard, which remained in place throughout the performance time in the city. Negotiations got under way for a special showing for Negroes. The first proposal provided that the Belasco Theatre, which was closed, could be used for a special showing that would give "all ranks of Negroes in the capitol" an opportunity to see the play in Washington. Negroes strongly objected to the plan, saying it was racial segregation of the rankest order. Stebbins realized such an arrangement would spell financial disaster. He worked assiduously to bring about acceptable accommodations for both sides, lest the revenue plan for the Washington performance might be disturbed. The Improved Benevolent and Protective Order of Elks, a black fraternal order that counted among its members some of Washington's professional men and a great number of minor governmental officials, agreed to sponsor a benefit performance at the National that would permit black persons to see the play in the National Theatre. The event was set for Sunday night, February 26, 1933, the third anniversary of the opening of *The Green Pastures* in New York. Reportedly, only a small number of Negroes attended the jim crow showing.

Notwithstanding the furor that the segregated appearance in Washington precipitated, Harrison was as cordially received there as he had been in New York, Chicago, St. Louis, Kansas City, Philadelphia, and all of the major cities in which he played. He had a much-publicized photograph taken with some members of the cast on the steps of the Lincoln Memorial. February 19, 1933, he spoke at the Sunday morning service at fashionable First Congregational Church at Tenth and G streets, northwest. The pastor, Dr. Allen A. Stockdale, preached on the subject *The Green Pastures*, and members of the production's choir sang. The next day the *Washington Post* reported that "an audience that tested the capacity of the auditorium and the galleries" came to see and hear Harrison. He spoke about the experience of playing "De Lawd" in the drama. Referring to the portion of the play that depicts the flight of the children of Israel out of Egypt, the article quoted Harrison as having said:

> I could sympathize with them for I belong to a race of men
> and women who have been led out of the house of bondage.
> They are on their way, not knowing whither they are going,
> but trusting in God. That spirit is the elemental simplicity of
> "The Green Pastures." It is to understand that elemental sim-
> plicity that many have returned more than once to investigate
> completely the unusual idea which prompted Mr. Connelly to
> write the play.[26]

Harrison and thirty-six members of the cast appeared before an interracial audience of students and friends of Howard University. Daniel Haynes sang a song that he dedicated to President Mordecai Johnson. In his remarks Harrison recalled some signal experiences of three years with the play. He introduced members of the cast as people who "worked toward an objective," with obvious reference to the tension the Washington performance had caused. He urged students in the audience to "be conscientious, honest, and unafraid of difficulties in their pursuit of success." In introducing Harrison, President Johnson recalled the privilege Howard had in conferring the honorary master of arts degree on him earlier. Albert Bushnell Hart, professor emeritus of history at Harvard, Jesse E. Moreland of New York City, and John H. Hawkins of Washington—all executive committee members of the Howard Board of Trustees—attended the event. No one mentioned Harrison's decision not to withdraw from the show because of the bitterness stirred up against him in Washington. Nor did the controversy end there. For the next several weeks Carter G. Woodson, founder of the Association for the Study of Negro Life and History and editor of the prestigious *Journal of Negro History*, wrote scathing columns in the *Pittsburgh Courier* about jim crow theater in America. And Kelly Miller, dean of Howard's College of Arts and Science, who wrote a regular feature for the Baltimore *Afro-American* newspaper, questioned whether black Washington should participate in a segregated inaugural ball for Franklin D. Roosevelt. Langston Hughes, young rising black poet and fiction writer, who had already published his first novel, *Not Without Laughter*, and had come to the attention of the literary public by winning prizes for his poetry in contests sponsored by *Opportunity* magazine, was among those who attacked Harrison for playing before segregated audiences. In his *Trouble with the Angels*, a brief short story, he explained in trenchant mock humor the story of the appeal of the play for white audiences. He sneered: "At every performance lots of white people wept."[27]

The traveling company put the Washington controversy behind them as quickly as they could.[28] It played in Wilmington, Delaware, and Reading, Pennsylvania, before going into Rochester, New York, and Buffalo for three-day runs in each city.

It played before its first British audience in Toronto for the week of March 20. R. E. Knowles commented on that historic event in his review of the play. He added that Toronto was the most British of Canadian cities, suggesting that if the Parliament had permitted the play to be performed in England, it would have been well received.[29] Toronto journalists and drama critics were particularly adept at conducting interviews with Harrison and in writing fresh impressions of the drama. Knowles asked Harrison about the important people he had met since he started playing the role, and the actor answered: "I have even met several of the presidents of the United States—Presidents Taft, McKinley, and Theodore Roosevelt. And one night the present president, then governor, brought a party of 17 to our performance—and I had a little chat with him afterward." He was speaking about Franklin D. Roosevelt in the final remark, and he was referring to having met the other presidents long before he joined the cast of *The Green Pastures*. When he was asked, "Whom would you name, Mr. Harrison, as among the greatest benefactors of the colored race, themselves colored?" Harrison answered, "I should say Fred Douglass first. But educationally and industrially, the outstanding name is Booker T. Washington. I knew him well, and held him in high esteem."

When he was asked how he would account for the remarkable vogue of the play—"What is beneath it all?" Harrison responded:

> Because in these days of sinking sand, I believe the human heart wants something (or somebody) to hang on to. Even the educated. Even the cultured. Even the agnostic. The secret of the appeal of our play is that it makes vivid a superior power—even hearts who don't know it want something to convert them, to convert them from the way things are going.

When Knowles pushed further with, "Do you learn of actual concrete cases of people who have been helped, religiously, by the play?" Harrison answered without hesitation, "Indeed, we do. Many and many of them—that is one of my great rewards." Asked whether he observed any sign of religious influence on his associates, due to the play, Harrison said he had. Other members of the cast would never swear in his presence. When one does explode, he apologizes copiously for his incontinent language or action. Harrison also told Knowles, on being asked about it, of occasions other than the celebrated one in Madison, Wisconsin, when he was denied hotel accommodation because of race. He said he could recall only two cases: the Taft Hotel in New Haven, Connecticut, and one in Milwaukee. He explained further that at the Taft Hotel he was not actually denied a room, but the management stipulated that the cast should have meals brought to their rooms in order not to be seen as patrons of the establishment. They refused to accept those restrictions, and the hotel refused to withdraw its stipulations. "But I'm not resentful," Harrison continued. "Wherever I am, in these hotels, I always try not to make myself conspicuous. All of our people, I think, try to do the same." He hastened to add that all of the company were warmly accommodated at all hotels and eating establishments in Toronto. Harrison's attitude toward slights because of race he and the cast suffered in moving about the United States suggests his acceptance of the "accommodationist" attitude of which his friend Booker T. Washington was accused. The irony of a society in which the cast of a play so completely accepted in American theaters and auditoriums throughout the nation often found it could not be sure it would find boarding and lodging at commercial institutions in their native land stands out in bold relief throughout the odyssey of *The Green Pastures*. That dimension to the biography of the play and its cast is indeed a significant part of the story of American socioculture.

William Arthur Deacon, literary editor for the *Toronto Mail and Empire*, wrote about the two parts of the play: the first that "appears to be a musical comedy based on the Old Testament"; and the second that moves from a burlesque on the primitive theology of ignorant folk into "the triumph of the Negro spirit over the harsh Judaic God of Genesis." In it, he wrote, "the kindly human quality of the black man's heart, and his courage in adversity, and his fine, simple faith melt the wrath of the vengeful deity." Having been in bondage themselves, the Negroes understand the trials of the slaves and can comprehend the evolution of the doctrine of love and sympathy as a necessary partner with justice in a human world, is the way the insightful critic explained this theological interpretation of the play and the way it was performed. But it is not the only element the Negro race contributes to Connelly's mythmaking. It is that everything is Negroid, including the entire cast. There is the mellow quality of the voices, swelling in chorus after chorus of spirituals; the lively imagination that has dramatized the biblical scenes; the desolution of the deluge, the melodrama of Moses' contests with the plagues of Pharaoh, the death of Moses—all have a bright, sure quality only possible for people to whom these things are real. And what others had spoken of as the sheer theater of the chosen people marching through the desert became as one oppressed people playacting another oppressed people's travail centuries ago. The affinity between the two peoples passed through the audience, though not an implicit word of it was included in the spoken word, the singing, or the mime. The marvel of it all, the critic concluded, is "all that is attractive in the Negro nature has been gathered up into this interpretation of a religion given him by his white masters in a hand and tongue not his own."

Large audiences poured into the Royal Alexandra to see *The Green Pastures*, and there, as had been the case in American cities, Harrison was an attraction both on and off the stage. Praise for his acting was loud and constant. Civic groups and academic clubs invited him to address them, as did pastors of churches. Speaking before the Canadian Women's Press Club, he reminded them that his parents and other black slaves escaped from the United States and settled in Ontario at the invitation of Queen Victoria. He was, after all, a Canadian by birth, and Toronto was taking him to its heart. All the newspapers reported on his activities during the week the show played there. One would have to conclude that the appearance in Toronto was one of the most successful runs of the season.

Back into the states, the tour moved into Cleveland, Ohio, for a week, where it played to full houses at the Hanna Theatre, which had been dark for several months. Essentially, the season ended in Detroit, beginning for a week on April 24, 1933. Readjustments to the bookings brought the final playing in Easton, Pennsylvania. It closed in that town May 13, 1933.

Russel McLaughlin, writing the principal review in the *Detroit News,* used for its title "The New Play." "The theatre never saw anything exactly like this before," he wrote, "and it probably never will again because *Green Pastures* is the sort of thing which once done—superbly done—establishes a peak in theatrical history which it is precarious work to climb again."[30] True, it was three years old. And all the stagewise folk in the English-speaking world had already heard about it. But, in Detroit, "it is the same wondrous and astonishing spectacle which was unfolded before a skeptical New York three seasons ago." These were the usual comments, tailored for that particular city and that stage of the second long-range tour. But McLaughlin's review stands among those insightful comments about the play, for like the better of the critics, he tried to move into evaluation of the play as an American cultural document. It shows how the American Negro, "as the world knows," he wrote, "turned to the God of the Old Testament in his slavery and bewilderment, and here found peace." That peculiar event of acculturation saw the Negro slave interpreting the wonderful old stories in the light of his own essential simplicity and poetry. His "so-called spirituals" became the chief document on this "remarkable rejoinder of stern theology and pure, poetic worship." The slave took Christianity in its essence, without any of the doubts and complexities that had bothered his white brothers for nearly two thousand years, the critic wrote. And the value and the beauty of "the general baptism" had been incalculable. What James Weldon Johnson had called "the wide, wide wonder" in the creations of the black and unknown bards, McLaughlin called "something of extreme loveliness" that flowered on this continent. This was black American culture, a multifaceted artifact so uniquely black American that it would be blasphemy for a white man to essay a role in *The Green Pastures,* he wrote, reminding one that Al Jolson had made known his desire to play the role of "De Lawd" in another stage version or a film. McLaughlin thought that "sacrilege would fill the stage if a flock of Broadway actors attempted the stirring fishfry scene at which celebration the Lord decided to create the earth." One trembles at the thought of a Nordic comedian playing Gabriel too, he said.

McLaughlin saw the play as a capsule of black culture, ingeniously primitive in its content and masterfully professional in its execution. "Only the journeying of Jehovah brought forth by means of a turntable is a piece of stage sophistication." All other devices are those of "imprisoned simplicity and they are great and quite indescribable."

Surely, the critic understood the conception of the play. He understood the artistry in the pristine and never bothered himself with sentimental recollections of a childhood replete with blacks singing about their cabin doors, as many of the New York critics claimed, with respect to the time distance between themselves and the slavery period. This critic's words about Harrison were measured:

> Richard B. Harrison's venerable figure, saintly face, flowing white hair, dominate the fable. At the close of the evening one feels that for any other to attempt the part would be an imposture of a particular horrid kind. Mr. Harrison must have received some "sort of call" to play it.

This tour had not covered quite so many miles as the previous ones. It had started in Boston and ended in Pennsylvania. It had attracted large audiences after a slow start. The Washington, D.C., performance had gained the kind of notoriety neither management nor cast wanted—certainly not Harrison. Yet the matter had shown that the company could act as a catalyst for the nation's view of itself. Stebbins and Connelly would not have wanted this incident to happen. They tried all they could to prevent it. But they must have quietly enjoyed the benefits from the clash. There is no indication that box office receipts dropped as a result of the disputation, with the possible exception of the jim crow staging in Washington. Detroit and Toronto provided the most profitable stops, both financially and aesthetically. They are large cities, but they are also places that held special meaning for Harrison. Toronto considered him a Canadian, and Detroit remembered that he had worked there as a young boy when his family came to that city to seek a living after leaving London, Ontario. The play did well everywhere, though. Few road companies were getting beyond Chicago. Philadelphia and Boston were considered secondary stops. All other week stands or those that lasted for two or three days were regarded as "break mumps." Ohio was hardly profitable, owing to the ten percent admission tax, part federal and part state. Moreover, theaters were becoming outmoded. People were not accustomed to picture palaces. Long road tours were fast becoming obsolete. As soon as a show clicked on Broadway, film scouts cured it with money. Most producers, faced with that kind of offer, were willing to take the big money because they knew there was little to be gained from out-of-town engagements. The population was unable and unwilling to pay three dollars, or even two dollars, for tickets in most spots. Yet *The Green Pastures* did surprisingly well under these circumstances. Stebbins would hear nothing of turning his show into a film. His sagacity in keeping his play alive and in secure bookings throughout the nation at

these perilous times for the economy place *The Green Pastures* in a
special category among American works in the theater in the United
States.

During the 1932-33 season Stebbins and Connelly pondered whether
to take the play back to Broadway in the fall of 1933, to arrange a tour of
Europe, or to work out another national tour that would include the
American South. Charles G. Stewart, general manager of the company,
had come up with a plan the previous winter that seemed feasible.
Himself a Southerner, Stewart proposed inviting opinion-makers from
such Southern cities as Atlanta, New Orleans, Nashville, and Chatta-
nooga to see the play in Washington, D.C., and to comment on whether
The Green Pastures would play well in their particular sections of the
South. He knew many Southerners had seen the play in northern and
border cities and that they had liked it. But their reactions were
personal. No one knew just how the play would fare in strictly racially
segregated cities. For all the goodwill *The Green Pastures* had been said to
have promulgated on its first national tour into the border states, producers were unwilling to commit thousands of precious dollars to a show
that might fail because of a white paying public that refused to give good
money to attend a performance of scores of black performers in a play
that was far from minstrel or vaudeville. Seeing a black God on stage
was a new experience for all Americans. It might be traumatic for Southerners. Some said their racial bias would outweigh their respect for the
merits of the play. Clark wanted to go directly to the heart of the matter.
He convinced Stebbins to invite twenty-eight Southern journalists to be
guests of the management at a Washington, D.C., performance. He reasoned that newspapermen, sensitive to the sentiments of their communities, would be better able to render a valid opinion on the matter. And
they could help to promote it by writing editorials in their papers. Invitations were extended to journalists in fourteen cities in nine states below
the Mason-Dixon line. They were from Richmond and Norfolk in Virginia; Charlotte and Winston-Salem in North Carolina; Birmingham,
Alabama; Atlanta, Georgia; Louisville, Kentucky; Wheeling, West
Virginia; and New Orleans, Louisiana. William Fields, a publicist for the
management, wrote that "the response to the invitation was gratifying
beyond hopes." Acceptances were received immediately from sixteen of
the twenty-one persons who had been invited. Responses ran generally
along the line of that sent by Colonel Wade H. Harris, publisher of the
Charlotte Observer, who wrote an editorial that pleased Stebbins and
Connelly:

> This production by Rowland Stebbins, written by Marc Con-
> nelly, based on Roark Bradford's book, and commonly known
> as a Negro play, has been presented in every section of the

country except the South. For some reason, the producer has felt that it might be objectionable to Southern people, so he took advantage of the opportunity of a two-weeks' run in Washington to invite a party of Southern editors to witness it and "pass" on the proposition of bringing it South. The editor of the *Observer* witnessed the play last Monday night, and was moved to wonder why there had been any halting about bringing it South, for it is a play that would be best appreciated by Southern people, familiar as they are with the customs, traditions and peculiar religious notions of plantation Negroes. . . . In fact, we would regard avoidance of the South by a stage organization of this kind as an actual and unwarranted deprivation. Southern people would enjoy it more than the people of any other section.[31]

Alfred Mynders, chief editorial writer of the *Charlotte News*, wrote that the difficulties the play would find in the South, if there were any, would not be religious or racial prejudices, but in finding theaters big enough to accommodate the production. He rejected the idea that the South was not interested in worthwhile attractions, but that people had grown weary of going to buildings in which they could not hear what was being said. The editor of the *Winston-Salem Journal* wrote an editorial for his paper, agreeing that the South, of all sections of the country, would understand both the language and the music of the play. He ended his long editorial with the complaint that the South had a right to feel aggrieved that it has been slighted so long by the most popular group of Negro artists ever assembled in this country. He declared that they would be welcome in Dixie. Gladstone Williams, who was assigned by Clark Howell, editor of the *Atlanta Constitution*, to write that paper's editorial and response, wrote: "I see no reason why 'The Green Pastures' should not make a successful tour of the South and I believe it will be well-received in Atlanta." He admitted that he had seen the play in New York sometime earlier and was delighted with it.

Louis Jaffe, editor of the *Norfolk Virginian-Pilot*, whose anti-lynching editorial brought him the Pulitzer prize some years earlier, wrote that the play should have been presented in the South before being taken to New York. Only T. R. Waring, editor of the *Charleston* (S.C.) *Evening Post*, dissented out of those who had accepted the invitation. He characterized the plan an invasion of the South and a highly uncertain and perhaps hazardous venture. His letter to Stebbins is particularly interesting, inasmuch as he makes specific reference to Du Bose Heyward's *Porgy*, which had been fairly successful on Broadway. He wrote that he had discussed bringing Heyward's play to the South and that the producers rejected the idea, not because "our people are intolerant or unintelligent nor that there is any unkindly feeling toward the Negro." He said there were "peculiar problems" in presenting such a play as *The Green Pastures* in the South. He did not elaborate on that comment.

Stebbins originally intended to inaugurate the Southern tour in Richmond, Virginia; however, a combination of circumstances prevented him from carrying out his plans. Motion-picture interests that controlled the theaters in Richmond were unwilling to guarantee the arrangements that would be required to stage a play as big as Connelly's. The same problem arose when Stebbins tried to book the show in Norfolk and Lynchburg. Clearly, some racial issues arose, but they were not the principal problems. Roanoke was settled on as the location for the beginning of the fourth year of production and the long-heralded Southern tour. That town was excited about the coming of the hundred or so performers who had played throughout the nation on previous tours. The Broadway company was coming intact. The play was to play one- and two-nighters, with the understanding that some bookings might have to be changed because of stage requirements. The treadmill required eight hours to install. Hotel arrangements were being made by advance men, but everyone knew the South would present accommodation problems for the cast. Hotels and restaurants simply did not serve Negroes. But the larger towns provided black hotels and boardinghouses and eating places. In most cases, cast members, as their black fellow actors had done in the past, "stopped with" black friends and relatives who had set up a network of accommodations, actually since the company had left Chicago.[32]

Every seat was taken at the Academy of Music in Roanoke when the play opened its three-performance run there October 4, 1933. The management's apprehension was dispelled by the reaction to the appearance. Aside from the publicity by Stebbins' company, a local newspaper set the pattern that would be followed by every location where the drama would play in the south. The praise was effusive. "This city's appreciation of the Pulitzer prize winner was evident as much in the warmth of the reception as in the actual applause which left a very definite impression that the applauders had had an experience they would not have missed for anything," the piece in the *Roanoke Times* read. The play does what its author set out to do, the reviewer continued, "with an effect that is at once devastatingly powerful."[33] Because the eyes of the nation were on the South to see how it would receive the play, the *New York Times* carried a small news item about the Roanoke performance and added that it was the only Virginia town on the tour because adequate theaters could not be found in Norfolk and Richmond. Stebbins was able to get the cooperation of the entertainment media in dispelling any implication that the South would not want to come see a play in which a Negro plays God on the stage.

After three sold-out performances in Roanoke, the play moved to Greensboro, North Carolina. That city had a special meaning for Harrison. He was teaching dramatic art to teachers at the agricultural and technical state college there the summers during the 1920s when he went to New York to audition for *The Green Pastures*. When the Southern tour was being planned, Greensboro had been considered the place for the premiere in the South because Harrison had been so well known there. President Ferdinand D. Bluford, chief executive officer of that black state college, had met Harrison some years earlier when the actor was appearing regularly on the dramatic readings circuit. The college was all male then and was the black land grant institution for North Carolina. Its summer sessions were becoming increasingly popular, though, for in-service teachers. President Bluford engaged Harrison to conduct a summer course in drama for in-service teachers and to produce one or two plays at the school.[34] He was popular there. Today the principal auditorium on the campus bears the name of Richard B. Harrison, as does the college drama society. In Raleigh, North Carolina, the original Negro branch of the public library is still called the Richard B. Harrison Branch. Greensboro would have been a good choice of a place for launching the foray into the South, but Stebbins wanted to take advantage of the large audiences that he thought would be possible in the cities of Virginia.

During his appearance with the play in Greensboro, Harrison was honored by the city and the college. In a most unusual event for that time and place, he addressed the Greensboro Civitan Club, with the presidents of the several white and black colleges and universities of the area in the audience. The principal of the white high school, who was also president of the Civitan Club, and the white superintendent of schools were also there. Harrison was given a key to the city. At commencement time A. and T. College conferred on him his first honorary degree, the doctor of humane letters. Harrison pleased the natives when he said he considered himself on leave from the college and that he planned to return to Greensboro to make his home when he left the stage. The local press paid high praise to one they considered a returning hometown celebrity, although Harrison's only relationship to Greensboro occurred during the six summers he taught there. Local reviewers made significant observations about the play that had not been made previously. Were it not for the musical element, *The Green Pastures* would never have had a hearing, one wrote. The music makes the play akin to opera—"an opera with dialogue"—some said, and an indication of the start of American opera premised distinctly on American folk music. The reviewer pointed out the contrast between reading the play and witnessing a performance of it in the theater. In the armchair the mind is occupied with the remarkable dialogue, "the swift changes from buffoonery to genuine tragedy." But in the theater, "to one not tone-deaf, the spirituals rendered by an unusual choir often present themselves in such a manner as to dominate the production." Although it is true that the spirituals cause the biblical episodes to "hang together," the work itself causes one to wonder when the great American opera on American themes by an American composer will be written. The answer to that question, the critic suggested, might lie in *The Green Pastures*.[35] Also in Greensboro, the media began the often-repeated reaction heard throughout the South: that Southerners regarded the play religious. Note this part of the review:

> But if there were among the audience those who saw in its humor, in its fantasy, in its homeliness of de Lawd Gawd Jehovah and the figures on high any semblance of sacrilege, it was because of their own insufficiency. . . . Southern audiences, if members of the cast do not already know it, take their religion, the religion of their Negroes, seriously, reverently. There was in the theatre last night what one might term a holy atmosphere; a tribute of silence far more effective than thunderous applause. Applause came at the end of the first act and again at the conclusion, when Richard B. Harrison, Doe Doe Green as Gabriel, and Daniel L. Haynes as Adam took curtain calls; but even then it was a dignified, restrained ovation. Southerners do not applaud in church; and "The Green Pastures" seemed strangely like church.[36]

Strange, indeed, for Connelly would not have thought this play about the simple beliefs of American rural Negroes could have impressed a sophisticated, largely white audience as "church" for them too. Another writing about it called it marvelous grandeur and beautiful simplicity, "a religion—real religion."[37] The Southern tour was off to a good start. At Greensboro it had solved the mystery of how the Bible Belt South would take to a biblical miracle play whose cast were all Negroes, the social outcasts of the religion. *The Green Pastures* was beginning to take on a unique meaning there.

The attraction continued into the deepest places in the South, except for the state of Mississippi. The bigger cities reacted to the drama and to Harrison much in the fashion of the cities in other parts of the nation. Atlanta, as much a center for Negro culture in the South as Washington was for the Middle Atlantic region, gave him high honor. White and black institutions reacted in the same manner. During the time between the eight performances scheduled for Atlanta, Harrison was pressed with invitations far beyond the possibility of acceptance. On the one Sunday he was in the city, he appeared three times before large audiences. Two hundred white and black college students heard him at Central Congregational Church in a meeting arranged by the Interracial Student Council. An hour later a crowded house greeted him at Big Bethel African Methodist Episcopal Church. That evening he addressed the largest audience ever assembled in Druid Hills Methodist Church, South, one of the leading white churches in the city. According to press accounts, every seat was taken and every inch of standing room was occupied upstairs and down, the vestibule was packed, and people looked in from the outside steps through two sets of opened doors.[38] The principal review in the *Atlanta Constitution* the morning after opening night posed two "slight feelings of puzzlement." First: "Whatever made the producers of 'The Green Pastures' ever hesitate, for one moment, in sending it South?" Second: "How could anybody by any stretch of mis-apprehension, dream there is anything sacrilegious in this tremendous spectacle?" The reviewer's own answer to the first question was tradi-tional: The South fully understands its Negroes, whom they have lived among and admired. The second was more valuable in understanding the force of the drama on the American cultural intellect. For as the writer agreed, much after the fashion of the attitude expressed in Greensboro, "if 'The Green Pastures' is sacrilegious, then all the writ-ings and stories and plays about sacred things are sacrilegious." For none can possibly do more than interpret according to the imagination of those who read or hear, and this is exactly what the play does. It interprets according to the imagination of its people. On the Sunday after the last performance, the Reverend R. M. Ashby Jones used for the subject of his sermon at the morning service *The Green Pastures*. He sought to address some of the questions that had arisen: Is it a sincere representation of the religion of the primitive Negro? Is there a close analogy to the religion of the primitive Hebrew? Has the play a genuine religious portrayal of these issues? These reactions to the appearance indicate that Connelly's play and Harrison's portrayal of his principal character, in particular, were fostering serious thoughts about art and religion.

From Atlanta the company appeared in small cities and towns, including sold-out performances at the Grand Theatre in Macon. The company holding the contract for hauling the scenery had its greatest challenge in three years. The firm worked all week on reconditioning a forty-foot trailer to carry the sets from the railroad cars to the theater. Only one route could be used because of the size of the truck. Reporters remembered that Roark Bradford had worked at one time on the *Macon Telegraph*, the morning daily newspaper, and that he had been fired, allegedly, for spending too much time among Negroes, from whom he was collecting folklore. This incident added interest to the performance in Macon.[39] Throughout the fall and winter the drama moved into prac-tically every town and city in the South that could accommodate it.

One of the most memorable of these performances was the one-night stand at Tuskegee Institute, Alabama. Harrison insisted on including that performance in the itinerary, although the logistics of playing there were almost prohibitive. There in the school for black youth founded by Booker T. Washington in 1881, Harrison found unusual acclaim. And he was particularly gratified for the appearance. Charles Winter Wood, understudy for the role of "De Lawd," had taught English and drama and served as librarian there for nearly thirty years before he joined the cast of *The Green Pastures*. Harrison was feted as he had been everywhere the drama played. At Tuskegee he was the houseguest of President Robert Russa Moton, Booker T. Washington's successor as chief executive officer of the school. In an interview the venerable old actor was asked how long he expected to continue in the role, and he replied with a smile: "De Lawd is everlasting. I expect to go on and on, from everlasting to everlasting." And in a more serious vein he said, "I expect the play to run at least three more years."[40] He expressed his pleasure with the reaction his play received at Tuskegee, especially, he said, "in view of the fact that of the 3000 present, I understand half were students." As he stepped into the car waiting to take him back to the railroad station on the morning after the performance, Harrison said once more he was "more proud that the students of Tuskegee liked his performance and the play than of any applause he had received at Times Square." He might very well have been remembering his own days as a teacher in a small black college and the many years he traveled and made his living giving dramatic readings to black college students. At Tuskegee they had helped the stage crew erect makeshift settings for the stage that was far too small to accommodate the elaborate scenery. Students there took pride in working on the sets. In another sense Harrison was giving his tacit approval once more to Washington's self-help philosophy that had been the guiding force at Tuskegee. They both had come along the way of the black Horatio Alger mode of the late nineteenth century and the early years of the twentieth century. Further, this was probably the largest all-black audience ever to see the play.

While *The Green Pastures* was breaking box office records in Texas for a traveling legitimate company, Laurence Rivers, Inc. (the trade name for its management) began to advertise for its 1934-35 season. The vexing problem of finding suitable theaters in the small and medium-sized cities of the South and Midwest had been solved by using auditoriums. This development gave new impetus to promotion. A notice in *Variety* used a letter from the manager of the auditorium in Memphis, Tennessee, to solicit engagements. It read in part:

> During my lifetime in the show business I have written many letters from which I have derived pleasure, but I would like to say to you frankly that I believe I am getting more pleasure from

this letter to you than any I have written. . . . It has taken us
five days to get our "feet on the ground" following the engagement of "Green Pastures," in addition to the fact that it is
the greatest attraction from a financial standpoint that we
have ever had in the building. . . . I have been in the business
over twenty-five years and I will venture to say that I have
never seen a road attraction handled more perfectly and with
such harmony as "Green Pastures." From the front door to
the back, things run like clock work, and I have never come in
contact with a manager who was so willing to do things and
work so hard to make an engagement successful as Mr. Clarence Jacobson. . . . To my way of thinking, it is absolutely
marvelous the manner in which this attraction is being received in the South and the attitude of the Southern people
towards it.[41]

But New Orleans was disappointing. The press made copy about the
city being the hometown of Roark Bradford. Charles P. Jones, writing in
the *Times Picayune* on the eve of the opening, wrote: " 'The Green
Pastures' is opening at the Tulane this week, finally brought South, after
all these years, to the town of its birth." Bradford, he claimed, "takes
rank among the few prophets who are not without honor in their own
country, and his famous play will be presented in the town where a
literary genius walked the earth like a natural man." Bradford made one
of his few appearances in the theater during any one of the tour appearances at the Tulane Theatre in New Orleans. Reviewers liked the play.
They could hardly help praising it and the performance. But they took
uncommon pride in claiming it for their native son. Somehow it had
come as a valedictory for one of their own, who had written about what
they all know only too well, had gone to Broadway to show the folks up
North what he knew about Negroes, and had returned home to finally be
appropriately honored. No matter how high its plaudits, or how wild the
enthusiasm with which it is greeted, one critic wrote, "the fact that we
liked it last night, that to a New Orleans audience it was the theatre's
highest expression, a work of art, will give its authors the most genuine
satisfaction there is—to make good with the folks back home."[42] Still, the
performances were not sold out there as they had been in most major
cities.

Outside New York, few cities paid as many tributes to *The Green
Pastures* as did Dallas. Joe Line, writing in the *Times Herald*, claimed per-
fection for the play. He considered it a high mark in the theater, one that
will keep the country's playgoers "in a state of watchful waiting until
they might again witness anything worth a comparison." Lavish praise
perhaps, but the reviewer defends his evaluation; for, to him, "so

flawless is its writing, so completely realized is its execution, that it is easy to imagine Mr. Connelly wondering to himself whether it is not the peak of his career, that anything he produced thereafter would appear anticlimactic."[43] Another wrote about the extraordinary technical demands of the play and the drastic change required to transpose the Melba Theatre stage from a "picture sheet" to a living picture of three dimensions. It had to make room for the three motor-driven treadmills, and the orchestra pit had to be remodeled to hold members of the choir. The rainbow required five experimentations before a successful one would be realized. It and the waves that were supposed to recede when Noah's flood subsided refused to work on opening night in New York. But they were perfect for Dallas. Most theater buffs had heard of these feats that Robert Edmond Jones accomplished in his sets for *The Green Pastures*. They went to performances to see how the miracles of staging would accomplished in their local houses. This certainly was the case with reporters in Dallas, who saw the play in a theater that had not housed a stage attraction since vaudeville was discontinued there in 1926. Melba was a motion picture house when Connelly's extravaganza played there in December 1933. The *Dallas Morning News* dedicated a full page to its impressions of the play the day after Christmas. John Rosenfield, Jr., sought to explain it as "a study of sociology." It was superficially "a slumming party to North Hall Street," for it brought downtown the exhibition of what was said to be the religion of the Negroes who lived elsewhere in town. Essentially, though, "it is the most thorough-going and lucid exposition of sociological processes ever introduced by the drama," not excluding Shaw and Ibsen. For it is the story of anybody's religion, with the naive conceptions of the illiterate rural Negro as its clinical material. Rosenfield thought of the play's anthropomorphosis of God as the patriarchal Uncle Tom, with every-thing else in the Old Testament matching in such a fantastic manner that white civilization can view it objectively. Obviously, he did not consider Uncle Tom as a pejorative metaphor. Through Connelly's dramatic method, the critic continued, white civilization "can find the clue to what the King James Bible and three centuries of Sunday school lessons have done in our imaginations." If the ecclesiastical imagery of *The Green Pastures* is the Bible translated in terms of the menial Negro's experience, then "our own imagery grows out of our more varied experi-ences against a background of Renaissance oils and etchings." Con-tinually in his sociological approach to interpreting the play and what it means to Americans—especially those who saw it in the Dallas theater—this writer reminded his readers that they, and he, have constructed a picture of the Pearly Gates from some Elysian suggestions, even as Mr. Deshee's Bible class in New Orleans visualizes the entrance to heaven as a wrought iron grille in the French Quarter. Sophisticated whites might think of eternity in terms of an Italian sky, Texas clouds, Irish harps, Raphaelite wings, and nightgowns of A.D. 1200. And in their Negroid fantasy the costumes are much the same, but the activities run to eating fried fish and drinking "b'iled" custard. Rosenfield adds the note that Harrison, whose mother was a slave to the famous Chouteau family, played in Dallas in a theater for which Azby Chouteau had been manager as part of the old Interstate Vaudeville circuit. Harrison was, to him, "a shaded counterpart of William Jennings Bryan and Henry Ward Beecher," whose massive poise, inescapable magnetism, and ready and rotund oratory is everything a benevolent Negro of the nineteenth century would expect God to be. He is, the critic judged, the successor in the theater to Booth and Barrett.[44]

As the company continued its 1933-34 tour, it moved into Oklahoma, Tennessee, and Texas on the Southern leg of the itinerary. Devastating floods along the Mississippi River forced cancellation of several engagements. Big Springs, Texas, provided the smallest box office receipts—merely six hundred dollars. The most jarring note to break into the harmony the company took along with it in its swing through the South came in attempts to arrange a performance in Lubbock, Texas. The management approached the *Lubbock Morning Avalanche* and *Evening Journal* about sponsoring an appearance of *The Green Pastures*. Apparently, the process used in securing the cooperation of Southern editors for the more Eastern portion of that section of the country did not work in Lubbock. The editor and publisher of the papers there explained that he did not turn down the offer on solely racial grounds but because the city's only auditorium that could accommodate the production was the new $650,000 senior high school building and he did not "cotton" to Negroes using the school's dressing room and then expecting the sons and daughters of white citizens to use them thereafter.[45] *Time*'s editorial note to the letter sent by the Lubbock journalist added that the play's management had offered to erect its own dressing room tent outside the school because of the objection. No such arrangements were possible to be made. Miami, Florida, was a location in which racial ordinances prevented the playing of the drama. City law barred black performances from stages where the audience is composed exclusively of whites. The ordinances were said to be needed to keep Miami audiences unmixed in color.

Five performances in Dallas, Texas, registered a gross business of fifteen thousand dollars—the record for the South. Oklahoma City was a close second, and Houston, Texas, finished third in box office sales. Most disappointing of the cities played, both from the standpoint of financial return for a location of its size and for lack of enthusiasm for the play, was Louisville, Kentucky. There, during a full week's engagement, the intake amounted to only $12,934. In Austin, Texas, Governor Miriam ("Maw") Ferguson was in attendance at the appearance at the University of Texas-Austin and added her voice to the thousands of students and faculty who applauded the performance.

Newspaper announcements about the two-day run of *The Green Pastures* in Little Rock, Arkansas, place one "inviolable rule" on access to Harrison. It applied to the director, actor, and stagehands alike. During the half hour before the curtain rises, the sixty-nine-year-old actor was to be left to himself in order that he may read and reread his lines. That was the fourteen hundredth performance, but the rule had been "imposed" by Harrison, as the report goes. Actually, part of the reason for it was that wherever he went, people from many walks of life descended on Harrison and made heavy demands on his time. He seemed never to tire of meeting people and was always gracious, but the constant performances and the grueling travel schedule were taking a toll on him. He had never missed a performance, but he was cautious.

The morning after the opening there January 5, 1934, newspaper reports told of the approving audience that had filled the Arkansas Theatre. A journalist wrote:

> Whoever doubted the reception this version of the Negro's Heaven would receive in the South had only to sit in the packed house at the Arkansas last night to watch the emotions play over the faces of the audience, most of them Southern born and Southern bred, and to listen to the response at the close of the play, to have all the doubts dispelled.[46]

A day later the Sunday edition of the same newspaper carried a story about Sir Edmond Roblin, a former premier of the province of Manitoba then living in Hot Springs, Arkansas, who had come up for the performance. Both he and Lady Roblin had looked forward to seeing the play. "Nobody can understand," he said, "just how they dared to bring it South, but the Southerners seem to be liking it." These comments indicate the full acceptance the play had received in the South, despite some serious apprehensions. Also, Little Rock was the final stop on the first Southern tour. From there the play's company would head north into the wintry Midwest.

When *The Green Pastures* left the South at Little Rock, Arkansas, January 6, 1934, it penetrated the Midwest as far north as Sioux Falls, South Dakota. It had not played that city on the first national tour. Interest was slight then, and the production managers had not become quite so adept at arranging national tours as they were a year later. This season Sioux Falls, the only city of any size in South Dakota, was included in the itinerary. When Harrison received members of the press, previous to the two-day engagement there, he remarked that opening night, January 20, 1934, was the fourth anniversary of his having joined the cast. The play went into rehearsal that day and opened five weeks later. Sioux Falls was fascinated with Harrison. Newspaper accounts went far beyond the advance publicity and wrote impressions of "De Lawd."[47]

In one week the company appeared on Monday and Tuesday at Fort Wayne, Indiana; played Wednesday and Thursday in Lexington, Kentucky; on Friday and Saturday in Charleston, West Virginia. Within less than nine hours of striking the scenery there, the company opened ninety miles away at Athens, Ohio, where it celebrated its fourth anniversary with a one-night stand at the Memorial Auditorium. An audience numbering twenty-seven hundred persons from southeastern Ohio and neighboring West Virginia braved the icy, winding roads on that February night to come to Athens. Ohio University sponsored the performance, but there was no theater on the campus large enough to accommodate the show. In his review of this performance, Tom Byrne wrote in the local newspaper:

> The fame of "The Green Pastures" preceded the play, itself, to Athens by nearly four years. Because they had read the famous religious drama, or had heard from the lips of local pilgrims the spirit of the production, 2,700 persons witnessed last night's performance at Memorial Auditorium and were prepared for many of the beautiful, humorous, poignant scenes. . . . Playgoers had heard of Richard B. Harrison, "The Lawd." But to see the inspiring, dignified, benevolent old man move through the Old Testament; to hear the voice that is firm and fascinating despite Mr. Harrison's seventy years; to feel the conviction behind his every action—this was the new experience of the audience last night.[48]

As he had done on countless occasions, Harrison gave interviews to students and reporters and played his other role as principal promoter for the play whose leading part he had played, by that time, in twenty-one states since this particular national tour had begun in Roanoke, Virginia, the preceding October.

Other performances were held during February and March in Zanesville, Youngstown, and Akron, Ohio; in Bradford, Pennsylvania; and in Jamestown, New York. By the time *The Green Pastures* opened in Buffalo, New York, at the Erlander Theatre for eight performances in early March 1934, audiences were not quite so enthusiastic about seeing it. On opening night in Buffalo, the house was only half full. It was warm in its praise, however. Rollin Palmer, writing in the *Buffalo Evening*

News, noted that the play had won critical praise, popular acclaim, and a Pulitzer prize in the three years since it opened at the Mansfield in New York City. But "a lot has happened to its prospective patrons." They have been troubled by wars, earthquakes, and bank holidays, the critic wrote. And these "cumulative harassments" probably have the audiences in an especially appreciative mood for the play. "Surely, never have Buffalonians so generally felt in the need of the consolation of a religion," he claimed. And because *The Green Pastures* is a religious play, it "falls on ears that are more than ever ready to hear."[49] The point here seems to be that although the nation knows the play well and thousands had chuckled over its humor and left no stone unturned in giving justifiable praise to the drama itself, the music of the choir, and the superb acting of the cast, witnessing the play took on a new focus as the Depression deepened. Even writing about it posed new challenges. Almost everything had been said. But the critic from Buffalo wrote in hushed contemplation—not in the usual currency of the drama review—as he mentioned a play that is "a little elusive of analysis"—one told with a simplicity that produces a "steady bubbling of amusement" but also with "a deep and genuine religious significance between the surface."

From Buffalo the cast moved to Rochester, Utica, and Syracuse, New York, and into Toronto for a scheduled week's run beginning March 19, 1934. The season ended within a few days and canceled plans to go into Montreal owing to a strike of Canadian stagehands. Efforts were made to book performances in London and Hamilton in Ontario, but theater managers in those cities said they could make more money from motion pictures than they could from stage shows. The season ended, quite short of the day it was planned, March 23, 1934.

Writing from Baltimore toward the conclusion of the last road tour, Harrison reminisced over highlights of his role as "De Lawd." The curtain had rung down on the 1,642nd performance. It was time for reflection. He spoke of his pride in being called "Daddy" of the play's company and mentioned some incidents that stood out in his memory. He referred to some as pleasant and some that were not so pleasant. No doubt he was thinking about the bitter controversy one year earlier when, playing in Baltimore the first time, he had been confronted by ministers and community leaders from Washington, D.C., who urged him to cancel the engagement at the National Theatre because that house barred Negroes from its audiences. But as was characteristic of Harrison, he chose to write more fully about the pleasant experiences. "We try to remember only those that are agreeable," was his way of expressing his recollections. One was his birthday, September 29, 1934, when the fourth tour and the fifth year of performance began at Norfolk, Virginia:

> I had just reached threescore and ten years, and very early in
> the morning I was awakened by a messenger who brought me

a lot of telegrams, probably twenty, on the first delivery. Among them were messages from the presidents of fourteen leading colleges and universities throughout the country. Later in the day I received telegrams from the Governors of seven states. I could not quite believe they were for me. I didn't know "Green Pastures" had grown so popular as to attract the attention of such distinguished personages. It is hard for me even now to realize the wires were for me, yet I have them. Right now I am wondering if I am living up to the confidence of the people who so graciously sent me the telegrams.[50]

Although he did not say so, Harrison must have remembered Norfolk particularly because it was there that he was finally given top billing for the play. From Norfolk the company traveled the short distance to Hampton Institute, another institution that had been highly respected among Negro people. Its administration and most of its faculty were white at the time, but the choirs had enjoyed renown—along with those from Fisk and Tuskegee. The president of Hampton gave a reception honoring Harrison's birthday anniversary. *The Green Pastures* choir sang some numbers at that festival.

Perhaps the single most thrilling experience of the final tour—if not of the entire traveling experience for Harrison—occurred on October 28, 1934, the day when the Canadian Pacific train rolled into London, Ontario, carrying the cast for a performance in Harrison's place of birth. He recalled that on the platform were the mayor, aldermen, and members of the black community. The next day at noon Harrison was presented the "Freedom of the City" by the mayor at a Rotary Club luncheon. The Reverend William Harrison, his brother from Windsor, Ontario, was in the company of greeters, together with three members of a baseball team he and his brothers had played on when they were boys. The pastor of Beth Emanuel British Methodist Church, the parish in which Harrison was christened, acted as chairman of a combined welcoming home and church service honoring the returning celebrity. Local newspapers carried several stories about Harrison, including biographies that showed how his family had escaped slavery in the United States into Canada. In his characteristic manner Harrison wrote about that experience in London that day.

It was a great day in my life when I stepped off the train in London. There was my brother Tom and my brother Will—he's a sort of jack-leg preacher—and my sister Victoria—she was named for Queen Victoria and never got over it—she has all the dignity of a queen in everything she does—and there was a mayor and the city fathers, to escort me to my hotel.

After the performance there was a supper and reception in the little church where my mother and father who escaped from slavery in the South had been married in 1854. The town gave me a fine picture of my mother with a little brass plaque on it to commemorate the event.[51]

He had not lived in London since he was seventeen years old, Harrison recalled, and he wondered whether anyone there would remember him. From that city he traveled with the company into Michigan and to places in Detroit he remembered when he worked there in a hotel and went to the theaters to see the best-known American and Canadian actors perform.

Now he was pleased to be returning to New York after the arduous travel throughout so large a portion of the nation on the last tour. As he anticipated the second opening in New York City, Harrison wrote from Baltimore that he hoped Broadway would be as kind on the return of the cast as it had been when the first 640 continuous performances had played there during the 1930-31 season. "How glad we will be to shake hands with old friends," he wrote. And, in summarizing the relationship between *The Green Pastures* cast and the United States of America, he added:

> It is indeed a source of great satisfaction to know that we have broken important records. We have met the most prominent people in America, including the president of the United States. On the eve of our New York return I remember the words of the little ebony-hued schoolboy who was asked what message the class had for the Board of Education: "Tell 'em we's a'rising."

NOTES

1. " 'The Green Pastures' Special," *Chicago Defender*, 12 September 1931, p. 7.

2. "The Week," *Chicago Defender*, 5 September 1931, p. 1.

3. "The Armchair Dramatist," *Sunday Tribune*, 6 September 1931, p. 6.

4. " 'De Lawd' Back with Neighbors on the Southside," *Chicago Tribune*, 20 September 1931, sec. 7, p. 4.

5. " 'Green Pastures' Opens at American Theatre Monday," *St. Louis Argus*, 26 February 1931, p. 4.

6. "Aldridge Players Honor the 'Green Pastures' Cast with an Unique Program," *St. Louis Argus*, 11 March 1932, p. 4.

7. "Profound Drama and Comedy Mark 'Green Pastures,' " *St. Louis Star*, 1 March 1932, p. 4.

8. " 'The Green Pastures' Fine Negro Fantasy," *St. Louis Post-Dispatch*, 1 March 1932, p. 3B.

9. " 'Green Pastures' Starting Second St. Louis Week," *St. Louis Globe-Democrat*, 6 March 1932, sec. 4, p. 1.

10. "Connelly Folk Pageant Opens Here," *San Francisco Chronicle*, 17 March 1932.

11. These observations appear in George C. Warren's review, "Success of 'The Green Pastures' Repeated in Its Engagement Here," *San Francisco Chronicle*, 22 May 1932, p. 8.

12. John Williams, "Anent 'Green Pastures,' " *California Eagle*, 15 July 1932, p. 4.

13. "Harlem Hails Cast of 'Green Pastures,' " *New York Times*, 3 August 1932, p. 8.

14. "Recounting the Labor of de Lawd," *Tuesday*, 6 September 1932, p. 4.

15. Ibid., p. 10.

16. "Richard B. Harrison Reviews Negro's Contribution to Stage Before Boston Audience Race Relations Sunday," *New York Age*, 14 February 1931, p. 6.

17. William Fields, " 'De Lawd' of 'Green Pastures' Discounts Ability as Actor," *Baltimore Sun*, 19 January 1933, sec. 1, p. 1.

18. " 'The Green Pastures,' " *Baltimore Sun*, 7 February 1933, sec. 1, p. 1.

19. "Protest Row on 'Green Pastures,' " *New York Times*, 16 February 1933, sec. 8, p. 6.

20. "Negro Ban Lifted on 'Green Pastures,' " *New York Times*, 10 February 1933, sec. 8, p. 4.

21. Ibid., p. 5.

22. "Washington Theatres," editorial, *New York Age*, 18 February 1933, p. 4.

23. " 'Green Pastures' and Black Washington," *Crisis*, April 1933, p. 24.

24. "A Curious Question," an editorial, *Commonweal*, 1 March 1933, p. 481.

25. " 'Green Pastures' and Black Washington," *New York Daily News*, 15 February 1933, p. 6.

26. "From the Front Row," *Washington Post*, 20 February 1933, p. 6.

27. The story is included in *Something in Common and Other Stories* (New York: Hill & Wang, 1963), pp. 201-7.

28. For a more detailed discussion of this incident, see Walter C. Daniel, " 'The Green Pastures': The Washington Performance," *Negro History Bulletin*, April-May-June 1979, pp. 42-43.

29. "Kegs of Liquor for Noah Hit in Play, Says 'De Lawd,' " *Toronto Daily Mail*, 20 March 1933, p. 7.

30. Russel McLaughlin, "The New Play," *Detroit News*, 25 April 1933.

31. This portion of the editorial is reproduced in William Fields, "Southern Journalists Approve Dixie Tour for 'Greeen Pastures,' " *New York Herald Tribune*, 25 June 1933, sec. 5, p. 2.

32. See " 'Green Pastures' Plays at Roanoke," *Lynchburg* (Va.) *News*, 22 September 1933, p. 4; " 'Pastures' in 4th Year, Goes Deluxe," *Variety*, 22 September 1933, p. 50, and 12 November 1933, p. 52.

33. " 'The Green Pastures' Enthralls Audience at First Performance," *Roanoke Times*, 5 October 1933, p. 2.

34. See Walter C. Daniel," 'Absolution,' an Unpublished Poem by Richard B. Harrison," *Negro History Bulletin*, October/November 1974, pp. 309-11 for one incident related by Mrs. T. E. McKinney, Sr., one of the participants in these

workshops. The article centers around one of the orignal poem-dramas Harrison wrote for class.

35. " 'Green Pastures' Is Regarded as Opera," *Greensboro Daily News*, 5 October 1933, p. 5.

36. A. D. Jones, "Highest Praise Is Given Play," *Greensboro Daily News*, 5 October 1933, p. 5.

37. A. D. Jones, "Highest Praise Is Given Play," *Greensboro Daily News*, 5 October 1933, p. 7.

38. " 'Green Pastures' Comes Home," *Interracial Review*, 6 (December 1933):214.

39. "Roark Bradford in Macon," *Variety*, 5 December 1933, p. 51.

40. "The Morning After," *Tuskegee Messenger*, December 1933, p. 3.

41. "Letter from Memphis," *Variety*, 5 December 1933, p. 54.

42. " 'Green Pastures' Charms Audience," *New Orleans Times-Picayune*, 26 November 1933, sec. 2, p. 1.

43. " 'Green Pastures' One of Truly Great Theatrical Offerings for Dallas Drama Followers," *Dallas Times-Herald*, 26 December 1933, p. 6.

44. "Dallas Drama Followers," *Dallas Times-Herald*, 26 December 1933, p. 6.

45. "Letters," *Time*, 18 March 1935, p. 6.

46. " 'Green Pastures' Justifies Praise," *Arkansas Gazette*, 6 January 1934, p. 6.

47. See " 'De Lawd' Likes Nice Day," *Sioux Falls Argus Leader*, 19 January 1934, p. 4; "Stagehands Get Scenery in Place Without Any Help from 'De Lawd,' " *Sioux Falls Argus Leader*, 19 January 1934, p. 4.

48. " 'Green Pastures' Comes to Athens," *Athens* (Ohio) *Messenger*, 27 February 1934, p. 6.

49. See "Erlanger Patrons Delighted by Play," *Buffalo Evening News*, 13 March 1934, p. 6.

50. " 'The Green Pastures' Comes Home," *New York Times*, 24 February 1935, sec. 8, pp. 1-3.

51. " 'De Lawd' Comes Home to London," *London* (Ontario) *Advertiser*, 23 February 1935, p. 4. For additional stories about Harrison's visit to London, see " 'De Lawd' Will Always Remember Kindness of London Citizens," *London* (Ontario) *Free Press*, 25 October 1934, p. 2; "Richard Harrison Returns to His Native City of London, *London* (Ontario) *Free Press*, 29 October 1934, p. 5; "Richard B. Harrison in His Home Town," *London* (Ontario) *Advertiser*, 27 October 1934, p. 47.

7

RETURN TO NEW YORK AND VALEDICTORY

When the cast returned to New York from Baltimore on February 20, 1935, they had reached the conclusion of the fifth season and the final national tour. Harrison came back to his tiny corner room in the 135th Street YMCA in Harlem and was immediately whizzed away by taxicab to meet Mayor Fiorello La Guardia in a formal reception for his return to the city. When Mayor La Guardia asked him if he thought he (the mayor) was going to meet any politicians in heaven, Harrison responded with his dignified humor, "What I'm worrying about, Mr. Mayor, is whether the politicians are going to meet you there." The old actor had played his role in 203 cities and towns, never missing a performance or a cue. "Even bein' de Lawd ain't no bed of roses," he quipped in the interview with reporters that February morning, throwing his head back and revealing once more the ease with which he slipped into his part in the play that had become the nation's enjoyment. He said that was perhaps his best line, but that he remembered his most dramatic scene as that in which he leads the old, blind Moses up Mount Nebo and tells him, "I'm a-gonna show you a land a million times nicer than the land of Canaan." He remembered that quiet scene had either drawn tremendous applause or none at all around the country. "In the silent houses you can hear sniffles and a few sobs," he recalled. That day Harrison was wearing the original wide-brimmed black felt hat, the original Prince Albert suit, and the original shoes. He said the hat had been blocked about twenty times, the suit had been cleaned dozens of times, and the shoes had had new half soles and rubber heels once. "The Lawd does a good deal of walking about, you know," he added.

The cast was coming home to perform the play for the 1,653rd time. Whitney Bolton wrote in the *New York Telegram*:

> This grand old Negro, I dare to think, has awakened more humans to the frailties of their souls than a host of thundering from the pulpits. Compassion and understanding and forgiveness shine in his face, his every gesture and intonation is one of gentle consideration. He looks upon the gift of his faith as something to share with all mankind. There is a constant temptation to abandon all restraint when considering this majestic old gentleman. In one black person there is encompassed all that any of us ever have been taught.[1]

Harrison was seventy-one, and Oscar Polk, the new Gabriel, who only joined the show a few days earlier in Baltimore, created attention. Polk, who was six feet four, had been in New York since coming there at the age of seventeen from his native Magnolia, Arkansas. He seemed a little perturbed that two persons before him had played the role of Gabriel, and both of them had died literally in performance. On the day of the new opening at the 42nd Street Theatre, photographers were taking a minute and twenty seconds worth of the first newsreel shots ever made of *The Green Pastures*. Marc Connelly was presiding over the preparation for the night and of the photography session. "Oh, it will be a much better production than it was when New York saw it last," he exclaimed to a reporter. And he explained that a fine performance is one that must be simple. Acting had to be edited just like writing. "Its chemistry is so delicate that holding a pause too long may be as wrong as using the wrong verb."[2]

Connelly was the director, after all. He had long since stopped traveling with the show on a regular basis, but he had seen a performance about ten days earlier in Savannah, Georgia, he said. In this fifth year, he made it a habit to see the drama about once a month while it was on the road on the theory that an actor who plays in it every night gets too close to the play. He gets to the point where he can't see the woods for the trees. Roark Bradford was also at the dress rehearsal that day. He had come in from New Orleans with his wife to celebrate the play's return to New York. He said he had seen it "two or three dozen times" at various places around the country. *The Green Pastures* was scheduled to play at the 42nd Street Theatre for three weeks on the return engagement. Then, after a summer vacation, the company would begin a six months' tour of the Canadian Northwest. Four principals had died in the five years of performance, but the mass of the large cast had remained intact. The only states in which they had not performed were Maine, New Hampshire, Vermont, New Mexico, Wyoming, Arizona, Nevada, and North Dakota. It had played the largest number of towns in Texas and Pennsylvania—fifteen and twelve, respectively.

Next morning after the opening, Brooks Atkinson was as exuberant in his praise for the play as he had been five years earlier, when he was the first New York critic to heap praises on Connelly's play, Jones' sets and costumes, Richard B. Harrison's acting, and the singing of the Hall Johnson Choir. "Count it as one of the major blessings of theatre-going that the humble little drama Marc Connelly made of Roark Bradford's Negro Bible stories and presented hopefully five years ago last night has lost none of its inner beauty." Those were some of the words he used in his review. And he was not the only one who felt that way, for Atkinson noted that on opening night during intermission, as had been the case on the other opening night in 1930, the lobby of the theater was full of people who felt the old glow once more and who were congratulating one another that *The Green Pastures* is still the seat of the theater's affection.[3] The popularity continued, Atkinson wrote, largely because "five years is nothing to a story that is already a few thousand years old" and because of Harrison's acting. "Although the grand old man who embodies its finest emotion has added five years to his life at a time when years become precious, he is still the glory," Atkinson wrote. Harrison was still drawing out of people a "reverence and a wonder that we do not often feel toward mortal men; and so long as he walks the earth like a natural man but with a serenity that now distinguishes him from his fellows, sheer goodness will continue to seem like a miracle." Continuing his canonization eulogy, the eminent critic and principal voice of Broadway wrote:

> What moves us to tears in the theatre is the sight of that kindly, gentle old man and the sound of his resonant voice. "The Green Pastures" has enriched him. His performance has grown in the simplicity and warmth of his spirit.

Richard B. Harrison walked the earth like a natural man for only a few days after Atkinson's words of praise. Three days later he collapsed as he prepared to go on stage for the 1,659th performance. Too tired to perform in the matinee on March 2, 1935, he was found in his dressing room in a "state of super-weariness." He was sent to the Fifth Avenue Hospital in a private automobile. A newspaper story reported that it was said that Harrison would be back in the theater by the next Monday. But Dr. M. J. Raisbeck, his physician, said that while he could not make any prophecy in that regard, he did not believe Harrison would be able to return quite so soon as that. "Harrison is not ill," he said. "He's just tired out. He has seen a lot of one-night stands and all that sort of thing and he's not as young as he used to be." The doctor said Harrison needed rest. His heart was perfectly all right; he was just tired out.[4] When Connelly heard about Harrison's collapse, he hurried to the theater. He was pleased to find that Charles Winter Wood, Harrison's understudy and close personal friend, was ready to go with the part. Reports said that although Connelly fully understood the substitute was "not gifted with the special benignity of Harrison," he was prepared to play reasonably well. For this matinee performance, Wood was applauded for a long time at the final curtain. At least for the time being, the audience seemed to want to assure Wood it would support his taking over the role from the disabled man who had made himself the metaphor for American acting. Connelly seemed moved by the sudden illness of his principal drawing card, for whom he had maintained a high but austere respect through the years since they first met early in 1930 as the playwright was looking feverishly for someone to enact the demanding role he had written into his new play. He told reporters the recent tour had been strenuous for Harrison. Although he had made an effort to alternate a series of one-night stands with a solid week of performance, Connelly said, it had not been possible to make that accommodation. Even in the few days since returning to New York, there had been many rehearsals to break in the new angels and other minor characters. Despite his advanced age, everyone thought Harrison was in good physical condition. Until the day of his collapse he had stood up well under the rigors of the production on tour and his own personal appearances before scores of groups of people wherever he played. He had survived three Gabriels, two Moses, two Noahs, two archdeacons, and a number of cherubs and seraphims who had to be replaced because their voices changed and they outgrew their parts.

Two weeks after his initial attack, Richard B. Harrison died. One newspaper account carried the news simply:

> The world was assured that Mr. Harrison indeed would be presiding again over the famous fishfry scene before long. His ailment was diagnosed simply as a tired heart. But Wednesday night he became very uncomfortable and called a nurse just before his fatal attack. She saw that the old actor's pulse was failing and called the physician, Dr. M. J. Railsbeck of 1155 Park Avenue. Mr. Harrison was dead by the time the doctor arrived at his bedside. The star of "The Green Pastures" had died of acute coronary occlusion, Dr. Railsbeck said.[5]

Only Doe Doe Green, who had played the part of Angel Gabriel for the past two and a half years, would say he had seen Harrison failing. "De

Lawd" started to waver toward the end of the performance in Jackson-ville, Florida, on January 30, he noted. From that incident Green hovered close to the grand old actor in order to catch him should he fall. But Harrison would not admit fatigue until the day he left the show for good.

On agreement between black and white Episcopalians in New York City, Harrison's body lay in state in St. Philip's Church in Harlem before being transferred to the Cathedral of St. John the Divine at the suggestion of Bishop William T. Manning. Bishop Manning and the Reverend Mr. Shelton Hale Bishop, rector of the Harlem church, conducted the funeral. The body was carried then to Chicago for another service and interment. Symbols of the personal accomplishment of Richard B. Harri-son as a man and as an actor abound in the many reports of the funeral. A principal story in the *New York Times* captures the essence of Harrison's meaning to those Americans who could not be present for the funeral in New York:

> Tremulous organ music, rich-timbered Negro spirituals, the faint scent of many floral wreaths and the mystic light of breeze-blown tapers awed more than 7,000 mourners yester-day afternoon at the funeral service for Richard Berry Harri-son in the Cathedral of St. John the Divine.
>
> Bishop William T. Manning probably never looked down from his pulpit on so mixed a throng as listened in deep silence to his solemn eulogy of the venerable Negro who for five years had played the role of "de Lawd" in "The Green Pastures."
>
> Every foot of space, even the area around the communion rail before the great white altar where candles flickered against a background of scarlet drapery, was filled with sorrowing Negroes and white admirers of the old actor. They flowed into the chapels and even into the street.[6]

After a prelude of music from the great cathedral organ, the procession "moved past the coffin between the rows of gleaming candles: the crucifer, the black-gowned choir, the clergy in white vestments tipped with purple and scarlet and black; then the honorary pallbearers, Paul Laurence Harrison, the son of "De Lawd," and the cast of *The Green Pastures*. As members of the procession found their places on either side of the chancel, Dean Milo H. Gates pronounced the sentences that opened the service. The choir sang the hymn "The Strike Is O'er, the Battle Done." Bishop Manning ascended the pulpit and began, "We are gathered here in this cathedral to commit to its rest the body of Richard B. Harrison and to commend his soul to the care and loving kindness of the God and Father of us all." The bishop spoke briefly about Harrison's life and the example it reflected on his own race and on mankind and his qualities of "soul and character" that gave dignity and greatness to human life everywhere. "His experience of life was truly remarkable, reaching from the humble beginnings to a phase unique in the history of dramatic art," Bishop Manning said. The Reverend Shelton Hale Bishop spoke of the simple man who had been "De Lawd." "This service," he said, "is the simple Christian tribute of an adoring populace to a man who walked upon the earth and touched men like himself in a mystical way that made them feel that they had been with God."

Charles Winter Wood, the new "Lawd" of the play, went into the pulpit and told of Harrison's death. "Terrified, I saw him stricken," he told the grieving audience. "He looked up. 'Charlie, old man,' he said 'hold me, Charlie old man, old man. Don't let me down. The world needs this play.' " Wood ended his tribute with the traditional words: "We thank Thee, O God, for the victories and the triumphs of Richard B. Harrison." Then Hall Johnson, director of the famous choir bearing his name that had sung the spirituals in the first New York run of *The Green Pastures*, lifted his arm, stood facing the white altar with his back to the candles and the coffin, and led the choir in singing "The Blind Man Stood on the Way and Cried," "I Am Seeking for a City," and "Sometimes I Feel Like a Motherless Child"—all favorites of Harrison's. The Reverend Adam Clayton Powell, Sr., pastor of Harlem's famous Abyssinian Baptist Church, read from the fifteenth chapter of First Corinthians.

After the bishop's benediction and singing of a final hymn, the mourners filed out of the cathedral. The coffin was covered with a blanket of 1,657 blossoms spelling out "Green Pastures" in white carnations and red roses. More than a hundred policemen kept the crowds moving, but thousands stood still in the March sunlight as the black-robed choir assembled around the hearse. Paul Laurence Harrison and the new "De Lawd" climbed into the coach. Harrison would accompany his father's body to Grand Central Station and then to Chicago for the burial.

As impressive as the funeral at the Cathedral of St. John the Divine had been as a tribute to Richard B. Harrison, the outpouring of people and respect in Chicago was even more so.

Chicago was home to Richard B. Harrison. He had made it so as early as his brief association with the Columbian Exposition in that city in 1893. As we have seen, he and Paul Laurence Dunbar established a home there, although Harrison spent most of his time on the road, both in professional performance and as a worker on the transcontinental railroads. He bought two houses in Chicago, and his wife and children were established there while the actor toured with lyceum programs and with *The Green Pastures*. His coming back to Chicago as a final resting place, then, was a highly emotional experience for many persons who had known Harrison close up. His body lay in state there in his home from the time of its arrival in the city until the funeral service. Police estimated that nearly fifteen thousand persons had filed through the home by the time the body was moved to St. Edmund's Episcopal Church for an 11 A.M. service on March 18, 1935. The body was clad in the long frock coat and costume of "De Lawd." Men and women of social prominence, government officials, celebrities of the stage, educators, and clergymen thronged the nave of the church. Outside, hundreds of others stood in silence, including many who had served as Pullman porters and waiters with Harrison. A report of the Chicago funeral noted:

> Marching down the aisle, the Reverend Samuel J. Martin, rector of the church, chanted the opening sentences of the service. Before him were eight flambeaux, two crucifers, and two acolytes, clad in long white albs, and the vested choir. Behind him followed the coffin, covered with a huge spray of lilies, Mr. Harrison's favorite.
>
> Bishop George Craig Stewart, who confirmed Mr. Harrison in special services a year ago, and a chaplain, the Rev. Garland McHorter, entered.
>
> There followed the solemn celebration of the high Episcopal Requiem Mass. The music was the "Plain Song" of Canon Douglas. Anthems of the Anglican Church were sung, John Green, the Negro baritone, sang "Missa de Angelis," and Abbie Mitchell, a soprano, was also heard.
>
> Bishop Stewart pronounced the absolution. The litany of the dead was sung and the rites of asperges followed.[7]

Harrison's wife and daughter, although they had been hospitalized at the time of his passing a few days earlier, were able to attend the funeral. At the graveside in Lincoln Cemetery in Chicago, they lay the blanket of 1,657 roses sent as a tribute from the members of *The Green Pastures* cast. Marc Connelly, author of *The Green Pastures*, who was in California and did not attend either of the funeral services, sent the following tribute that was widely publicized:

> Richard Harrison was not an actor in the conventional sense. Up to the production of "The Green Pastures" his life had been largely spent in teaching elocution and poetry in Negro schools. He was a gentle, simple man, whose mellowness evidenced itself in the little Harlem theatrical agency where I was casting the play. We were a little afraid he would forget some of his lines the opening night, but to the surprise and

delight of us all it was he who helped Gabriel out in a moment of forgetfulness. Every one loved him, and with him I feel that a great deal of sheer goodness has gone out of the world.[8]

Appropriately, Harlem honored Harrison with a memorial service at the Abyssinian Baptist church, 132 West 135th Street. Two thousand friends and others sat in silence as Charles Winter Wood, lifelong friend and for five years his understudy, told the story of his long friendship with "De Lawd." "He was one great outstanding man who did the things he wanted to do for his people and for the art of his people," said Wood. "He lived in his vision of beauty and love and art, and no man can live that way and really grow old." The Reverend Dr. Adam Clayton Powell, Jr., assistant pastor of Abyssinian, presided. His father, the senior pastor, presented a picture of the life of Harrison as "a divine miracle." Harrison, he said, "imbibed the gentleness, the peace, the love and the compassion of God." *The Green Pastures* choir, now directed by Evelyn Burwell, sang several spirituals, including Harrison's favorite, "City Called Heaven."[9]

Richard B. Harrison and Marc Connelly owed each other a deep debt of gratitude. Without the role in *The Green Pastures*, Harrison would not have been a household name in the United States. Conversely, without his role in the play and his ability to relate favorably and significantly to all types of Americans off the stage, Connelly would not and could not have become a household name in the theater. Notwithstanding the unexpected, phenomenal success the play enjoyed, it was not until the beginning of the fourth touring season that Harrison's name appeared as the top item on marquees and in the public announcements advertising the play. Publicity copy usually began with "Laurence Rivers, Inc. Presents: THE GREEN PASTURES." And reference was made to its having won a Pulitzer prize, as well as to Marc Connelly's having written a play "Suggested by Roark Bradford's Book." On the occasion of the seventieth anniversary of Harrison's birthday, he was given top billing in public notices. Stebbins, actually the Laurence Rivers of the production company, announced in September 1933: "Henceforth all advertising will read like this: RICHARD B. HARRISON IN *THE GREEN PASTURES*, instead of *THE GREEN PASTURES* with Richard B. Harrison."

One indication of Harrison's significance to black Americans may be seen in the following column note about his funeral:

> In my fifteen years of reporting here are three Harlem funerals that for size, impressiveness and solemnity stand out, and all were funerals of stage stars. First, there was the passing of the late Bert Williams, who was honored in death with a service by a white lodge of Scottish Rite Masons. Then,

there was the late Florence Mill, whose passing Broadway and Harlem joined in mourning. And finally, there was the funeral of Richard B. Harrison, to whom all New York paid reverent tribute from the Cathedral of St. John the Divine last Sunday.[10]

More than passing interest lies in the comment that Harlem had given its biggest funerals to stage stars. This historic fact lends credence to the honor black Americans give to those who, they believe, represent the race on the stage. Each name mentioned above transcended the usual limits placed on black performers as mere scenario material for American stage drama or pure entertainment. Bert Williams was a comedian, but his consummate talent reflected dimensions far beyond the characterization of the "Stage Negro." Florence Mill endeared herself by using all the theatrical possibilities available to her in her time. Tributes to them in their death represent these performers' role as a principal metaphor of honor for black Americans. They have known and do know that their own economic clout can hardly place black talent in a position for national and worldwide recognition. They need the backing of white Americans. But they have and do maintain their claim on their stars. The high and low among the race feel a vicarious honor in the accomplishments of one of their own. They illustrate that kinship and honor in their reaction to the death of black luminaries. Despite some adverse comments about Harrison and his inclination to follow what some black spokesmen call "accommodationism," he enjoyed their love and respect. And he gained it primarily through his role as "De Lawd" in Marc Connelly's *The Green Pastures*.

Of the dozens of death notices and obituaries written about the passing of Richard B. Harrison, one appearing in the *Christian Century* seems particularly impressive and representative of the major sentiments about the actor's accomplishment among American religious scholars:

> Richard B. Harrison has laid his burdens down. . . . It is not easy to go on from there. He was my friend. For that matter he was a friend of thousands. He belongs perhaps no more to those who knew him off stage than to those who saw him only as "De Lawd" of "The Green Pastures."
>
> He belongs to the Negro race and to the white race, to the North and to the South. He lived in both sections of the country, and as "The Green Pastures" touched the thoughts and emotions of more than two million, Richard Harrison gained the affection of all the people, regardless of race or geography, and that of Frederick Douglass who believed in him and, it is said, inspired him with a sense of mission, but

> he belongs in a true sense to all races. To many he was more
> than merely a man or an actor; he was a symbol. Of what he
> was a symbol can only be answered when we answer the
> question, What is "The Green Pastures?"[11]

And that writer goes on to capture the essence of Harrison's importance to the American stage of the time and to the success of *The Green Pastures*. It was no ordinary play, he wrote. "It had a phenomenal run of five years and is still drawing large audiences." Its universal appeal that transcends race and creed and contemporary religion gave it its high value. More importantly, the play provided the perfect "vehicle for Harrison's talents"; for "it is no less true that the old Negro's dramatic powers, immeasurably enriched by his attitude of mind and heart toward the play itself and the part he had to play, provided, in turn, a perfect vehicle for the play's deeper and truer meaning."

On the matter of Negroes who would like to get away from plays that presented the race "in its lowliest and more primitive manifestations," this critic considered Harrison beyond reproach. He was too big to be hypersensitive. He could tell a dialect story himself. He loved Dunbar's poems best and recited them regularly from the lyceum platform, giving them a hearing and raising them to dimensions of dignity few other readers could lend them. There was something special about Harrison in this respect:

> There was nothing of the parvenu about him. Nevertheless, it
> would have been understandable had such a man rejected a
> play about heavenly fish-fries and stout and tender angels as
> misrepresentative of the race he was proud to call his own.
> On the contrary, he made of the part offered to him an opportunity to be an ambassador of his race, to promote mutual
> understanding, dignifying the race in the minds of those who
> saw the play, and caught the poetry of its oldest lines and
> scenes. It was poetry reflecting the rhythm and imagery of
> Negro speech, but it was more than that.[12]

Harrison provided the clear enunciation of the hint of theological evolution in the play, "even in the least controversial and most inclusive sense, of humanism." "De Lawd" undergoes change and development, just as the conception of God in the Bible changes and develops. The philosophical lesson, so aptly enacted by Harrison in "the thing done," makes clear the point that men who conceive of their God after their own images undergo a change of conscience.

Clearly Harrison's role in the theater at the height of the devastating Depression and at a time of uncommon racial strife in the nation taught lessons of mutualism and mercy, human kinship and human divinity in his role. He considered himself an instrument in advancing better understanding between races.

Another theologian separated the play, the role of "De Lawd," and Harrison the man in writing:

> It was, I think, not so much the extraordinary success of the play, nor even the astonishing achievement of the actor in portraying the role of "De Lawd" in the theater without seeming sacrilegious, that called forth this tribute. It was the character of the man revealed in his triumph. I met him personally and conversed with him intimately on two or three occasions, and was impressed with the singular combination of genuine humility and personal dignity which characterized him. I also arranged with him to speak on "How It Feels to Play 'De Lawd' " in Joseph Bond Chapel at the university and afterward to take lunch with the faculty of the divinity school at the Quadrangle Club and all were impressed with the quality of the man and with the reverence with which he regarded the role. He viewed his task as a genuine religious ministry. And so it was.[13]

Praises were legion. Black Americans hailed Harrison as their actor who had brought dignity, at last, to the theater when a stage is entirely peopled by Negroes. Theologians lavished encomiums on him for the personal goodness that shone through his role. Drama critics fully understood that Harrison had been the essence of *The Green Pastures*. John Mason Brown captured some of the rapture and the humor of Harrison and the play when he wrote:

> Most of us cannot think of the grand old gentleman's passing up the gangway of another Lord without secretly hoping that when our time comes a Lawd very much like Mr. Harrison's will be presiding over the heavenly fish fry all of us would like someday to attend.[14]

Brown expressed what thousands of Americans felt about Harrison as they met him in Connelly's play. He brought forth from hundreds of audiences both the tear and the smile. His regal bearing alone brought a visage to the stage that was, after all, pretty close to what many Americans thought God would be like if they tried to picture Him on the stage of their minds. Many had never thought of Him graphically before perhaps, but *The Green Pastures* formed the image for them and they believed it for the two hours they were in the theater. His kindliness, His

ameliorated wrath, even when He had every reason to be vengeful, His
fussing over the smallest detail of His heaven and His earth lay on a
delicate line between buffoonery and divinity. Harrison's demeanor and
his voice kept the role in the realm of the latter. He brought a peculiar
symbiosis to concepts of white God and black God in America. Few sophisticated theatergoers had thought of black Christianity as more than a
caricature of what took place in the white churches far across town and
far across some religious dividing line. The "old black Preacher" had
become a ready image for disdain and low comedy used by creative
artists and men and women on the streets. Not so in *The Green Pastures*.
By a stroke of genius Marc Connelly had envisaged a role and had
directed into execution a stage personality that was hardly part of his
regular acquaintance. His imaginings brought it into being, together with
some direct observations. He did not write the part with Richard B.
Harrison in mind, nor any other black preacher-type actor. No models
existed.

In a fortuitous coming together of events that was unique in American
theatrical history, a playwright with an unusual script and a resourceful
bankroller found in black American culture an uncommon talent of
acting and singing that transcended the minstrel convention and found a
responsive chord deep inside the psyche of native audiences. The play,
as written by Connelly, as enacted by Harrison, and as sung by Hall
Johnson's choir, was native American to the core. Drama critics might
debate—as they do some fifty years after the play appeared regularly on
stages throughout the country—the merits of *The Green Pastures*. They
recognize it as a document on the scholarly progression of the Judeo-
Christian concept of God and His relationship to Man. Connelly's accomplishment as a playwright was to present that development in a new key
that could be called "a divine comedy."

No other person came close to reaching with *The Green Pastures* the
heights of theatrical accomplishment Richard B. Harrison attained. The
play was essentially his. When he died the vitality of *The Green Pastures*
died—not only because no one could match his acting in the role and his
amazing interaction with American people, but also because the times
changed radically. By the time the play was revived, it could not achieve
success again. When it was filmed, one could see immediately that
motion picture technology could not come close to "De Lawd" on the
stage.

Richard B. Harrison was *The Green Pastures*.

When *The Green Pastures* was revived in 1951, some two decades after
it had first appeared and traveled throughout the country with Harrison
as "De Lawd," it could not regain its original popularity. Theophilus
Lewis, writing in *Interracial Review*, explained the change of the national

perception as well as anyone when he wrote: "Almost precisely 20 years after Harrison's death the play was revived, and once again was acclaimed by the critics. But for some mysterious reason the public did not respond to their enthusiasm. Perhaps it was because when Harrison died the play died with him."[15] Lewis went on to recall his own reaction to the play when it first came to the stage. His comments are important in any biography of the play and Harrison's role in it:

> I was an agnostic at the time, and also a kind of southpaw racist. My chauvinism and skepticism were both offended by the play. I confused its reverence with superstition and its humor with blackface comedy without cork. By the grace of God, I have outgrown my intellectual infirmity; and my friends don't mention it anymore. In my first review I wrote, "It will be interesting to see just how the Bible-belt folks will react to the proposition that after all is said and done, God is merely a pretty fair colored actor who forgets his lines too often." In spite of my disapproval, "Green Pastures" was a hit.

From the perspective of twenty years, Lewis was able to write in 1951 that the play's success was well deserved because it was one of the finest in dramatic literature. God is the leading character, and He is portrayed by Marc Connelly as a wise and benevolent colored preacher with a fatherly interest in the world He created, Lewis explained. He had originally thought the scenes in Pharaoh's court and in Babylon ribald and sacrilegious, intended to show Negroes are clowns even when worshiping God. "I know now these scenes of bawdry and revelry, in the context of reverence, are intended to suggest God's inherent patience with His wayward world," he wrote. Still, it was, to Lewis, "an actor-made play."

The *Daily Worker* took a different approach to the revival in 1951 from Lewis'. That publication's recitation of the history of the play on Broadway in the 1930s was less than accurate. It mentioned prominently that it was produced by a Wall Street financier after three well-known producers had turned it down and that religious circles "questioned Marc Connelly's motives for writing the play." Claiming it was condemned by the Washington, D.C., NAACP "as fraud" goes against the truth of the controversy over the performance in Washington as detailed in chapter six. In giving the play serious evaluation in 1951, the *Daily Worker* stressed the nation's current focusing

> too deeply about fundamental problems of a very earthly if not earthshaking nature to be long bothered with Marc Connelly's fraudulent message of folk whimsy from heaven by a

cast of Negro actors and singers who, in order to work, have no alternative but to perform in what is offered: plays like "Green Pastures" which have no relation whatsoever to life as they know and experience it.[16]

The columnist pointed out that the cast of the revival presents a radically different attitude toward the play's material from that of the original actors. Some of the language has been changed "and references insulting to Negroes have been deleted or changed, except for the murder and the gambling scenes." Thus, the new version "has more formal dignity than the original." All this is to the good, the analysis continued, since it is not possible to deal with the problem of the Negro actor in a vacuum. It is plain that more is being achieved by direct participation of some of our best Negro talents in the play than would be achieved by remaining outside it. The principal difference between Harrison's role and the new central character was important to the *Daily Worker*:

> The "Lawd" of today portrayed by William Marshall is not the "Lawd" of the 1930s. He's really angry with the world and in a different manner. He walks the earth with tolerance and dignity that befits a great man. The first person he meets is the young Negro woman, Zeba (Vinie Burrows), strumming a ukelele. He rebukes her for carousing on the Sabbath. She is the only woman character in the play treated with any delineation, but she is an immoral person of disrepute. Marc Connelly will protest that this is a fable, that this is harmless entertainment based on the "simple" beliefs of a childishly simple people, meaning Southern Negroes. Which means ultimately Negroes.

William Marshall portrayed "De Lawd" "like a man really concerned with the problems of a real world," the critic concluded. Whether he ever saw Harrison play the role is not clear, but "De Lawd's" concern for His world seemed to be a common topic for most critics.

Brooks Atkinson's reactions to the new cast and the revival become significant here. He who had never ceased to praise the drama as American theater at its finest—especially the acting of Richard B. Harrison—recalled that when the venerable old actor had been asked to play the role, he was afraid the play would turn out to be sacrilegious; that the late Bishop Herbert Shipman persuaded him that, on the contrary, it was a devoutly religious play. "And, thanks largely to Mr. Harrison's spiritual radiance, it was," Atkinson wrote. His visage counted. For "an elderly man, he looked as though he had found his mercy through a lifetime of suffering." One difference, then, between the two performances of "De Lawd" lay in the essential difference between the two men who played the role. "Since William Marshall is a much younger man, he lacks the spiritual wisdom that a long life had stored in Mr. Harrison's soul," Atkinson concluded. At the same time he noted that Marshall's "Lawd" has a nobility of its own. "He is an enormous man who towers over the angels and the people and he has a big voice," Atkinson explained. He was sincere, however. He was not sanctimonious, and he conveyed love, and the pain and the selfless responsibility of the fatherly character. He was no Richard B. Harrison, nonetheless. Atkinson began his review of the new production with the candid observation that reasserts his judgment of Harrison's indispensable playing in the drama:

> Although Richard B. Harrison has gone to his reward, "The Green Pastures" remains green, disarming and moving. William Marshall plays the Lawd in the beautiful new production which opened at the Broadway last evening. Old Mr. Harrison was an inspired man, ripe with years and dedicated to a mission. There will never be his equal in Marc Connelly's incomparable play.[17]

Two weeks after the opening, Atkinson used his column to praise the drama and to try to explain to skeptics that it does have a lasting and significant value. He wrote about some visitors from overseas who were unhappy during the intermission. They called the play sacrilegious. He considered their attitude perverse. For "those of us who already knew the play from having seen it repeatedly twenty-one years ago" still regarded it a profoundly moving religious work that captures the faith of mankind in a God of compassion. Most of the old-timers, he wrote, "have an affection for its purity and exaltation." Once more he explained, as he had done years earlier, that the real genius of *The Green Pastures* does not emerge until "De Lawd" learns about mercy through suffering from the impregnable faith of Hezdrel. But the thing that gives the play immortality in the literature of the stage is the fact that it has a theme, Atkinson declares. The signals are clear: "Adam's happy and hopeful acceptance of the world into which he has been created and which seems too halcyon at the time, the resolute flight of the children of Israel and their brief, touching expressions of devotion to Moses, and finally de Lawd's humble scene with Hezdrel amid the agonies of the battlefield." These expressions of faith give the drama its eminence "because they keep unbroken the line of men who have done God's work through the horrors and inequities of the centuries."

Notwithstanding the *Daily Worker*'s trenchant criticism that the play demeans the Negroes who enact its parts, no critic made that argument in quite those words while *The Green Pastures* captured the affection and imagination of the nation. It did not make that same impression on audiences in Europe, where traveling casts met with only moderate success in the Scandinavian countries. The Lord Chamberlain of England forbade its performance on the single ground that English custom forbade personification of the Deity on the theater stage. Even Harrison could not overcome that prohibition. Popular sentiment in the United States was actually unfavorable to such representation too. Its acceptance of *The Green Pastures* in practically every state of the Union and by widely varying societies within the nation attests to the recognition of the themes and identifications Atkinson wrote about. Prejudice against Negroes, rather than rejection of the drama as native theater, created the greatest problems for national tours.

The Green Pastures was essentially an expression of American perspectives of its time. It provided a balm for a nation facing the unsettling problems of social and economic revolutionary thought and action at home and the darkening clouds of world military conflict in Europe. Its successful life was Richard B. Harrison's successful stage career. The two beloved American institutions died together. In later years *The Green Pastures* could become a literary critic's discussion piece. Its place in national theatrical history had been made between February 1930 and March 1935.

NOTES

1. "The Stage Today," *New York Telegram*, 28 February, 1935, p. 8.

2. " 'Okay, Gabe!' cried 'De Lawd,' at Reopening," *New York Herald Tribune*, 27 February 1935, p. 9.

3. Brooks Atkinson, "The Play," *New York Times*, 27 February 1935, p. 16.

4. " 'De Lawd' Tuckered Out," *New York Herald Tribune*, 2 March 1935, p. 16.

5. "Richard B. Harrison, 'Green Pastures' 'Lawd' Is Dead," *New York Herald Tribune*, 15 March 1935, p. 18.

6. *New York Times*, 8 March 1935, p. 14.

7. *New York Times*, 20 March 1935, p. 21.

8. *New York Times*, 16 March 1935, p. 18.

9. This service was held after the funeral and burial, *New York Times*, 22 April 1935, p. 17.

10. William E. Clark, "In the Name of Art," *New York Age*, 3 March 1935, p. 5.'

11. Frank L. Hayes, "De Lawd," *Christian Century*, 27 March 1935, p. 399.

12. Ibid.

13. Charles T. Holman, "Richard Harrison Combined Humility with Dignity," *Christian Century*, 3 April 1945, p. 452.

14. *Two on the Aisle: Ten Years of the American Theatre in Performance* (New York: W. W. Norton & Co., 1938), pp. 243-44.

15. "About 'The Green Pastures' 21 Years Later," *Interracial Review*, May 1951, p. 79.

16. *Daily Worker*, 30 March 1951, p. 10.

17. "First Night at the Theatre," *New York Times*, 16 March 1951, p. 8.

BIBLIOGRAPHICAL
ESSAY

Stages of the development of the drama as a genre of American literature can be understood clearly by reading the kind of details presented in Arthur Hobson Quinn, *A History of the American Drama from the Civil War to the Present Day* (New York: Appleton-Century-Crofts, 1936). It was an old-fashioned book that gives little attention to the period that saw *The Green Pastures* find its way to the stage. But it relates titles of plays, their authors, synopses of the works, and the national milieu in which such works were written and performed. Less comprehensive coverage but emphases of the themes and works from what the author calls appropriately the most productive years of the American drama, Alan S. Downer's *Fifty Years of American Drama* (Chicago: Henry Regney Co., 1966) adds considerable insight and information to a work like Quinn's by discussing "theatricalism" and the movement toward drama in American stage art through romance, reality, folk drama, and comedy through the first half of the twentieth century. Joseph Wood Krutch, in *The American Drama Since 1918* (New York: George Braziller, 1957), undertakes "to offer both a connected account and some critical evaluation of playwrighting in America since the World War." His is one of the liveliest narrations of the beginnings of what can be called an American drama, including several pages about Marc Connelly's collaborations in the theater with George Kaufman, which gave him the visibility among theater people before he wrote *The Green Pastures*. While Walter J. Meserve's *An Outline History of American Drama*

(Totowa, N.J.: Littlefield, Adams, 1965) is basically an outline, its arrangement of material, details about playwrights and works, and comments on the prevailing trends in the several periods it covers make it a useful document for understanding the richness of the development of American drama.

Because *The Green Pastures* might be considered a "Negro" play, in that it is part of and concludes that period in which white playwrights succeeded in bringing plays about black America to the commercial stage, one needs to look at Fannin S. Belcher, Jr., "The Place of the Negro in the Evolution of the American Theatre, 1767-1940" (Ph.D. dissertation, Yale University, 1940) for the classic study on its subject. It is encyclopedic in its covering of the earliest attempts by black Americans to stage drama, the subject of black American personalities and affairs as represented on the stage by white playwrights, and the handful of plays written by black playwrights that had reached the commercial stage by the time covered by the study. James Weldon Johnson's *Black Manhattan* (New York: Atheneum, 1969), is a reissued version of the 1930 publication in which Johnson, as cultural historian, writes about theater and music among black New Yorkers. It is popular history, but it contains program details and some biography that is essential. Frederick W. Bond's *The Negro and the Drama* (Washington, D.C.: Associated Publishers, 1940) performs much the same purpose as Belcher's work, although it is considerably more limited in scope. Moreover, it contains details in the development of drama among black Americans from religious ceremonies to minstrelsy, musical comedy, the legitimate stage, and little theater. Both black and white authors are reported in the book.

Twenty-five years after the Belcher and Bond works appeared, Loften Mitchell's *Black Drama: The Story of the American Negro in the Theatre* (New York: Hawthorn Books, 1967) adds data that the earlier works could not have discussed. Mitchell's book, together with the unusually significant *Black Drama of the Federal Theatre Era* (Amherst: University of Massachusetts Press, 1980), written by E. Quita Craig, provides a careful examination of materials that have recently become available to scholars about that period of dynamic activity in the drama that immediately followed the end of the five-year run of *The Green Pastures*. This book is one of the few pieces of writing that analyzes Hall Johnson's *Run Littl' Chillun*, a play written by the black playwright who also scored the vocal music and trained the chorus for *The Green Pastures*. In addition to these works on the black drama, its actors, and its authors, Doris E. Abramson's *Negro Playwrights in the American Theatre 1925-1959* (New York: Columbia University Press, 1969) brings the reader up to the beginning of the Black Consciousness Drama of the 1960s.

How *The Green Pastures* fits into what has been referred to as the "cultural paternalism" tradition in American drama can be studied by details presented by Harold Cruse in his *The Crisis of the Negro Intellectual: From Its Origins to the Present* (New York: William Morrow & Co., 1967). This somewhat revisionist book on the dilemmas of the black intellectual and creative artist during the Harlem Renaissance is rich with details of personalities and events that shaped that period in Afro-American culture, which the author considers highly overrated. He provides history about the little group of free-thinking intellectuals who developed a colony on the tip of Cape Cod that became the generating force for the Provincetown Players and Theatre, Mabel Dodge's famous Fifth Avenue Salon as the meeting place for those liberal journalists and authors, and James Weldon Johnson's relationships with those white "shakers and movers." Eugene O'Neill, Ridgely Torrence, and Paul Green, as well as Robert Edmond Jones, were members of this group. They became also the men whose reputations in the theater were made through their decision to exploit subjects about black Americans for the stage, and thereby to change the direction of the development of American drama. Daniel Aaron's *Writers on the Left* (New York: Harcourt, Brace & World, 1965) provides excellent biographical data on these Americans and their professional and artistic activities. Anecdotes about the liberals who came to Mabel Dodge's Salon can be found in Lois Palken Rudnick, *Mabel Dodge Luhan* (Albuquerque: University of New Mexico Press, 1984).

Those playwrights most closely associated with the "cultural paternalism" of the 1915-30 era are discussed in important works, including Arthur Gelb and Barbara Gelb, *O'Neill* (New York: Harper & Row, 1962); John M. Clum, *Ridgely Torrence* (New York: Twayne Publishers, 1972); Frederick Carpenter, *Eugene O'Neill* (New York: Twayne Publishers, 1979); Vincent S. Kenny, *Paul Green* (New York: Twayne Publishers, 1971).

A book that is the biography of a role in a play as it was conceived and created by a playwright and executed by an actor depends largely on newspaper and magazine reviews written by drama critics. Those reactions to the play, both in its Broadway runs and on its tours of the United States and parts of Canada, were provided by many periodical references, as well as by interviews with living persons who were associated with the performances or who witnessed them. *The Green Pastures* is a play about religion, however. One could argue that Connelly wrote it, to some extent, as a response to the prevalent questions about religion of the times. Whether that claim would be true or not, even a cursory glance at titles of articles and editorials in *Christian Century*, a liberal Protestant journal, during the 1929-30 period would be informative.

"All Christians Equal Before God," an editorial that appeared in the 29 October 1929 issue (p. 1306), supported a Christian unity conference, called at St. George's Protestant Episcopal Church in New York City, that sought to de-emphasize denominationalism. "Two Meetings," a news story in the 2 April 1930 issue (pp. 429-30) describes the bitter confrontation between persons who came to a meeting called by Bishop Manning of the New York Episcopal diocese for a service of prayer at the Cathedral of St. John the Divine and a counterbalancing mass meeting called by William Z. Foster, the Communist party standard-bearer who had recently been released from jail for his part in a demonstration by the Friends of the Soviet Union. The two meetings referenced the one called by Foster at Madison Square Garden to detract attention and attendance from Bishop Manning's. This article and many items in the *New York Times* show clearly the challenges conventional Christianity was facing at the time. "How Can We Find God?" in the 28 February 1929 issue of *Christian Century* (p. 291) is typical of the kinds of questions about God and practices of the Christian religion that were pervasive throughout the nation. Other subjects during the same year and in the same periodical were titled "The Church and Social Actions," 29 May 1929, pp. 702-4; "A Workable Idea of God," 14 February 1929, pp. 226-8; "Nationalism: The New Religion," 8 May 1929, p. 613; "Man and Humanism," 5 March 1930, pp. 299-300. All indicate the questioning climate about religion of the decade that followed the end of World War I.

INDEX

About the Author

WALTER C. DANIEL is the Director of the College of General Studies, University of Missouri, Columbia. He is the author of *Images of the Preacher in Afro-American Literature, Black Journals of the United States* (Greenwood Press, 1982), and articles published in the *Negro History Bulletin* and the *Journal of American Culture*.